Postdramatic Theatre and
the Political

Methuen Drama Engage offers original reflections about key practitioners, movements and genres in the fields of modern theatre and performance. Each volume in the series seeks to challenge mainstream critical thought through original and interdisciplinary perspectives on the body of work under examination. By questioning existing critical paradigms, it is hoped that each volume will open up fresh approaches and suggest avenues for further exploration.

Series Editors

Mark Taylor-Batty
Senior Lecturer in Theatre Studies, Workshop Theatre,
University of Leeds, UK

Enoch Brater
Kenneth T. Rowe Collegiate Professor of Dramatic Literature and
Professor of English and Theater, University of Michigan, USA

Forthcoming Titles

Theatre in the Expanded Field: Seven Approaches to Performance by Alan Read
Replay: Classic Modern Drama Reimagined by Toby Zinman
Rethinking Brecht: Theatre, Theory and Performance by David Barnett
Howard Barker's Theatre: Wrestling with Catastrophe edited by James Reynolds and Andrew Smith
Rethinking the Theatre of the Absurd: Ecology, the Environment and the Greening of the Modern Stage edited by Carl Lavery and Clare Finburgh
Ibsen in Practice: Relational Readings of Performance, Cultural Encounters and Power by Frode Helland

Postdramatic Theatre and the Political

International Perspectives on Contemporary Performance

Edited by
Karen Jürs-Munby, Jerome Carroll and
Steve Giles

Series Editors
Mark Taylor-Batty and Enoch Brater

BLOOMSBURY
LONDON • NEW DELHI • NEW YORK • SYDNEY

Bloomsbury Methuen Drama
An imprint of Bloomsbury Publishing Plc

50 Bedford Square
London
WC1B 3DP
UK

1385 Broadway
New York
NY 10018
USA

www.bloomsbury.com

Bloomsbury is a registered trademark of Bloomsbury Publishing Plc

First published 2013

British Library Cataloguing-in-Publication Data
A catalogue record for this book is available from the British Library.

ISBN: HB: 978-1-4081-8570-4
PB: 978-1-4081-8486-8
ePub: 978-1-4081-8516-2
ePDF: 978-1-4081-8588-9

Library of Congress Cataloging-in-Publication Data
Postdramatic theatre and the political : international perspectives on contemporary performance / Jerome Carroll, Steven Giles and Karen Jürs-Munby.
    pages cm. – (Methuen drama)
    Includes bibliographical references and index.
ISBN 978-1-4081-8486-8 – ISBN 978-1-4081-8570-4 – ISBN 978-1-4081-8516-2 – ISBN 978-1-4081-8588-9 1. Theater–Political aspects. 2. Political plays–History and criticism. 3. Performing arts–Political aspects. I. Carroll, Jerome, 1972- editor of compilation. II. Giles, Steven, (Professor) editor of compilation. III. Jürs-Munby, Karen, editor of compilation.
    PN1643.P67 2013
    792–dc23
    2013020298

Typeset by Newgen Knowledge Works (P) Ltd., Chennai, India
Printed and bound in India

Contents

List of Figures vii

Introduction: Postdramatic Theatre and the Political 1
Jerome Carroll, Karen Jürs-Munby and Steve Giles

1 Towards a Paradoxically Parallaxical Postdramatic Politics? 31
 Brandon Woolf

2 Performing Dialectics in an Age of Uncertainty, or:
 Why Post-Brechtian ≠ Postdramatic 47
 David Barnett

3 Political Fictions and Fictionalisations: History as
 Material for Postdramatic Theatre 67
 Mateusz Borowski and Małgorzata Sugiera

4 A Future for Tragedy? Remarks on the Political and the
 Postdramatic 87
 Hans-Thies Lehmann

5 Spectres of Subjectivity: On the Fetish of Identity in
 (Post-)Postdramatic Choreography 111
 Peter M. Boenisch

6 Christoph Schlingensief's *Rocky Dutschke, '68*:
 A Reassessment of Activism in Theatre 129
 Antje Dietze

7 Postdramatic Reality Theatre and Productive Insecurity:
 Destabilising Encounters with the Unfamiliar in Theatre
 from Sydney and Berlin 147
 Ulrike Garde and Meg Mumford

8 Postdramatic Labour in The Builders Association's *Alladeen* 165
 Shannon Jackson

9 Acting, Disabled: Back to Back Theatre and the Politics of
 Appearance 189
 Theron Schmidt

10 Parasitic Politics: Elfriede Jelinek's 'Secondary Dramas'
     Abraumhalde and *FaustIn and out*   209
     Karen Jürs-Munby

11 Phenomenology and the Postdramatic: A Case Study of
     Three Plays by Ewald Palmetshofer   233
     Jerome Carroll

12 Performing the Collective. Heiner Müller's 'Alone with
     These Bodies' ('Allein mit diesen Leibern') as a Piece for
     Postdramatic Theatre   255
     Michael Wood

Notes   273
Notes on Contributors   309
Index   313

List of Figures

2.1   Brecht's *Herr Puntila und sein Knecht Matti*, directed by
       Michael Thalheimer   60
9.1   Nicki Holland and Rita Halabarec in *Food Court*   198
9.2   Nicki Holland, Sarah Mainwaring and Rita Halabarec   201
10.1   Gotthold Ephraim Lessing's *Nathan der Weise* with
       Elfriede Jelinek's *Abraumhalde*, directed by
       Nicolas Stemann   223
10.2   *Faust 1–3* with Elfriede Jelinek's *FaustIn and Out*,
       directed by Dušan David Pařízek   229

Introduction

Postdramatic Theatre and the Political

Jerome Carroll, Karen Jürs-Munby and Steve Giles

This volume of essays emerged from an international conference on 'Postdramatic Theatre as/or Political Theatre: Representation, Mediatisation and Advanced Capitalism', held at the Institute of Germanic and Romance Studies in London in September 2011. The term 'postdramatic theatre', systematically introduced by Hans-Thies Lehmann since the 1990s, has by now gained international currency. Since the original publication of *Postdramatisches Theater* in 1999 the book has been translated into twenty languages. Lehmann had deployed the term as an alternative to the then ubiquitous term 'postmodern theatre' in order to describe how a vast variety of contemporary forms of theatre and performance had departed not so much from the 'modern' as from 'drama', that is they no longer conformed to the idea of mimetically enacting a dramatic conflict in the form of a story (fable) and dialogue spoken by characters in a fictional universe. The London conference set out to explore how postdramatic theatre – in terms of both Hans-Thies Lehmann's theoretical approach and the diverse contemporary theatre and performance practices that are subsumed under this term – could be considered political, given that its modes of political engagement are significantly different to what has previously been considered 'political theatre'. Questions surrounding postdramatic theatre's relationship to traditional twentieth-century 'political theatre', to politics or 'the political' were – and still are – certainly on the agenda, both for theatre practitioners and academics. Thus, a symposium held at the end of 2008 at the Künstlerhaus Mousonturm in Frankfurt am Main explored how the German independent theatre scene (*freie Theaterszene*), whose emergence had been inseparably connected to the political movements of the 1960s, had developed new forms of engagement with the political in theatre, performance and dance since then. Similarly at a conference on 'Dramatic and Postdramatic Theater: Ten Years After' held in Belgrade, Serbia in 2009 the discussion repeatedly turned to the ways in which postdramatic theatre was still or was no longer political. In his own contribution at this Belgrade conference, Lehmann observed that in the ten years since the original publication of his book in 1999 there had been an impulse, at least in German theatre, to 're-open the dialogue between theatre and society by taking up more directly political and social issues'.[1] He stated that

> [T]he motives for a certain re-entry of the political and social dimension since then are rather obvious: Nine-Eleven 2001, new wars, the rise of rightist populist leaders in Europe, the whole ideological and political field after the 'Wende' [the 'turning point' marked by the fall of the Berlin Wall], and last, but not least new social problems of different kinds. Theatre definitely felt and feels a need to deal more directly with political issues, even if there are no solutions or perspectives to offer.[2]

Arguably, even in the short time since this assessment there have been further urgent motives for politically motivated theatre: the almost global recession in the wake of the collapse of the US debt market in 2008, leading to increasing unemployment, the Eurozone crisis and the threat of bankruptcy to national governments in the West, as well as a widening gap between the rich and the poor; the worsening global climate crisis and food crisis; the 'Arab Spring' and the brutal attempts at its repression by Arab regimes, to name but a few. Yet, in Belgrade and elsewhere Lehmann also reiterated that '[u]nderstandable as the desire to "thematize" social and political issues may be, we must not forget that the truly social dimension of art is the *form*, as the young Georg Lukács observed.[3] He asserted that 'postdramatic strategies continue to be seen by many theatre practitioners as more suited to dealing with social issues (unemployment, violence, social isolation, terrorism, issues of race and gender) than the traditional model of socially engaged drama.'[4] So the question continues to be: what are these new forms and strategies of postdramatic theatre and how can they be considered political?

Certainly the case studies that make up the core of the chapters in this book leave barely any aspect of conventional dramatic theatre unchallenged. In several the dedicated theatre building has long since been abandoned, with the action taking place for instance as a staged demonstration on the streets in front of the theatre, or in a Berlin hotel, or in a lecture hall, or in the site-specific location of a Gdansk shipyard, highly charged with national-cultural memory. Likewise, character is largely dispensed with, the stage (where it is still employed) peopled by vestigial figures, 'text bearers', characters without coherent psychological 'interiority', or characters who – for instance through being surrounded by a chorus – have multiple or collective identities. We will also encounter 'real' people, who bring aspects of their real-world identity into the theatre, unadorned with fiction or character: disabled performers, as well as untrained actors who stand as witnesses and whose testimony evades and challenges 'imposed, official history'. 'Experts of the everyday' (Rimini Protokoll) are put on the stage, a term which includes both recognised 'experts' such as air traffic controllers and individuals 'lower down' the socio-economic scale, such as call centre staff and migrant workers. Sometimes character makes way for a focus on the body, in what might be taken as a revalorisation of the 'material' components of theatre, or of 'appearance' divorced in some way from 'meaning'. Causal or 'generative' action[5] is also often dispensed with: in some works there is no play at all, but what we have is always still 'theatre'. All of these ways in which the usual building blocks of theatre are dismantled also involve a thoroughgoing reconfiguration of the relationship between stage and audience, predominantly in ways that aim at generating audience participation or involvement. This participation can happen indirectly, for instance by being confronted with thoroughgoing indeterminacy of meaning of what happens or what is said on stage, or directly, when for instance the audience members are given the task of reading out sections of text. These are the kinds of approaches to theatre that have been called 'postdramatic', as Hans-Thies Lehmann puts it:

> When it is obviously no longer simply a matter of broken dramatic illusion or epicising distance; when obviously neither plots, nor plastically shaped dramatis personae are needed; when neither dramatic dialectical collision of values, nor even identifiable figures are necessary to produce 'theatre' [. . .] then the concept of drama – however differentiated, all-embracing and watered down it may become – retains so little substance that it loses its cognitive value.[6]

As this quotation makes clear, rather than simply dispensing with one or more of the components of stage, character and action/plot, postdramatic theatre thereby also absolves itself of the traditional (at least during the eighteenth and nineteenth centuries, although key aspects go back to Aristotle) requirement or expectation that the stage should generate what Elinor Fuchs calls 'a fictional world that aligns all dramaturgical elements into a synthetic whole'.[7] And indeed the guiding thread in this discussion of the concepts surrounding the practice of postdramatic theatre is that, at a certain level, issues to do with postdramatic theatre and performance might usefully be cast in terms of the concern among directors and practitioners to break out of the straightjacket of *re-presentation*, which is to say, of the obligation to reproduce an already written story, even a series of historical events, and beyond that a 'fictive cosmos' that is governed by pre-ordained conventions – perhaps even 'laws' – of psychological motivation, causal connection, and coherent conceptual meaning more generally. This obligation of representation may be seen to relegate the phenomena of theatre to an always 'secondary' status, rendering them 'only ever [. . .] less real and less significant than the event itself', as Joe Kelleher puts it.[8] The apotheosis of this mode of representation is to see the stage as the site for the more or less faithful reproduction of the authoritative dramatic text. By contrast, one way of looking at theatrical practice that we can call 'postdramatic' is that it seeks to secure for itself something 'primal' or 'direct' in the generation of meaning. The kinds of authenticity claim that are made – whether implicitly or explicitly – for onstage activity are of course varied. So-called verbatim theatre takes seemingly direct recourse to historical reality by using authentic historical documents or accounts, as it were *short-circuiting* the representative relationship. The aforementioned use of 'experts of the everyday' in productions is in a similar vein. In other cases practitioners put the emphasis on generating an *event* or *situation* whose uniqueness and validity do not derive from a re-presentation of reality but rather from what Lehmann refers to as 'the situation, the relation, the social moment which theatre as such is able to constitute.'[9] In his chapter in this book, Lehmann reconceptualises the tragic in these terms, as a transgression of cultural norms, a 'destabilising of the basic grounds of our cultural existence' (Lehmann), a moment in which the audience is shocked out of habits of thinking. He argues that this can only happen once standard patterns of representation have been abandoned – for instance, in the absence of a dramatic conception of theatre – in which the audience's response is no longer insulated by standard patterns of meaning or in aesthetic appreciation of the performance, no longer 'confined to an experience which remains in the framework of consuming an aesthetic reality', but is more 'real'. The fact that Lehmann elsewhere refers to postdramatic performance as allowing an 'irruption of the real' suggests a Lacanian dimension to his thinking, although when he conceptualises postdramatic theatre as 'more process than product, more manifestation than signification' he seems to be invoking the reality of the performance itself.[10] Delineating the conceptual issues that attend the postdramatic in these terms of 'representation' versus 'real' is inevitably crude and reductive, and in what follows we hope to move beyond this dichotomy, but it does serve a useful purpose, namely framing and setting some parameters for the discussions that follow, both in this Introduction and in the chapters that follow.

This issue of the 'reality-status' of a performance is often central to claims about the political value or force of theatre that eschews drama. In some respects this association of postdramatic performance with politics might appear counter-intuitive, insofar as postdramatic theatre has in recent years been taken to reject the modes of conventionally dramatic and even Brechtian 'political' theatre. These modes are seen as involving 'critical' plays with obvious political 'engagement',[11] which usually takes the form of dealing more or less discursively with 'important themes', articulated by characters with more or less coherent psychological interiority and varying degrees of effective agency, motivated by politically charged situations. So for instance, in her survey of the wave of 'realist' political theatre in Germany in the last two decades of the twentieth century, Birgit Haas lists issues such as the mass media, right-wing extremism and terrorism, as well as a focus on the impact of politics on the private sphere, which invoke a realism that she contrasts with   previous 'postmodern collages'.[12] Similar parameters are apparent in Jan Cohen-Cruz's sketch of US theatre in the last four decades of the century, with civil rights and anti-war protests in the 1960s giving way to 'identity-based political theatre' in the 1970s and documentary-based dialogues in the 1990s.[13] By contrast, contemporary modes of performance that eschew the conventions of 'dramatic' theatre – and in some cases go some way to abandoning discursive, conceptual meaning *in toto* – tend to approach political issues in a way that is fundamentally different. As Lehmann again puts it, 'it remains essential to acknowledge that the truly political dimension of theatre has its place not so much in the thematising of politically burning subject matters [. . .] as in the situation, the relation, the social mǫment which theatre as such is able to constitute.'[14] In this respect, the postdramatic mode overlaps with what has been called the 'social turn' in contemporary art.[15] Moreover, for some this trading of thematics for the 'social moment' ultimately makes a political point concerning the very nature of politics.

As such, the main characteristics of postdramatic performance that we have already registered point to the key claims about postdramatic theatre's distinct approach to 'the political', centring on the newly conceived relationship between performance and audience, which is directly linked to the aforementioned issue of the reality-status of the performance, and the new approach this takes to theatre's conventional representative function. Along these lines, it may be useful to distinguish between *social* and *semiotic* aspects of the political quality of postdramatic performance – as long as one does not lose sight of how intertwined these aspects are. The social dimension refers to the collective, and even democratic quality of the performance, in terms of both production and reception. At one level such claims are based on new collaborative working practices – or in Marxist economic terms: new conditions of production – among all those involved in a theatre project. As Jan Deck puts it, 'the classic division of labour in the production of plays is overcome.'[16] Brandon Woolf in his chapter in this book traces the politics of this reconfiguration of production back to Walter Benjamin's insistence that the political force of the work of art derives from the sense that it is no longer satisfied with the essentially bourgeois task of 'represent[ing] individual experiences', but rather must work towards the 'functional transformation' (*Umfunktionierung*) of the '*forms* and instruments of production'

(Woolf). And when now, to take The Builders Association's *Alladeen* as an example, the training of actual call centre workers is documented and mimicked in a postdramatic performance, this also serves to demystify a largely invisible industry and give cause for reflection on labour conditions in a globalised world, such as that of the 'immaterial labor' of the outsourced 'tech support' that serves as 'the new "base" supporting global citizenship', as Shannon Jackson argues in her chapter in this book. The performer's role is also expanded beyond that of simply being an actor who disappears behind a character. In his discussion Woolf points out Benjamin's debt to Bertolt Brecht, and the latter's *Lehrstück* is one of the key lineages for this transformation in the status of theatrical production: in its theoretical conception at least, the performers in the *Lehrstück* do not require an audience, but are spectators and students of their own action. This focus on production does not simply step away from the task of representation, as the Benjamin quotation above indicates, but also goes some way to unpick the seams of representation, by virtue of the sense in which production is 'both hidden from and necessary to the operations of illusion' (Jackson). In the *Emancipated Spectator* Jacques Rancière underlines the political point here with his characterisation of the spectator role as traditionally involving an assumption of, or at least feigning of, ignorance – 'viewing is the opposite of knowing' – and in particular an ignorance – or at least a feigning of ignorance – of the production process.[17] The point is that this focus on production also has implications for the audience, insofar as an important aspect of the political force of this transformation is the concern in many performances to make the new working conditions and processes *visible*, a concern that has its 'prehistory' in Brecht's concern to make the theatrical apparatus visible.

It should also be apparent here that an important aspect of these developments is a blurring of the boundary between production and *reception*. The new conditions of reception that are seen to be fostered by postdramatic performance, the aforementioned 'social turn', are equally important to its political force. In this respect postdramatic theatre capitalises on a relationship that is unique to performance, what Rancière calls 'bodies in action before an assembled audience',[18] or what Erika Fischer-Lichte calls the 'bodily co-presence of actors and spectators'.[19] The concern here is precisely to close the gap between production and reception, between actor and spectator, in as much as interpretation by an 'active' spectator is recognised as being integral to how the 'meaning' of any performance is generated. Implicit in the political investment here is the recourse to what Helen Freshwater has called 'one of the most cherished orthodoxies in theatre studies: the belief in a connection between audience participation and political empowerment'.[20]

It is these changes in conditions and understandings of production and reception that Jan Deck – presumably conscious of the debt to Heiner Müller[21] – refers to as 'making theatre in a political way', as distinct from the more conventional activity of 'making political theatre'.[22] This focus on 'making' theatre taps into what is arguably the other unique quality of performance when compared with any other art form: its status as an *activity*. In the postdramatic mode the crucial factor that characterises this activity is its indeterminate nature, which is to say the way in which fundamental aspects of it are not *pre-ordained*. In some cases this indeterminacy is apparent in a relinquishing of control on the part of the artist or director over what actually happens in the performance event. In this book, for instance, Lehmann relates the experience of participating in Egyptian artist Laila Soliman's 'No time for art', in which audience members are invited to take turns reading out letters addressed to the International Court of Human Rights regarding particular real-world human rights violations. Whether they choose to do so or not is of course no longer in the hands of the artist or the director. In other cases this indeterminacy happens at the level of the text, at the level of words and meaning, for instance where textual indeterminacy destabilises any straightforward relations of signification. This unpicking of expectations about meaning can also happen at the level of genre norms, and it is in this vein that Michael Wood in this book reads Heiner Müller's poem, *Alone with These Bodies*, as a piece for postdramatic theatre. Both cases would seem to be instances that prioritise what Kelleher refers to as the inherent 'instability and unpredictability' of the theatrical event.[23] Rancière is getting at the same point when he calls for performance to overcome 'identity of cause and effect, which is at the heart of stultifying logic.'[24] Not least significant in this process is the fact that the text is relegated from its position as authoritative source to that of 'material.'[25] Moreover, this indeterminacy is central to the specific political investment in the new 'situation' of theatre – what Lehmann calls an 'uncommon situation'[26] – the value of which is variously ascribed to its social quality, to the fact that it is in some sense separate from external reality, as well as its status as a practical 'forum' for experiment, or as a 'temporary space for public discourse.'[27]

This final reference to discourse reminds us that the political claims about this social space turn primarily on questions of *meaning* and the production of meaning, the 'semiotic' aspect indicated above. This 'politics' of meaning is addressed in various ways in theoretical reflections on performance, probably most commonly in the aforementioned terms of the resistance performance offers to the order of representation, where, as Kelleher puts it, politics is 'figured as a continuing process that eludes representation.'[28] Of course, this poses the question what is meant by 'representation'. We have referred to the notion that this representative function relegates the phenomena of the stage to a secondary status, where the stage itself is reduced to a (mere) conduit or mouthpiece for ideas and states of affairs that originate elsewhere. A further aspect of this concept of representation is its shorthand for a certain hegemonic conceptuality, a more or less rigid ordering of material: Rancière's 'stultifying logic'. We have already encountered the usual terms of this kind of ordering in the theatrical situation: action, character, thematic meaning. In response to this, performance has been valued for its capacity to resist or unsettle these frameworks of meaning, generating what Lehmann calls a 'conjunction of the heterogeneous',[29] a theatre that ensures it 'is in no way translatable or re-translatable into the logic, syntax, and terminology of political discourse in social reality'.[30] Both of these quotations appear in Brandon Woolf's chapter in this book, which discusses Lehmann's ideas in the context of Theodor Adorno and others' conceptualisations of aesthetic autonomy.

This reference to aesthetic autonomy also suggests the common ground with certain strands of European modernism, one aspect of which, as Joseph Wood Krutch has argued, implies a rejection of rationality assumptions that had been dominant in Western culture since the Renaissance.[31] Others have drawn attention to this anti-rationalist aspect in the postdramatic. Jenny Spencer characterises it as a turn against 'fact-based' theatre's assumption 'that the audience's opinions, actions, and political views are rationally driven'.[32] Jan Deck makes the same point when he insists that the goal in such a performance is not comprehensibility: 'One might grasp much from the complexity of a performance, but complete understanding is not required.'[33] This kind of loosening of onstage phenomena from conceptual, referential, representational logics is what is being denoted in the preference for 'presentation' over 'representation' (see David Barnett in this book). Sometimes this anti-conceptuality is expressed in terms of generating a renewed experience of the sensory, in some way liberated from the strictures of conceptual, determinate meaning or messages. Lehmann in this vein, citing Jean-François Lyotard, refers to 'energetic theatre', which 'would not be a theatre of meaning but of "forces, intensities, present affects"'. He cites the example of Einar Schleef's 'chanting and moving choruses', whose import we would not grasp by 'searching exclusively for signs and "representation"'. As such, energetic theatre is taken to be 'theatre beyond representation, [. . .], not governed by its logic'.[34] Deck likewise characterises performance as responding to the conception of 'politics as a production of meaning' (*Sinnproduktion*) by 'producing the sensory' (*Produktion des Sinnlichen*).[35]

These kinds of claims about collectivity, non-conceptuality, and the reality-status of performance are not unprecedented. We have already noted the continuity with Adorno's conceptualisation of aesthetic autonomy, which is to say that the value of the aesthetic derives from the resistance it offers to conceptuality, and instrumental thinking more generally. Nor are they without specific epistemological assumptions, grounded in a conceptual scheme of some sort. Arguments for the revalidation of collective and sensory experience often rely on the critique of representation within post-structuralist philosophy, whereby their reality-status derives from the fact that sensory experience breaks out of *received* patterns of representation that otherwise distort or repress it. The obvious precursor here is Antonin Artaud, whose proposed 'theatre of cruelty' was intended to disrupt the audience's unconscious and pulverise their sensibilities by developing a new theatrical language beyond the written word – concrete, physical, incantatory, ecstatic. Artaud's critique of Western culture, in turn, is grounded in Nietzschean vitalism, a point that reiterates the common ground between the postdramatic mode and certain strands of European modernism, whose political and aesthetic force derived in large part from its destabilising of norms of language and representation. In terms of modernist theatre, the primary norm of theatrical representation since the late eighteenth century is mimetic illusionism, and one might trace its undermining – along with the picture-frame stage that mediates it architecturally – from the moment when the ringmaster in Frank Wedekind's *Erdgeist* fires his pistol into the auditorium, thereby shattering the theatrical equivalent of

Émile Zola's transparent realist screen, via August Strindberg's dream plays, German Expressionism and Luigi Pirandello's *Six Characters in Search an Author*, to the early epic theatre of Erwin Piscator and Brecht. Central to these transformations is the focus on audience receptivity, which had been fostered by formal innovations in theatrical presentation since nineteenth-century realism and naturalism, gaining a different critical momentum in the course of the twentieth century with epic theatre's techniques of montage and interruption, the central aim of which is to re-activate the audience. Even some of the more radical arrangements and techniques that are seen to foster this active spectatorship in recent postdramatic theatre have their precursors, for example, taking the spectator out of the comfort of the theatre, which might be traced back to experimental performances like Vsevolod Meyerhold's *Storming of the Winter Palace* (1920) or the 'indigestible' 'happenings' and *Aktionen* of the Dadaists.[36] This is a debt that Lehmann indicates in *Postdramatic Theatre*, where he registers that 'Dada, Futurism and Surrealism demand an intellectual, mental/nervous and also physical attack on the spectator.'[37] This brief sketch is enough to indicate that the contemporary trend of postdramatic theatre and performance needs to be set in the context of a development beginning at the end of the nineteenth century that sees drama as traditionally defined as in a state of crisis. In its most radical form, it asserts that drama is in crisis because it is no longer dramatic – so that the much disputed 'modernity' of modern drama can itself be construed as the determinate negation of drama. This prehistory of the postdramatic is underlined by a prophetic statement by Krutch, writing in 1953:

> What would be the effect upon the drama if the theories and the procedure of both Chekhov and Pirandello were universally adopted by playwrights and carried to their logical conclusions? [. . .] Offhand I cannot think of any analyst who has maintained

that you could have a play without either action on the one hand or the revelation of character on the other. Yet Chekhov gets rid of action and Pirandello gets rid of character. One is tempted to suggest somewhat light-mindedly that whatever else we may or may not be able to predict about the future which lies across the chasm one thing seems fairly certain: There will not be any plays in it.[38]

All of this raises the question of what is specifically new – aesthetically and politically – in postdramatic theatre. Does it really constitute a fundamentally new direction in twentieth-century avant-garde theatre, or is it simply the latest manifestation of a century-long trend? If the latter, is it no more than a belated realisation of the theoretical precepts developed by Artaud in his writings on theatre of cruelty, especially as mediated by Jacques Derrida? Certainly Artaud's account of theatre of cruelty anticipates virtually all the characteristics of postdramatic theatre identified by Lehmann in *Postdramatic Theatre*, such as the shift away from adherence to the dramatic text, from individual psychology, and from the referential connection to external reality through mimesis.

At the same time this Nietzsche-inspired association of theatre with some unmediated or at least anti-conceptual 'reality' also needs to take account of the recurrent insistence, made in the context of discussions of postdramatic performance, that theatre is always in some decisive sense *not real*. Lehmann for instance is adamant that what happens in theatre is not 'real' politics. Sometimes comments of this kind simply state the inevitably 'secondary' nature of the theatrical phenomenon, as registered by Kelleher, who also points out that the very fact that the theatrical performance is 'put together in a particular way' makes it distinct from theatre-external reality, 'even if the "same thing" happens in both'.[39] This difference is of course a truism, but it is of interest here because this quality of performance as distinct from everyday reality is seen by some to be crucial to its capacity for social or political critique. Sometimes this quality is couched in the same 'anti-rational' or 'anti-conceptual' terms that we have noted above. Lehmann for instance insists on theatre's status as 'aesthetic' and theatrical, as something that is not reducible to or measurable according to the norms and standards of discursive meaning. But conversely some commentators draw attention to a specifically *cognitive* component to this difference, for instance insofar as a play 'invit[es] us to pay attention to a peculiar type of appearance'.[40] This idea of 'pay[ing] attention' suggests a more complex response, involving some role for our conceptual, cognitive faculties, raising the question of how this might compare to Brecht's idea of theatre as an exercise in 'complex seeing'.[41] What is evident is that many commentators perceive a connection between performance's status as 'not real' and its latitude for critical distance, or in the parlance of aesthetics, its autonomy, however this is exactly characterised. In Lehmann's view it is this distance from reality, but within a situation that is somehow real, that allows for a postdramatic 'politics of perception'.[42]

Some, however, see this issue of the reality-status of the stage as *divorcing* the stage decisively from external reality. Emblematic of this is the concern expressed in some quarters that the 'dialectical' generation of meaning between stage and audience (see Woolf in this book) displaces another dialectic from the stage, namely the historical dialectic of the individual and society (see David Barnett in this book). In these terms, the emphasis on 'perception', 'appearance', and seemingly immediate 'sensory' experience that is associated with postdramatic performance might be characterised as a kind of *formal* or *reflexive* turn, inasmuch as they relate to the connection between the 'components' of theatrical presentation and the reconfigured relationship with the audience, or the turn against representation, sometimes seemingly at the expense of (thematic) reference to phenomena in the 'external' world. This is in keeping with Lehmann's conviction, referred to above, that 'the truly social dimension of art is the *form*'. In most cases it is not so much an either/ or choice between formal innovation and thematic statement, but a question of the degree to which formal and linguistic innovation still accommodates more or less determinate reference to 'external' social, economic or political factors. In this vein Barnett's chapter contrasts Einar Schleef's (post-Brechtian) production of Brecht's *Herr Puntila und sein Knecht Matti* with Michael Thalheimer's (postdramatic) production. Certainly in terms of its referential technique Schleef's version moves from 'denoting' to looser 'connoting', but it still imparts the idea that Puntila is a product of society, that 'somehow, somewhere, everything's connected to class consciousness and the class struggle' (Barnett). In Thalheimer's 'postdramatic' production this semiotic openness is taken further, with even less concern to generate a fictive cosmos. Figures and onstage activity are largely 'atmospheric', with states or situations preferred to causal connections. In particular, Thalheimer's Puntila is largely divorced from history and politics. Another sceptical voice in the volume, that of Mateusz Borowski and Małgorzata Sugiera, insists that even the meaning of an individual performance must derive in part from individual history. They ask whether Lehmann's essentially 'synchronic panorama' of postdramatic theatre can make room for this contextual role of (external) history.

So what is the nature of the connection that postdramatic theatre makes with the world outside the theatre, and what is the 'political' aspect of this connection? In the case of conventionally dramatic, 'thematic' theatre, as noted above, the relationship is obvious: basically a mimetically referential one whereby what is enacted and said on stage refers to – and *defers* to – social and political realities outside the theatre. Conversely, the political force of postdramatic theatre has been conceived – at least in its theorisation by Lehmann, and others following him – as precisely deriving from the ways in which it takes issue with this thematic and content-based approach to political meaning. There are several aspects to this. In part such performance is read as a critique of the circular nature of conventional 'political' theatre, which – it is suggested – reaches only a self-selecting minority and preaches to the converted in any case. At the same time there is a sense that any seemingly assured portrayal of political realities or representation of action is problematic, for a number of reasons. The first concerns the nature of our experience of reality: such an assured approach is seen to rest on an ideological basis the coherence of which does not do justice to the complex nature of contemporary reality: 'The representational form "drama" is available but grasps at nothing when it is meant to articulate experienced reality.'[43] What Lehmann seems to be stating is that we do not do justice to that 'experience' by trying to make it *comprehensible*: 'The theatre of sense [or meaning, *Sinn*] and synthesis has largely disappeared – and with it the possibility of synthesizing interpretation.'[44] There is a clear parallel here with Brecht's well-known scepticism, expressed in the *Dreigroschenprozeß*, about our ability to coherently make sense of complex interrelations of advanced capitalism via the techniques of conventionally 'mimetic' representation.[45] The difference is that Brecht thinks that these difficulties do not absolve art of the challenge to make these interconnections more comprehensible than they are in our immediate everyday experience, which he thinks epic theatre can achieve by adopting more complex representational strategies. Thus he proposes an aesthetic founded in an abstract realism which, via techniques of interruption and estrangement, encourages the spectator to attain cognitive understanding of late modernity.[46] Fundamental to this cognitive understanding is the sense that, for Brecht, such interruption and complication takes place in the context of a *Fabel* – the crucial aspect of which is a causal link between the action and socio-economic factors. Perhaps overlooking the ways in which Brecht's approach takes issues with traditional models of self and action, however, Lehmann aligns Brecht with a dramatic approach that he thinks is outmoded, in an era in which economic developments such as globalisation entail that 'the historical preconditions of the dramatic mode are disappearing in a more fundamental way'.[47] This is no longer primarily about our experience, or about discourse, but about the fundamentals of reality in advanced capitalism. He gives no specific examples in that essay, although presumably the key issue here is political and/or economic agency: the extent to which we can or cannot comprehend and *intervene in* the social, political and economic order. In these terms representing reality in terms of traditionally dramatic personalised protagonists and antagonists is clearly anachronistic. Moreover, Lehmann thinks that the basis of any such cognitive, discursive understanding needs to be undermined, in part as a response to what he sees as the denuding of political discourse, which has become 'clichéd' and even 'deceptive'.[48] This brings us to the third reason for Lehmann's rejection of a thematic approach, namely that he sees political discourse itself as corrupted, as part of the problem. This corrupting of discourse and the erosion of the public sphere occurs in its co-optation or 'privatisation' by vested interests, but is seen most palpably in the mediation of social and political discourse by organs of the mass media, whose significance for both Lehmann and Rancière's understanding of the value of postdramatic theatre would be hard to overstate. Both refer in this regard to Guy Debord's concept of the spectacle, whose crucial quality is the separation of production and reception: 'What in fact is the essence of the spectacle for Guy Debord? It is exteriority. The spectacle is the reign of vision, and vision is exteriority – that is, self-dispossession.'[49] Rancière adds that this spectatorial attitude characterises our basic subject position in mass media society: 'Being a spectator is not some passive condition that we should transform into activity. It is our normal situation.'[50] Lehmann refers to the status of the spectator in similar terms: 'If we remain spectators/viewers, if we stay where we are – in front of the television – the catastrophe will always stay outside, will always be objects for a subject – this is the implicit promise of the medium.'[51]

Theatre's position here is ambivalent. On the one hand, Rancière sees the conventional hierarchies of the theatre, as well as its traditional thematic-discursive mode of representation, as ultimately complicit in this separation. This is expressed in his characterisation of the traditional theatre audience's ignorance and passivity. The traditional 'sender-message-receiver' model of theatrical communication[52] involves a hierarchy whereby knowledgeable playwrights 'explain to their [ignorant] audience the truth of social relations and ways of struggling against capitalist domination.'[53] As we have registered, for Rancière this mutual exclusion of seeing and knowing rests in large part on the mechanism of illusion at the heart of drama, which insists on an assumption of ignorance of the production process.[54] At the very least, the spectatorial hierarchy insists that 'what the spectator *must see* is what the director *makes her see*.'[55] And this spectatorial position is seen not just to exclude the audience member from knowing, but from acting as well: 'What human beings contemplate in the spectacle is the activity they have been robbed of.'[56] On the contrary, theatre is seen to have the capacity to overturn this ignorance and passivity, and the separation of which they are the symptoms, and it is seen to do so by virtue of the ways in which it is able to precipitate an 'activity' that is collective, and that is not 'pre-ordained', as discussed above. It is in this vein that Rancière refers to theatre as 'an exemplary community forum', and an event paradoxically 'without theatrical mediation', 'without spectators.'[57] As Peter Boenisch has recently characterised it, '[t]rue emancipation of the spectator for [Rancière] necessitates shaking up the underlying spectating relations and their implicit hierarchies.'[58] Lehmann likewise thinks theatre responds inadequately to the dilemma of the spectacle if, by virtue of its strategies of representation – for instance, treating the stage as thematic mouthpiece of the author or as a faithful mirror of external reality – it perpetuates the spectatorial hierarchy. He sees theatre, and postdramatic theatre in particular, as offering a more democratic 'situation', in which the production of meaning is shared:

> Instead of the deceptively comforting duality of here and there, inside and outside, it can move the *mutual implication of actors and spectators in the theatrical production of images* into the centre and thus make visible the broken thread between personal experience and perception. Such an experience would be not only aesthetic but therein at the same time ethico-political.[59]

This claim of 'mutual implication' is not just a reference to the 'social' situation in the theatre, namely that the audience situation places beings in a room together, but also its 'semiotic' aspect: Lehmann characterises theatre's response as operating 'at the level of sign usage itself'.[60] But the question remains what implications this focus on signs, perception and the emphasis on intra-theatrical collectivity have for the question of theatre's connection to realities outside the theatre. Are we dealing with two distinct – and possibly incompatible – concerns or motivations here? First, that the performance event should in some way adequately reflect or reflect on decisive aspects of contemporary existence: this concerns referentiality, or the stage-reality connection. Secondly, that the onstage activity should allow for some input on the part of the audience, presumably depending on some degree of semiotic freedom or interpretive indeterminacy: this relates to the audience-stage connection. It may be that these two aspects of performance are, to paraphrase Adorno, two halves of a shattered whole that do not add up: doing justice to one may inevitably preclude doing justice to the other. This much is implicit in the concern expressed by some (see Barnett) that there is a decisive gap between the kind of collective 'reality' that postdramatic theatrical situation seeks to generate, and external 'reality' – or to put it more prosaically, the decisive forces that govern our experience – which are located elsewhere, beyond the stage. In other words, does the focus on signs and perception set us in some way apart from decisive elements in material reality – for instance economic and political relations and inequalities? Conversely, the political force of some performances may be better understood in the light of the shift in awareness heralded variously as the 'linguistic', 'semiotic' or 'hermeneutic' turns in the course of the twentieth century, which point to the mediation of reality by language, meaning and interpreation. Pertinent here is Ernesto Laclau and Chantal Mouffe's objection to Louis Althusser's still Marxist conviction that reality is determined 'in the last instance by the economy'.[61] In her chapter in this book, Shannon Jackson insists on the need to take such post-Marxist revisions seriously, in a way that 'qualifies and complicates the weight that any critic might give to either material or immaterial registers' (Jackson). So in what sense do the formalist, anti-conceptualist orientations or the turn against representation that we have associated with postdramatic performance operate with a definitively different sense of what the basis of any political analysis is?

Perhaps the first point to make here is that those instances of theatre that might be classified as postdramatic constitute a broad field, ranging from Robert Wilson's dreamlike use of sound, light, space, time and movement to Rimini Protokoll's interactive call centre play, *Call Cutta in a Box* (premiere 2008). While perceptual, semiotic and representational experimentation plays a dominant role in the former, the latter more clearly engages with traditionally 'political' themes: globalisation and economic inequality. Moreover, the corollary of the post-Marxist focus on 'immaterial registers' associated with Laclau and Mouffe above is that the 'collective' or 'democratic' aspect that Lehmann and others see as theatre's response to the hierarchies and exclusions generated by the mass media is not characterised in terms of simple accessibility, but rather in the – in some ways opposite – terms of a *disruption* of the governing discursive norms. For both Rancière and Lehmann theatre's genuine democratic force is felt not in the harmonious assembly of consent but through practices that make room for disruption or dissent (*dissensus*), suggesting that the political value of performance is not found in an uncritical 'collectivity'. This is not least because Lehmann views this kind of guerrilla intervention as theatre's best hope of influence on our grasp of reality, in the face of the 'massive superiority of the structures [of the mass media]'.[62]

We might reiterate that this disruption occurs 'at the level of sign usage', but the reference to Laclau and Mouffe above should indicate that this is not to be taken to minimise its significance. The aforementioned 'semiotic' and other turns have brought the understanding that our experience of 'reality', whether that be the reality of actions and words that are made and uttered on the stage or those in everyday reality, is up to a certain point mediated by predispositions, attitudes and values in the form of language and discourse. This is at odds with the (Nietzsche- or Artaud-inspired) concern to break through received patterns of representation to something concrete or authentic. At a certain level, transgressing cultural norms, even where this is taken to 'destabilis[e] the grounds of our cultural existence' (Lehmann), happens within the realm of representation. As Woolf puts it in his chapter: 'any move beyond the representational entails a deep engagement with representation itself'. We might infer, moreover, that the underlying sense of a 'fictive cosmos', generated for instance through character (psychological interiority) and action (agency), is not the only way that the stage connects with 'external' reality. Rather, these links are also made through continuities of language and discourse, and through them (sometimes unconscious) socially grounded norms and values to do with selfhood, equality, justice, and so on. That is to say, a whole range of expectations and predispositions are brought into the performance space, not left at the cloakroom with our umbrellas. At a very basic level this persistence of norms and attitudes makes a nonsense of any clear separation between intra-theatrical and extra-theatrical experience, of real and representation. Woolf cites Lehmann in this regard: 'Theatre is a practice [. . .], which like no other forces us to realise "that there is no firm boundary between the aesthetic and the extra-aesthetic realm."'[63] And it is also the pervasive force of such norms of discourse that is crucial to some of the political claims made for postdramatic theatre, because it is precisely the assumptions and governing norms that *we* bring into the theatre, both about representational conventions of theatre and about wider cultural attitudes, that 'genuinely' political theatre is reckoned to disrupt.

Moreover, while the characterisation of postdramatic theatre as collective and democratic reaches its apotheosis in claims that this semiotic dismantling is essentially 'utopian',[64] it is worth noting that 'utopian' here need not denote a paradoxically unobtainable alternative reality, for instance the fleetingly 'collective' theatre situation. Rather it might refer to the way that norms of discourse and representation are disrupted, opening up a space for alternative realities to come into view, for the (also perhaps fleeting) emergence of new political subject matter or voices that have no representation yet. As Lehmann asserts, with reference to Derrida:

> Theatre that breaks through its aesthetic limitations by following its political responsibility to let in other voices that do not get heard and that have no representation within the political order, and in this way open the site of theatre for the political exterior/outside.[65]

Peter Boenisch also usefully registers that while such norms are necessarily social, their interrogation and disruption in performance inevitably also depends on the moment of *individual* sense-making.[66] This understanding that the theatrical experience also operates at an individual level, combined with the fact that our own (albeit socially and culturally informed) attitudes and beliefs are brought into the performance, gives us the wherewithal to conceptualise spectating as an act of *self-implication*. This aspect of audience activity is common to several of the chapters that follow, where the discussion turns on the ways in which our own attitudes are played out in performance: attitudes to disability in Theron Schmidt's discussion of *Food Court* by Back to Back Theatre, and attitudes to immigrants, asylum seekers and service workers in Meg Mumford and Ulrike Garde's chapter. In his chapter, Lehmann insists that this audience involvement is not to be taken as simple 'participation', which in an era of game and reality shows has lost its critical potential. Rather, the performance event gains its political force largely by virtue of its capacity to generate a 'situation' that precipitates a 'concrete questioning of the self' (Lehmann). Importantly, as far as the issue of representation is concerned, this self-questioning 'dismisses the scheme of separating reception and presentation' (Lehmann). Moreover, this idea of self-implication – and the combination of contribution, interruption and reflection it involves – may suggest a way of conceptualising how we might come away from a performance with better insights than – or at least a different perspective on – the norms and attitudes we go in with, without subscribing to any simple thesis of ignorant audience and knowledgeable writer/director, of the kind that Rancière militates against.

This sense that theatre engages with and disrupts attitudes and expectations also suggests a more subtle interplay than may be accommodated by a binary account that opposes the representative/thematic/conceptual to the corporeal/bodily/sensory/'real'. This is a point that is central to Jerome Carroll's reading of three plays by Ewald Palmetshofer, in which he takes issue with aspects of Lehmann's theoretical position where the political force of theatre depends on a clear demarcation between the theatre and external reality, subjective experience and historical reality, social and political norms and their disruption in art. In their place Carroll argues that a phenomenological approach to theatre as a 'discipline of the imagination' avoids such dichotomous views and marries 'external' political norms and the theatrical event in more subtle ways. This way of engaging with attitudes is also apparent in what Elinor Fuchs has called the 'layered [. . .] cosmos of the imagination'. Referring to Elevator Repair Service's *Gatz*, Fuchs does not see the performance as presenting 'a shattered fictive cosmos' but rather 'a layered one'. In her view this layering is typical of what persists in recent ostensibly postdramatic performance, in the form of the 'story', or the 'affective life'.[67] Whether or not one agrees with Fuchs that such layering amounts to a coherent fictive cosmos, this concept of layering seems to be a useful one for analysing what is going on in some postdramatic performances. It is one mechanism that precisely enables reflection on norms, attitudes, assumptions and ideologies.

In the chapters in this book there are several examples of a persistence of coherent normative, conceptual or imaginative frameworks, and their layering for critical effect. Antje Dietze analyses Christoph Schlingensief's re-enactment of the activist practices of the 1960s left-winger Rudi Dutschke as offering the spectators the chance to actively participate in a communal experience – outside the theatre, and outside the norms of dramatic representation – as well as deliberately confounding easy political messages. One of the defining features of the performance, according to Dietze, is the 'strategic ambiguity' whereby the performers provide 'neither a clear rejection nor a simple affirmation of their activist role models'. Rather the performance opens up a space of ambiguity in which the audience must themselves critically reassess the inheritance of the activism of 1968, for instance the movement's failure to achieve most of the activists' main goals, such as radically changing the existing political system, and also the ongoing potential of such activism. Karen Jürs-Munby sees the staging of Elfriede Jelinek's 'secondary dramas', texts which are designed to be performed alongside classical canonical dramas such as Goethe's *Faust* or Lessing's *Nathan der Weise*, as having the potential to disrupt political consensus, such as the unquestioned belief in (male) human progress or in religious tolerance. Jelinek's strategy, she argues, can be seen as a form of deliberately 'parasitic politics' where the secondary drama simultaneously feeds off the classical drama and contemporary reality. The political 'dissensus' here takes place in the liminal space opened up between the classical drama and contemporary reality by the parasitic 'secondary drama'. Documentary theatre is another case in point. Its use of authentic texts and personages is self-validating, in the sense that its legitimacy is vouchsafed by direct link to external reality made by the use of authentic material. This is apparent from Peter Weiss's *The Investigation* to the more recent revival of documentary theatre, where this authenticity is seen as an important critical intervention in the face of obfuscation by mass media or 'deliberately misleading information' from governments.[68] But in their postdramatic variant, documentary performance and other forms of reality theatre do not sustain a presumed authenticity in representation by means of the faithful and direct presentation of material, not least because such recourse to external, reliable, authentic reality is assumed to be unavailable. In this vein, Ulrike Garde's and Meg Mumford's chapter discusses the semiotics of authenticity on the reality theatre stage, which they argue is made volatile by postdramatic theatre's eliding or destabilising of fact and fiction. This volatility is seen to encourage or force the audience to navigate sociopolitical issues, for instance social exclusion or perceptions of and attitudes towards otherwise 'invisible' people, such as migrant workers in Lola Arias's and Stefan Kaegi's performance installation *Chambermaids*, and asylum seekers in the tribunal and testimonial performance *CMI (A Certain Maritime Incident)*, by the Sydney-based company version 1.0. That key protagonists are largely absent from the scene – in *Chambermaids* the audience, wandering through specific rooms in the hotel, become partially familiar with the protagonists of real-life cleaners via films, voice recordings, letters and photographs – is interpreted as allowing more latitude for this exploration of underlying attitudes and assumptions relating to the ways in which we make sense of contemporary social, economic and political realities. Shannon Jackson's treatment of The Builders Association's *Alladeen* (2003) brings out another instance of layering for critical effect. In the course of the performance the Western audience's privileged, dislocated and disembodied experience of the call centre is set alongside and problematised by the material reality of the labour relations in the call centre industry. At the same time the play cuts across the real/representational divide, insofar as it points up the role key elements of theatre play in the real-world service industry: rehearsal, performance, voice training, role playing, 'us[ing] of the hyperbolic capacities of theatrical performance to underscore the unregistered capacities of everyday performance' (Jackson). Meanwhile the theatrical stage itself, in which figures appear on a vast projector screen, all but dispenses with live performance, 'staging technology' (Jackson) all the more authentically by denying theatre its usual foundation of bodies in a room together.

It is a small step from this idea that our everyday grasp of reality is informed by (potentially shifting) assumptions and (potentially exchangeable) roles, to the notion that reality is in large part an 'appearance', which is to say that reality is not understood to be 'real' in any objective, empirically grounded way but is a question of how things 'appear' to us. This epistemological attitude is crucial to Dietze's analysis of Schlingensief, in which the focus is not so much on the 'real' Dutschke or his ideas, but on iconic images of Dutschke as part of collective memory. This issue of how things appear is also central to Theron Schmidt's analysis of Back to Back Theatre's *Food*

Court, which argues that postdramatic theatre is political not so much by eschewing representation and embracing the real (for instance in the employment of disabled actors), but precisely by embracing the theatricality of theatre and its play with appearance. 'Rather than suggesting that the political potential of postdramatic theatre depends on its capacity to resist or refuse the machinery of representation, I am interested in the political relevance of artistic practices that invest in and explore theatre as an apparatus of appearances rather than realities' (Schmidt). Here the 'flickering of appearances and representations' is not valued for the resistance it offers to 'reification' or 'conceptual predetermination', associated with Adorno above, but rather implicates and challenges the individual audience member's attitudes, thereby giving the performance its critical force.

Getting beyond this binarism of real/representation also takes on board the fact that theatre, even where it dismantles, cannot entirely do without norms, structures and subjectivities. These elements persist, but theatre in particular allows them to be experienced in their status *as* appearance. In this vein Peter Boenisch discusses the Hungarian dancer-choreographer Eszter Salamon's performance, *Tales of the Bodiless* (2011), whose title indicates the fact that the stage is empty, populated only by 'spatial sculptures formed of fog, smoke, and light', apart from a brief scene in which two immobile figures appear. This bodiless dance might seems to involve a typically postdramatic shift from meaning to energy, which Boenisch characterises as the 'end point' of a process in which 'movement, music and other theatrical means had been granted full autonomy'. But the fact that this absence of bodies is combined with audio narration and dialogue allows Boenisch to identify Salamon's work as redeploying a story and reengaging with the historical past, in a way that allows normative structures – of ideology, language, discourse, identity, subjectivity and agency – to persist. These structures however are understood to have been largely dismantled, 'always already deconstructed, seen in a dialectic vision that no longer suggests origins and foundations but asserts their "essential contingency"' (Boenisch). In Boenisch's view, this sense of contingency offers one way out of the dead end of agency that the post-structuralist dismantling of the subject had lead us into. So one is left with the sense that theatre's connection to politically charged issues persists in the performance pieces that make up the case studies in this book, even in the wake of drama's demise: issues like the nature of political activism, the status of enlightenment values like tolerance or progress, or social attitudes to disadvantaged groups – those who are physically or mentally disabled, those who migrate for economic or political reasons, those who bear a greater share of the human costs of the globalised economy. The postdramatic quality of the performances is evident not so much in a blank refusal of discursive or determinate meaning, but perhaps more so in the way that these issues are inseparable from questions about the nature of discourse, perception and value, in ways that are conveyed in the form of underlying attitudes or implied audience responses, as much as they are by explicit statement or agency on the part of characters. The point here is not to question the validity or usefulness of the term 'postdramatic', which is attested by the resonance it has found in the last ten years or so. Rather it is to acknowledge that its potential for illuminating much of the performance work in recent decades has also cast a shadow: not least this is apparent in the tendency in its reception to separate theatre into binary oppositions, in spite of what Lehmann himself has written on this: text-based/text-less theatre, verbal/physical theatre, discursive/disruptive theatre, representation/real. From our starting point of the latter two terms, we have also seen, however, that a strength of the case studies in this book is precisely the way in which, via the concept of the postdramatic, they are able to examine the political force of performance pieces taking full account of the sense in which this representative relation is not simply to be evaded, but is crucial to the richness of their critical insight.

We would like to take this opportunity to express our gratitude to the Modern Humanities Research Association (MHRA), the Lancaster Institute for Contemporary Arts (LICA), Lancaster University, the School of Cultures, Languages and Area Studies, University of Nottingham, and the Institute of Germanic and Romance Studies (IGRS) for their funding and support of the conference at which most of the chapters in this book were first given as papers.

1

Towards a Paradoxically Parallaxical Postdramatic Politics?

Brandon Woolf

Firstly: The political can appear only indirectly in the theatre, at an oblique angle, modo obliquo. And second: The political has an effect in the theatre if and only if it is in no way translatable or re-translatable into the logic, syntax, and terminology of the political discourse of social reality. What then follows, thirdly, is the seemingly paradoxical formula that the political of the theatre must be conceived not as a reproduction of the political, but as its interruption.[1]

Hans-Thies Lehmann, 'Wie politisch ist postdramatisches Theater?'

The summer and winter months of 2008 paid witness to an intensive transatlantic scuffle in the pages of *TDR: The Drama Review*. The subject-matter: the 2006 translation and increasing popularity of Hans-Thies Lehmann's *Postdramatic Theatre*. The contenders: Lehmann himself; Elinor Fuchs, author of a biting review of Lehmann's text; and Karen Jürs-Munby, translator of Lehmann's volume into English. Fuchs's review – which at times seems more like a personal assault – expends a good deal of its energy attacking Lehmann's legitimacy as progenitor of the term 'postdramatic'. She then goes on to question the quality of Jürs-Munby's translation due to its abridged length,[2] its prose style, even the typographical errors overlooked by the copy editors at Routledge. Surprisingly, Fuchs seems more interested in criticising an alleged 'scandal of ethics and oversight in academic publishing'[3] than she does in devoting critical energy to Lehmann's complex argument. One is left to wonder about her pre-existing aesthetic biases (toward the dramatic perhaps?) and about her personal and *political* motivations.

While much of the critical attention that Fuchs pays to the thrust of Lehmann's actual argument is laudatory, she does point to a seeming ambiguity in his text, which is the focus of this chapter. In many ways, Lehmann's volume is an ambitious attempt to come to terms with the *aesthetic* developments in American and European theatre and performance over the last three decades. How then, does Lehmann account for questions of the so-called *political*, which have been so integrally tied to both theories and practices of performance in the twentieth and twenty-first centuries? Fuchs writes:

> If in fact the 'dramatic' is destined [. . .] to be erased like a face drawn in sand at the edge of the sea, then all the social and political theorizing of the past quarter century so notoriously absent in his essay could be seen as mere flotsam on the ineluctable tide of an aesthetic life expectancy.[4]

Fuchs is frustrated by Lehmann's refusal to explicitly engage with questions of the 'political' in the body of his text. And while he does append an 'Epilogue' that addresses 'a few general reflections on the way in which one could theorise the relationship of postdramatic theatre to the political',[5] the writing is fragmentary, even aphoristic at times, and does not amount to a systematic appraisal. Perhaps that is just the point – but I move too quickly . . . .

In his invited response to Fuchs's review-cum-attack in the winter 2008 issue of *TDR*, Lehmann 'take[s] issue with' her substantive query. He writes:

> What kind of logic would deduce that a book offering an aesthetic approach to theatre necessarily denies the importance of the

political?! [. . .] Yes, I admit, I am tired of much social and critical theorizing that amounts to little more than circulating some supposedly critical notions. But, please, note in passing: questions of aesthetic form *are* political questions.[6]

I submit that Lehmann's 'note in passing' is anything but a transient side comment. In fact, I submit further that Lehmann's *Postdramatic Theatre* is deeply engaged with the 'political' – both in and beyond its 'Epilogue.'

I am most aware that it is by no means uncontroversial to engage in general terms with a concept like the 'political' in performance. However, because Lehmann invokes the term over and over again – and because it is invoked in the title of this book – my effort here is to greet (and close-read) Lehmann on his own terms. I attempt to tease out just what he means by such a term and, further, what is at stake – both to be gained *and* occluded – when such a term is deployed in (relation to) and by the postdramatic.

Ironically, Fuchs's own maritime metaphorics provide us with orientation. First, Fuchs encourages us to examine Lehmann's dialectical method – although she does not seem to grasp his method as dialectical. How does he understand historical and aesthetic progress? What is the means by which drama has become post-drama? Has the 'dramatic' been merely erased or overcome by the tide, leaving no trace of its previous inscription? Or does Lehmann work to unearth a more complex process in which the dramatic and postdramatic remain in constant, mediated relation? Next: Might it be useful to think of the 'social and political theorizing of the past quarter century' *as* flotsam, as wreckage, as (Benjaminian) debris that are *essential* for Lehmann? If we understand his narrative as other than strict 'erasure' – which it surely is – how does Lehmann incorporate (or account for) theories of aesthetics and politics in the last twenty-five years? And to move beyond Fuchs's quarter-century asymptote: how does Lehmann incorporate or account for the relations – if not dialectics – of aesthetics and politics that have long been so prominent in theatre studies and larger critical theory circles?

Before we can address the 'political' directly, we must understand the methodology by which Lehmann advances his conception of the 'post' in postdramatic. My intention is not – nor could it be – to fully explicate Lehmann's densely theoretical foray into the logic of dialectical relations (and a non-traditional dialectics at that) in order to postulate the transition between a dramatic paradigm and a postdramatic one. In fact, as Lehmann cautions, the movement from drama to post-drama is by no means neat and clean, and to speak in terms of a paradigm shift at all – as is so common in the sciences, for instance – presents a risk: 'Paradigm is [instead] an auxiliary term used here to indicate the shared negative boundary demarcating the internally highly diverse variants of the postdramatic theatre from the dramatic.'[7] It seems, then, that Lehmann conceives of a more 'negative' dialectic; he challenges the idealism of a simple transition between or overcoming of contradictions, and he denies the possibility of any grand sublation between poles in constant tension. The shift to the postdramatic is by no means a purely abstract negation, a 'mere looking away from the tradition of drama'.[8] Instead, Lehmann envisions a process of determinate negation, in which 'newly developed aesthetic forms allow both the older forms of theatre and the theoretical concepts used to analyse them to appear in a changed light'.[9] The process is one that resists conceptual predetermination and normalisation, and one that troubles a purely linear temporality. Lehmann invokes the language of constellations (hence my invocation of Walter Benjamin above) to help explicate the logic of this dialectical movement: '[I]t is only the constellation of elements that decides whether a stylistic moment is to be read in the context of a dramatic or a postdramatic aesthetics.'[10] Of course, the irony here – or perhaps it is the very point – is that Lehmann looks 'back' to Benjamin to justify his move 'forward'. In turn, we see how the dramatic is always already inherent in the postdramatic; the postdramatic is also – albeit somewhat paradoxically – inherent in the dramatic.

In light of Lehmann's constellatory language, we begin to understand the complexity of the 'post-ness' he is working to explain. We move, then, to the second aspect of Fuchs's metaphor: How does Lehmann make room – or does he? – within the postdramatic for that carefully crafted 'social and political theorizing', which, according to Fuchs, pertains to the dramatic? Although Lehmann engages with numerous prominent theoreticians of 'drama' throughout his text, I focus on Bertolt Brecht. The reason? One might argue – and this was explored at length during the conference for which this contribution was initially prepared – that Brecht's theory and practice of 'political theatre' was (and perhaps still is) the dominant reference point for so much thinking on the conjunction of aesthetics and politics in the twentieth and twenty-first centuries. Any theory working to track the political in performance must – at the very least – consult Brecht before moving on. Lehmann does just this – all the while remaining sensitive to the complexity of his own understanding of what it means to 'move on'. Lehmann posits that, despite popular conception and despite Brecht's own distinctions between 'dramatic' and 'epic' theatre, Brecht's epic theatre must be counted as a part of the dramatic tradition. Lehmann explains: 'Brecht's theory contained a highly traditionalist thesis: the *fable (story)* remained the *sine qua non* for him.'[11] Thus, in spite of his effort to move beyond traditions of naturalism and in spite of the great innovations of *Verfremdung*, Brecht remained, Lehmann explains, committed to a 'theatre of stories', which structured time and an audience's experience of the 'fictive cosmos'[12] in a (more or less) teleological manner. In turn, Lehmann continues, Brecht can no longer be 'understood one-sidedly as a revolutionary counter-design to tradition.'[13] Instead, we must understand the epic theatre as a *'renewal and completion of classical dramaturgy'*.[14]

If Brecht remains rooted in the traditions of the dramatic, then perhaps the postdramatic theatre can be thought of as a post-Brechtian theatre.[15] As Lehmann explains, in a revealing passage:

> [The postdramatic] situates itself in a space opened up by the Brechtian inquiries into the presence and consciousness of the process of representation within the represented and the inquiry into a new 'art of spectating.' At the same time, it leaves behind the political style, the tendency towards dogmatization, and the emphasis on the rational we find in Brechtian theatre.[16]

Lehmann thus presents a number of rhetorical questions which emerge at the fore of this analysis: '[I]s there a political theatre after narration? Without a fable in Brecht's sense? What might political theatre after and without Brecht be?'[17] In other words, how might we (re)conceive of the 'political' in performance beyond commitment, beyond the primacy of *content*? We must return, then, to Lehmann's 'note in passing' to Elinor Fuchs. For it is in the primacy of *form* that Lehmann locates a postdramatic politics. And it is this emphasis on the *form* of postdramatic performance that will occupy my attention for the remainder of this chapter.[18]

If we are to take Lehmann's dialectic seriously, however, we must also remember that a post-Brechtian theatre can never *fully* abandon Brecht – just as the postdramatic can never fully abandon the dramatic. Thus, we are poised to ask: What *formal* Brechtian elements remain most prominent in the realm of the postdramatic? Lehmann provides an interesting answer. He writes: 'Brecht's demand that authors should not "supply" the theatre with their texts but instead change it has been realised far beyond his imagination.'[19] Lehmann's reference here – although he does not provide a citation – also evokes Walter Benjamin's famous lecture on the 'Author as Producer', which he delivered to the Institute for the Study of Fascism in 1934. At the height of his most 'Brechtian' period, Benjamin explains that the 'bourgeois apparatus' is quite capable of assimilating revolutionary content. Artists must, in turn, be careful not to *supply* the apparatus; they must, instead, work to *change* it. Benjamin continues: 'Before I ask: what is a work's position *vis-à-vis* the production relations of this time, I should like to ask: what is its position *within* them? This question concerns the function of a work within the literary production relations of its time. In other words, it is directly concerned with literary *technique*.'[20] Thus, a full year before his most famous pronouncements about the possibilities of 'politicizing art',[21] Benjamin provides a cipher: the 'work of art' is no longer intended to 'represent individual experiences' as it is 'aimed at using ([and] transforming) certain existing institutes and institutions'.[22] The 'work of art' must achieve 'organizational usefulness'.[23] The 'work of art' – and here Benjamin most explicitly borrows from Brecht – must work toward 'functional transformation' (*Umfunktionierung*); it must work to transform the '*forms* and instruments of production'.[24]

It is thus Brecht-via-Benjamin's notion of *Umfunktionierung* that is front-and-centre in the movement from the dramatic to the postdramatic. And while Lehmann is not primarily concerned with bourgeois apparatuses per se, he is interested in the changing relations of *theatrical* production, interested in the 'new' theatre's almost exclusive focus on formal innovation, on functional transformation, on *technique*. Lehmann is interested in the new (aesthetic) forms that 'separat[e] the new theatre from those political forms that had dominated the experimental scene from the historical avant-gardes until the 1960s'.[25] Finally, Lehmann is interested in the ways these new (aesthetic) forms change our 'understanding of what politics in theatre can be'.[26]

Just what kind of *Umfunktionierung* of those older forms does Lehmann have in mind? He admits that his 'inventory' is in no way comprehensive; the amount of variety in such a vast – and diverse – collection of performances makes it hard to keep track of a systematic 'aesthetic logic'.[27] In a moment of condensational clarity, however, Lehmann recapitulates: '[I]t becomes more presence than representation, more shared than communicated experience, more process than product, more manifestation than signification, more energetic impulse than information.'[28] While I would argue that Lehmann's theoretical innovations help to secure *Postdramatic Theatre* as the primary text working to think through the aesthetics of contemporary performance, Erika Fischer-Lichte's *Transformative Power of Performance* is also somewhat helpful in categorising the formal transformations of the postdramatic. While Fischer-Lichte's admission criteria in *Transformative Power* are slightly different than Lehmann's – most notably in her penchant for performance art – the two texts share extensive overlap in the aesthetic criteria they consider. Like Lehmann, Fischer-Lichte is interested in performances that demonstrate 'contingency', 'participation', 'bodily co-presence', 'meaning that eludes linguistic interpretation'[29] and much more. Fischer-Lichte avoids adoption of the terminology of the postdramatic, however. Instead, she works to trace the primary '[functional] transformation'[30] of the so-called work of art into an *event*. According to Fischer-Lichte, the event-character of performance allows it to exist 'independent of its creator and recipient; instead, we are dealing with an *event* that involves everybody – albeit to different degrees and in different capacities'.[31] It is in these 'moments of enchantment', that the boundaries between artist and spectator blur, and all involved achieve a 'sudden deeper insight into the shared process of being in the world'.[32]

And what hints of the political reside in *Transformative Power*? In his 'Introduction' to the 2008 English translation of Fischer-Lichte's text, Marvin Carlson notes the seeming prevalence of the 'aesthetic' *over* the 'political'. As he explains: '[Her] approach, based as it is on what might be called the aesthetic side of theatre and performance, seeks the "meaning" or "purpose" of performance in what she calls its "specific aestheticity," a concern one would be most unlikely to encounter in an American performance theorist.[33] Writing from an American perspective, Carlson is quick to explain that this 'aestheticity' could seem foreign to those enmeshed in the interdiscipline of Performance Studies, 'with its close historical ties to the social sciences' and long traditions searching for the 'utility of performance in its ability to alter or at least alter the spectator's thinking about general and specific social situations'.[34] Here, Carlson's contextualisation also helps to explain Fuchs's objection. For Fischer-Lichte, however, the very form of performance *as* event constitutes politics in itself: the political is everywhere in her conception of performance. Fischer-Lichte's approach is most certainly Romantic – if not idealist. It is the blurring of 'roles', the 'bodily co-presence' of artist and spectator, of subject and object that works to overcome or 'collapse the ostensible dichotomy of the aesthetic and the political'.[35] Art, social life and politics: Fischer-Lichte believes that they 'cannot be clinically separated in performance'.[36] In and through its forging of concrete social situations, performance works to dissolve these strict binaries, so that all aesthetic work is inherently social, all social work is inherently aesthetic. It is in the *formal* construction, execution and experience of the *event* that one finds politics at the theatre. Fischer-Lichte explains further: 'Setting up art and reality as binary oppositions generated a whole range of other dichotomies, such as aesthetic vs. social, aesthetic vs. political, and aesthetic vs. ethical. As we have seen, such dichotomies have been collapsed demonstratively in performances since the 1960s'.[37]

Lehmann and Fischer-Lichte differ, however, in their readings of the political potential of the postdramatic. Lehmann is not interested in such an *easy* politics. His 'dialectical imagination'[38] commits him to a series of more complex and tenuous mediations between seeming binaries.[39] Performance does not merely *blur* lines. Performances do not merely *dissolve* dichotomies. While Fischer-Lichte's 'border-crossing'[40] is important for Lehmann, it is a necessary but not a sufficient condition. In a lecture at the University of California, Berkeley in March 2010, Lehmann explained – in an implicit critique of Fischer-Lichte – that conceptions of the postdramatic must extend beyond the mere *event*.[41] Instead, Lehmann contends that the postdramatic both embraces *and* challenges the fundamental differences (even contradictions) between art and reality. How does Lehmann envision the complexity of relations between Fischer-Lichte's 'dichotomies', between 'real' and 'representation', between the 'political' and the 'aesthetic'?

His answer is a complex one. On the one hand, Lehmann asks us to consider the dwindling role of 'representation' in the realm of the postdramatic. As he explains, 'real' conflicts of our own time no longer find 'truth' in the representational conflicts of the dramatic. 'The representational form "drama" is', Lehmann writes, 'available but grasps at nothing when it is meant to articulate experienced reality.'[42] For drama no longer rings *true* in its representation of 'action', of 'personal conflict', of 'reconciliation'.[43] Drama is no longer capable of representing the great 'contradictions' of our 'mediatised and globalised'[44] society – one replete with 'social and political conflicts, civil wars, oppression, growing poverty and social injustice'.[45] For Lehmann, then, the postdramatic reflects the *real* 'retreat' or 'unravelling' of the dramatic imagination: 'The theatre of sense and synthesis has largely disappeared – and with it the possibility of synthesizing interpretation.'[46] And in the place of 'realist' representation, Lehmann locates the postdramatic, a theatre of 'partial perspectives and stuttering answers that remain "works in progress"'.[47] Lehmann insists that he is not interested – like Fischer-Lichte – in a simple, unmediated one-to-one mapping of the 'real' and the 'aesthetic'. And yet, it is the postdramatic that brings us closer to the 'real', and to the 'political' – no longer by means of 'dramatic' representation, but by mediated 'reflection'. In other words, the 'real' has become a 'co-player'[48] on the postdramatic stage; a stage which – as David Barnett explicates Lehmann – has moved '*beyond* representation, in which the limitations of representation are held in check by dramaturgies and performance practices that seek to present material rather than to posit a direct, representational relationship between the stage and the outside world'.[49]

On the other hand – and as we have come to expect from Lehmann by this point – to move 'beyond' is precisely to undertake a simultaneous process of engagement with and differentiation from the very thing that is superseded. In other words, any move beyond the representational entails a deep engagement with representation itself. As Lehmann explains, 'Theatre is a practice [. . .], which like no other forces us to realise "that there is no firm boundary between the aesthetic and the extra-aesthetic realm."'[50] It is a practice that is 'at once signifying and entirely real'.[51] And while the postdramatic critically questions the representational status of the dramatic, and foregrounds 'real' elements, it also clings tightly to its aesthetic (or representational) status, foregrounding its 'signifying' elements, its 'fictive cosmos' – albeit a cosmos quite different from a dramatic cosmos.

Contrary to Fischer-Lichte, in whose work the 'real' emerges as the central and structuring tenet, the postdramatic develops an '*aesthetics* of the irruption of the real'.[52] It foregrounds 'the significance of the extra-aesthetic *in* the aesthetic'.[53] The signifying, the representational, the aesthetic remains an essential and constitutive element.[54] The postdramatic theatre remains theatre and continues to remind us – and itself – of this very fact. To make this point, Lehmann harkens back to those almost messianic leanings of another of his Frankfurt forefathers: namely Theodor W. Adorno on the mimetic quality of the artwork. Mimesis, for Adorno, does not consist of a dutiful copying of reality, a subsumption of the aesthetic by the real. Instead, the art object presents a 'becoming-like-something', always foregrounding its aesthetic-cum-mimetic character, its position as art *object*, and thus serving as a stopgap against an instrumentalising totality. Lehmann quotes Adorno: 'Art is no more a replica of an object than it is an object of cognition. Otherwise it would debase itself by becoming a mere duplicate of something. [. . .] Actually, what happens is that art makes a gesture-like grab for reality, only to draw back violently as it touches that reality.'[55] In so doing, in drawing back, art establishes its resistant, and thus its political character. By refusing to imitate the administered world, it indicates the possibility, albeit negatively, of another world that is not yet here; it 'postulate[s] the existence of what does not exist.'[56]

In an unexpected passage – one which was omitted from the English translation – Lehmann also begins to conceptualise the relations between the resistant relevance of the 'representational' in the postdramatic and the ways in which its re-functioned modes and apparatuses of production produce (or enable) such a potential politics. He writes:

> Nowadays, theatre does not – or only rarely – become political by directly thematising the political, but by the implicit content of its modes of representation (*Darstellungsweise[n]*). (These modes involve, by the way, not only certain [aesthetic] forms, but also particular modes of labour (*Arbeitsweise[n]*). This study has hardly mentioned such labour forms, but they merit their own investigation: how theatre is made, and how the political content of theatre can be grounded in the way it is made.) Theatre represents – not in theory, but in praxis – an example of a conjunction of the heterogeneous, which symbolises the utopias of 'another life'. In the theatre, mental, artistic, and physical labour, individual and collective praxis, are mediated. It can claim to be a resistant form of praxis already by dissolving the reification of actions and works into products, objects, and information. By pushing its event-character, theatre manifests the soul of the dead product, the living

artistic labour, for which everything remains unpredictable and [remains] to be invented tomorrow. Therefore, theatre is by means of the constitution of its praxis virtually political.[57]

Hopeful Adornian language abounds again in this enunciation, in which the postdramatic resists the active forgetting of reification (*Verdinglichung*), and thus resists the 'real' itself by foregoing outright political commitment (on the level of content) and forging new modes – arts – of labour, of collaboration, of imagination, of spectating (on the level of formal production). And while Lehmann admits that he has not allotted ample time to the analysis of these new 'forms and instruments of production', it is, it seems, in this praxis *and/of* representation of formal 'heterogeneity' that Lehmann understands the postdramatic as a '*promesse de bonheur*', looking forward to the 'utopia' of 'another life' that is – and will remain – *not-yet*.

One could argue that Lehmann works to maintain two seemingly incompatible positions here: a retreat from representation on the one hand, and an insistence on the theatre's 'aesthetic', 'mimetic', or 'representational' character on the other. However, the citation with which I began – from a 2001 essay – insists on this 'double-diagnosis'[58] (*doppelte Feststellung*):

> Firstly: The political can appear only indirectly in the theatre, at an oblique angle, *modo obliquo*. And second: The political has an effect in the theatre if and only if it is in no way translatable or re-translatable into the logic, syntax, and terminology of the political discourse of social reality. What then follows, thirdly, is the seemingly paradoxical formula that the political of the theatre must be conceived not as a reproduction of the political, but as its interruption.[59]

Postdramatic theatre thus 'obliquely' engages the political *real*ities of our 'mediatised and globalised' world by refusing to 'represent' a *real*ity which is no longer *really* representable as drama. Simultaneously, the postdramatic is a theatre that ensures it 'is in no way translatable or re-translatable into the logic, syntax, and terminology' of the 'real' world by embracing, foregrounding, insisting on its 'aesthetic' or 'representational' status, its status as not-conceptually-predetermined. How then does Lehmann propose we mediate this tenuous circumstance, this first *and* second? Lehmann hopes – albeit 'paradoxically' – that his constellatory dialectic makes this 'double-diagnosis' feasible.

And in this 'paradoxical' position, Lehmann is in good company. Over the last few years, a good deal of European performance scholarship – while not concerned only with the postdramatic – has turned sharply away from 'simple', 'unmediated' conjunctions of theatre and politics, of real and representation, and turned toward more nuanced, more dialectical readings of these relations. A number of critics have grown impatient with a theatre that wants to think of itself as purposefully and explicitly intervening in the realm of the political. In place of the content-based 'political theatre', critics have begun to explore theatre's (negative) political potential as much more indirect, much more unpredictable. Like Lehmann, Joe Kelleher, Alan Read, even Jacques Rancière have been re-reading Adorno (albeit implicitly) – and perhaps each other – and they come together in their understanding of a different kind of political potential for the theatre, an 'unintended politics of performance'.[60]

In *Theatre & Politics* Kelleher argues that 'theatre's value for political thinking [derives from] its seeming fragility and tendency to untruth rather than from the strength of its representations and the justice of its political messages'.[61] There is no guarantee that the 'committed' message of the theatre or its desired effect will be achieved, or understood in the ways they are intended. Rather, theatre 'remains unpredictable in its effects, given that its effects reside largely not in the theatrical spectacle itself but in the spectators and what they are capable of making of it'.[62] The potential inherent in the theatre is the 'unpredictable relationship'[63] between the event's very liveness, its there-ness, its ephemerality, and a public's (and performer's) aesthetic experience of performance.

Alan Read also issues a sustained polemic against any neat and clean, any *sublated* rendering of theatre '&' politics. In fact, it is only by *separating* theatre from the political, Read argues, that we can come to understand the ways in which theatre might function politically. 'The error', Read explains, 'has precisely been to leave these two terms bonded in a fantasy of expectation and hope while patronizing them both with the commiseration of a failure.'[64] If we examine the ampersand (&) used to bind supposedly related terms – like theatre & politics – we notice that the 'ampersand turns its back on theatre with its two ends binding politics to itself'.[65] This turn, notes Read, signals an ambiguity that must not be ignored or taken for granted. Only by troubling – by 'interrupting' in Lehmann's terms – the presumption that the two terms belong together can the 'consequences' of the conjunction be truly evaluated. Read does 'not seek an apparent symmetry between the theatre machine, its politics and more general political processes'.[66] Instead, he takes what he calls a 'parallax view'[67]: a view that asserts incompatibility and asymmetry where there was once a presumption of relation and congruence. The goal of this 'parallax' terminology is to posit a complex (negative) dialectic of sorts, one that thrives in its dissonance and not in its reconciliation, yet one that is unwilling to forego the possibility of some (eventual) (gradual) (accidental) identity, or relation, between its terms. Only by challenging a symmetry between theatre and politics can we understand how full of politics theatre actually is.

Similarly, Jacques Rancière in his *Emancipated Spectator* is interested in gradual experiences, accidental experiences, aesthetic experiences that are not conceptually predetermined. For with conceptual determination, he argues, comes a representational 'logic, syntax, and terminology' that has already been co-opted. Instead, aesthetic experience (of the theatre event) is oblivious to desired effects. And it is in this very denial of the 'real', of the here and now, of a world which is entirely bound by concepts that Rancière locates the political. Like Adorno, Rancière advocates a 'sensory rupture within the continuity of the representative cause-effect schema'.[68] He has no patience for 'critical art' which conceives of a straightforward, undialectical confluence of political aims and aesthetic means. Like Adorno, Rancière is resistant to any attempt to anticipate our common future. Instead, he is interested in new configurations unbound by concepts, by anything that could be anticipated. Like Adorno he puts faith in the theatre (and the aesthetic more generally) as a means of reconfiguring the 'landscape of the possible'[69] or, at the very least, providing a fleeting glance toward a different future.

We return finally to the explicitly 'political' 'Epilogue' to *Postdramatic Theatre*. Here Lehmann presents us with paradoxical, or parallaxical sentences like: 'Theatre can only ever be ambiguously "real."'[70] Or: '[T]heatre can never know whether it really "does" something, whether it effects something and on top of it means something.'[71] Or, finally: 'In the postdramatic theatre of the real the main point is not the assertion of the real as such [. . .] but the unsettling that occurs through the *indecidability* whether one is dealing with reality or fiction. The theatrical effect and the effect on consciousness both emanate from ambiguity.'[72] Somehow the postdramatic gets us closer to the 'real' than the dramatic could ever dream. Somehow the postdramatic must also resist the 'real' and refuse the status quo in order to preserve its critical, and thus political, edge. For Lehmann, it is this 'double-diagnosis' that permits a 'genuine relationship with the "political".'[73] For Lehmann, it is by means of this very uncertainty, this very tenuous and contradictory situation, this formal interruption of the predetermined logics of the political, that the postdramatic becomes an 'aesthetics of resistance', an '*Ästhetik des Widerstands*'.

Performing Dialectics in an Age of Uncertainty, or: Why Post-Brechtian ≠ Postdramatic

David Barnett

Early on in Hans-Thies Lehmann's *Postdramatic Theatre*, one finds an explicit connection between Brechtian impulse and postdramatic response:

> Postdramatic theatre is a *post-Brechtian theatre*. It situates itself in a space opened up by the Brechtian inquiries into the presence and consciousness of the process of representation within the represented and the inquiry into a new 'art of spectatorship'.[1]

The links Lehmann makes with Brecht are clear and certainly hold true, and by calling the postdramatic '*a* post-Brechtian theatre', he notes that the post-Brechtian may indeed have several manifestations on a contemporary stage. Lehmann's approach, as articulated in another essay, envisages many post-Brechtian theatres, defined in terms of what can be salvaged from various aspects of Brecht's formal arsenal.[2] That is, Lehmann understands the term as suggesting a process of decomposition, in which elements of Brecht's theatre persist in the present, having been taken up and/or recycled. He thus seeks to integrate elements of such a theatre into the umbrella term 'postdramatic theatre'. However, I will argue for a more holistic definition of post-Brechtian theatre, based on understanding its root, the 'Brechtian', as a dialectical performance philosophy rather than as a collection of formal components. While the post-Brechtian and the postdramatic share some broad common interests, as Lehmann notes above, fundamental differences between the two emerge when one probes the categories in detail, and these help to establish the two terms as separate paradigms. My emphasis on 'paradigms' concerns a frequent misconception regarding Brecht's theatre itself. While it is usually associated with key terms like *Verfremdung* (making the familiar strange) or *Gestus*, these devices are derived from Brecht's dialectical method of making theatre. Brechtian theatre is a method and not an aggregation of devices. A post-Brechtian theatre can thus be considered in terms of what happens to Brecht's method when it is put under pressure by the conditions that brought about postdramatic theatre. With this in mind, I will first set out what the Brechtian might suggest in performance before considering why it requires modification in the light of postmodern epistemology. I will then move on to consider two productions of the same play by Brecht, *Mr Puntila and His Man Matti*, to analyse the ways in which one may be called post-Brechtian while the other sits within the broad church of the postdramatic.

Brechtian theatre and the binary dialectic

Brecht's theatre practice is best understood in connection with the last seven years of his life when he returned to German soil and co-founded the Berliner Ensemble (BE) with his wife, Helene Weigel, in what would become the capital of the German Democratic Republic, East Berlin. Here he was able to interrogate his own ever-developing theoretical positions, which were mainly formulated in exile, under circumstances which may not have been ideal but which were certainly more accommodating than anything previously available to him. Brecht's work as a director, at its most fundamental, focused on staging materialist dialectics. The dialectical worldview sees individuals and society in a process of perpetual dialogue which, through contradiction, brings about change in perpetuity. This philosophy is political because it proposes that both human behaviour and society are unfixed, a relationship which affects the exercise of power. Thus, put rather simply, if human beings change society, they also change human beings, as the conditions under which people function will help to produce different behaviours. Consequently, Brecht's theatre practice was concerned with two issues: a critique of the innate, that is, the unchangeable in both human beings and society, and the articulation of contradiction, that is, the means through which change occurs.

Brecht's theatre was predicated upon realism, but a realism that was defined in contradistinction to the reproduction of everyday appearances as is the case when 'conventionally' staging plays by Anton Chekhov or Eugene O' Neill, for example. Brecht's realism was defined in the glossary of *Theaterarbeit*, the book that documents the BE's first six productions, in terms taken directly from Friedrich Engels as 'the reproduction of typical people under typical circumstances'.[3] This definition clearly exposes itself as primarily a philosophical rather than an aesthetic concept: one has to know what is typical and what is not for it to be 'valid' on the Brechtian stage. Brecht's solution to this problem was to be found in his emphasis on what he called the *Fabel*. The *Fabel* was the meta-narrative that informed the actions, deliveries and gestures (which could nonetheless productively jar within any given production to draw attention to themselves); it was the interpretive thread that guaranteed the realism of the production, and thus represented the materialist laws of any given society on stage.

The *Fabel* was the primary means of arranging dialectical tensions, but here one should note that the very nature of the dialectic itself was open to Brecht's interpretation. By 1954, Brecht had been profoundly influenced by Mao's essay 'On Contradiction', which posits a hierarchy of dialectical tensions, starting with a 'principal contradiction' to which all other contradictions defer.[4] While Meg Mumford notes that Mao himself viewed the 'principal contradiction' as changeable, Brecht made it the monolithic interpretive centre point of productions and thus constrained and pared down the dialectical material performed on stage.[5]

Brecht's is also a theatre of showing. The dossiers held in the Berliner Ensemble Archive consistently stress the importance of showing aspects of the dialectic clearly. One may then infer that a certain epistemological stability pervades this theatre. First, reality does exist, and secondly, it can be represented. The devices Brecht developed to realise his theatre were derived from his analytical method. In order to reveal the dialectical nature of reality, Brecht needed to find ways of getting behind the naturalising and universalising processes that perpetuate the dominant ideology. His solution was to develop key terms in practice that would reveal the processes behind everyday surfaces, like *Verfremdung*, *Gestus* and the epic. While I will not examine these concepts in detail, I will note that each one aims to challenge the spectator's perceptions of reality in a bid to reveal the truth behind the veneer: the dialectic. *Verfremdung* makes the familiar strange; *Gestus* reconnects the character to society through the body of the actor; the epic drives a wedge between the experience of the event and a reflection on it. All three denaturalize the performed material in a bid to make the spectator productive; that is, that he or she can process the realistic material and reach conclusions. So, Brecht's epic theatre was not in any way simplistic, yet its philosophical basis reduced the potential of the devices I have just mentioned.

Post-Brechtian theatre as a response
to a philosophical deficit

Brecht's materialist dialectic proved a powerful theatrical tool in the 1950s and, if the many reviews are to be believed, struck a chord with audiences in East and West Germany, as well as further afield in Paris, London and Moscow. This militant theatre offered a way of seeing the world that more character-based, 'bourgeois' theatres lacked. Over time, however, the means of Brecht's theatre were questioned and some of those making theatre politically felt constrained by the narrowness of the dialectic as Brecht interpreted it. This questioning, as manifested in productions by Ruth Berghaus, B. K. Tragelehn, Benno Besson, Manfred Karge and Matthias Langhoff around the early 1970s overlapped with early signs of the postdramatic as identified by Lehmann. That they coincided was, of course, no coincidence. Postmodernism, when viewed as an epistemological category, is founded upon the acceptance of modernist uncertainty, and it inflected many traditions of theatre practice with a grave sense of doubt.

The meeting of uncertainty and the dialectic is dramatised in Theodor Adorno's *Negative Dialectics*, first published in 1966. This huge work fundamentally interrogates the formal structures of the dialectic as expressed by Mao and other Marxists who went before him without doing damage to the idea of the dialectic as a mechanism that effects social and individual change. While I do not want to get bogged down in philosophical terminology, it is worth noting Adorno's basic position is concerned with banishing harmony from the dialectical process. In conventional dialectical thought, the thesis and the antithesis form a synthesis in which disparate elements are unified. Adorno the materialist makes a remarkable historicising observation here: the flattening of the dialectic marks the influence of capitalism on Marxist thought in the form of the law of fair exchange.[6] Capitalism seeks to convert the unequal into the equal to foster and promote the universality of capital. The negative dialectic is consequently a Marxist reclamation of its own theoretical arsenal. Adorno argues for a dialectic in which the heterogeneous elements of the thesis and the antithesis remain thus as change takes place. The very nature of the negative dialectic defies all attempts at order, as Adorno writes in his introduction: 'if one talks of anti-drama or anti-heroes in the latest aesthetic debates, then one could call the Negative Dialectic an anti-system'.[7] He heralds an uncomfortable, awkward dialectic, which does not move effortlessly from synthesis to synthesis but accrues contradiction upon contradiction. As such, each side of the dialectic, the thesis and the antithesis, contains material which cannot be reduced or reconciled to simply binary formulations. Instead, the dialectic becomes an unwieldy beast alive with contradiction and not harmony. This 'rich' or 'unfiltered' dialectic offered post-Brechtian theatre an openness in dealing with its material on stage which was no longer to be treated in knowing categories but to be left uninterpreted for the audience.

Brecht's 'knowledge' was provided by the meta-narrative of Marxism, and this was something the perhaps best known post-Brechtian, Heiner Müller, was keen to criticise: 'Every ideological gaze [. . .] is a false gaze and prevents seeing what is really there'.[8] Müller sought to remove the ideological straitjacket from the dialectic, to leave its components free to communicate with each other. The post-Brechtian sensibility thus touches that of the postdramatic in that material tends to be presented rather than represented. The meeting point between Müller and Adorno is that the dialectic in postmodernity is a site of uncertainty. It can no longer be articulated with the minutiae of knowable details; its elements are complex and do not submit themselves to harmonising hierarchical structures. These are the theoretical modifications applied to the dialectic in post-Brechtian theatre which retains dialectical structures but loses the reductiveness and simplifications of Brecht's philosophical approach.

Einar Schleef and the persistence of the dialectic

Brecht wrote a first draft of *Mr Puntila and His Man Matti* in 1940 as an exile in Finland, where the play is set, and revised it as a script which he could use for the world premiere in Zurich, in 1948. The play revolves around a central conceit that Mr Puntila, a wealthy Finnish landowner, is a vindictive capitalist when sober, but a reasonable, egalitarian fellow when drunk, which he is for the greater part of the play. He thus encapsulates the dialectical tension between a socially defined role and a utopian liberation from it in a single character. The plot follows his dealings with his chauffeur, Matti, who ultimately leaves Puntila's service in the epilogue, and Matti's relationship to Puntila's daughter, Eva. She forsakes her fiancée, the Attaché, for Matti, who then tests her suitability as a potential wife later in the play and finds her wanting: she does not understand how to 'change class' and marry a working man.

I shall first discuss a production of *Puntila* at the BE, directed by Einar Schleef, which premiered on 17 February 1996, as an example of a post-Brechtian reinterpretation of the play.[9] I will then move on to one directed by Michael Thalheimer, which premiered at the Thalia Theater Hamburg on 10 March 2007 and which then transferred to the Deutsches Theater Berlin on 30 October 2009, as an example of a postdramatic realisation. What unites both productions, among other things, is the radical shift in emphasis away from socially specific comedy into differing conceptions of the tragic. Both Schleef and Thalheimer overtly emphasised the centrality of Puntila as a tragic figure, yet, as we shall see, 'tragedy' itself is not a free-floating category and the different ways in which the two directors treat it signal a fundamental difference between the post-Brechtian and the postdramatic.

Heiner Müller invited Einar Schleef to direct *Puntila* at the BE, something which initially left him nonplussed.[10] Schleef was well known, at the BE at least, as the director of *Wessis in Weimar* (*Westerners in Weimar*) in 1993, a brutal confrontation between stage and auditorium in which large choruses bellowed texts on the subject of German reunification. His aggressive choral theatre appeared to have little in common with the dialectical humour of *Puntila* until he went to the archive and read one of Brecht's first versions, written in 1940, that is, shortly after the outbreak of the Second World War.[11] *Puntila* was inspired by the stories of Hella Wuolijoki but at this crucial historical phase, Brecht also looked back to the end of the First World War in Finland. At this time, the class struggle manifested itself in a bloody civil war between left-wing forces inspired by revolutionary Russia and right-wing militarists from Finland, the Protection Corps, who prevailed. Brecht's early drafts, then, emphasised Finland's traumatic and class-riven past and were thus no longer that light; by 1948, these references were much reduced. Franz Wille notes: 'Instead of the knowing comic look back to the victory over the disasters of war and Hitler in 1948–49, [one finds] the look forward from 1940 into the inescapable catastrophe.'[12] Wille's reading points to Schleef's materialist aesthetics: for all the formal precision and abstraction in performance, which I will discuss presently, the starting point was concrete and historical. As Ute Scharfenberg notes: 'Schleef's discovery of the play's "language of the exile" offers him an important point of departure for his production's rationale.'[13] That is, the earlier version allowed Schleef the opportunity to disorientate the audience by uncovering impulses later expunged and making them the basis for a new approach to the material.

In addition, Schleef was interested in the treatment of the female characters in the earlier version. He was keen to counter Eva's relegation as a mere appendage to the male leads in the later version and he contended that Eva was not always an Aunt Sally figure in the play: 'Eva is a Miss Julie with high ambitions for her own education. [. . .] But Brecht turned all the women into idiots.'[14] Schleef sought to reintegrate the female characters; he noted the importance of Puntila's housekeeper, Hanna, in the earlier version and viewed her as a concrete antagonist to her master. He also insisted that the two other female members of Puntila's staff, Fina and Laina, were on stage more frequently, often observing the action and maintaining their presence.

The other important change of emphasis, from a textual point of view, was the role of Matti, the usual antagonist. Günther Heeg writes that this conflict was in fact a convenient way of demonstrating proletarian superiority in the later version: 'The dialectic of master and servant is replaced by the cooperation between the author and a character who represents him in the play: Mr Brecht and his dramaturgical lackey Matti.'[15] Matti's superiority is ideological and loads the dialectic in favour of the oppressed underdog. A part of the post-Brechtian impulse, as noted earlier, is a desire to retain the dialectic while opening it up in all its complexity beyond the reach of ideological pressures. Schleef thus underplayed and re-functioned Matti's role as a privileged character. Eva and Hanna became more central figures, while Matti assumed a wholly different role.

The play itself was radically rearranged. Schleef divided it up into four sections, in which, for example, the first section included material from the standard version's first, third, fourth and eighth scene. The diffuse texts ran into each other without a nod to the spectators and consequently assaulted them as text rather than as the basis for a coherent plot. The logical unfolding of the *Fabel* gave way to the experience of the words, shouted or declaimed by Puntila for the most part or by the choruses, which I will discuss below. Such a presentation of the text opened it up for the audience – it became linguistic material, as one might expect in postdramatic theatre, yet here the dynamics of delivery were clearly demarcated; a power relation lay at their centre, and so the text did not float entirely freely as text, but was linked to the dialectical tensions at the heart of Schleef's reading.

The openness of the dialectic was also evident in the use of parataxis, the equal valorisation of the scenic action, a quality Lehmann also associates with processes of de-hierarchisation in postdramatic theatre.[16] The production had, for example, several finales, one was never sure quite when it was over. This extended to the encore when the cast, in strict formation, sang one of the songs from the play that did not appear in the production itself. One notes Schleef's deliberate obfuscation of what belonged and did not belong to the production, something that was echoed in his portrayal of the Puntila figure, as we shall see. Esther Slevogt found the following structure running through the production as a whole: 'Every image gives birth to its own counter-image.'[17] Yet the paratactical arrangement served in this instance not merely to offer a series of permutations to the audience; instead, the use of contrast highlighted the manifold possibilities of the dialectic that ran through the production.

Schleef's return to the more historically painful text was signalled from the opening of the production. Eva delivered an anecdote, usually told by Sly-Grog Emma later in the eighth scene 'Tales from Finland', before the safety curtain. The conventional prologue to the play consists of a speech given by the Milkmaid, which sets the scene, and perhaps the first verse of the 'Puntila song', which introduces the main character. Instead Eva told the story in the first person, not the third as in the text, of her visiting Athi, one of the Communists kept in a prison camp but who refuses his mother's food, despite his great hunger, because she had to beg for it from her mistress. It is clear that Eva is not the speaker of the text, because she herself is socially a 'mistress', and so the reliability of the signs onstage is destabilised from the very outset. That Eva delivers the speech, however, focuses attention on the character and confers an importance on her which she never loses. The short story also initiates themes that will recur throughout this version of the play: that social conflict has led to suffering, that class relations are defining categories, that the most wretched can still offer resistance.

Yet while Eva was important, Puntila was essential. Dressed in formal white tie, he controlled almost everything on stage with a series of gestures, dominating the production with roars and shouts. Consequently, even Puntila's more sympathetic speeches sounded forced and insincere. Schleef himself played Puntila, after his first choice for the role had to withdraw through injury, and so the character Puntila was conflated with a real director, who, on occasion, would also give directions to the actors around him. In more conventional meta-theatre, levels are clearly demarcated, such as in the play-within-a-play in *Hamlet* or the consciously fictional figures in *Six Characters in Search of an Author*. This meta-dramatic addition created instability in the central character and the production as a whole, as the audience was never sure who was talking or, rather, shouting. The grotesque presentation certainly registered with reviewers: 'Schleef performs himself. Not just as a loud mouth and a dry tee-totaler in a dinner jacket. Also as the generalissimo on the director's collective farm'.[18] The exaggerated figure acknowledged the reality of the theatre as well as the fictionality of the play in a portrayal that never settled in either place.

Puntila the individual was surrounded by choruses, as was often the case in Schleef's work. Matti was no longer one person but several and was presented as an instrumentalised extension of Puntila's will. At the beginning of the second section, the Mattis performed vigorous physical exercises which reviewers, and doubtlessly spectators, identified with Nazi military training camps for young people.[19] The Mattis dutifully obeyed, were visibly tired, fell over from time to time, and offered the audience the experience of real exertion that lasted for several minutes. 'Matti' was no longer Puntila's opponent, but traced a brutal masculine arc across class boundaries in which the worker was not imbued with an implicit immunity to his 'class enemy', but could be canalised for violent action. However, with the opening monologue in mind, we note that Schleef offered the audience contrasting positions and did not suggest an inevitability to the dialectic of servitude and defiance.

The women also formed choruses. In the first instance, they declaimed the speeches normally given by the women of the local area, but they also contributed, like the male chorus, to other dialogues, conveying collective power which, depending on the speech, may either support Puntila or act as a counterpoint. Both male and female choruses were also carefully choreographed so that a gestural language emerged, whose precision made it readable, in the same way as Brecht intended his *Gestus* to function. Yet here, the gestures did not necessarily have a referential relationship to reality. Instead, the language developed from the production itself, provoking the audience to make connections between the elements of a sign system that had been carefully formulated.

What emerges from this consideration of the production is that Schleef was very much concerned with political issues as articulated in dialectical terms. However, the components of the dialectic were given great freedom to show their myriad possibilities, something located in Schleef's systematic demolition of denotation in favour of connotation. This had the effect of withdrawing onstage value judgements from the performed material. More negative reviewers, for example, believed that Schleef was paying lip service to the far right: 'Brecht's *Volksstück* has become an antique and fascistoid motorway pile-up on a grand scale in a freestyle of Greco-Roman forms.'[20] Schleef did not limit the power of the fascist imagery he employed, but this was hardly a tacit expression of support. Instead, he allowed the full implications of such barbarity to be presented on stage. While one reviewer noted that 'somehow, somewhere, everything's connected to class consciousness and the class struggle' others were more specific.[21] Brecht expert Ernst Schumacher wrote that he considered the production 'the most radical realisation of an epic theatre [. . .]. In all [. . .], this production demands in the strongest of terms that one think anew about Brechtian performance, a task to which no other theatre is more especially called than the Berliner Ensemble.[22] A 'radical' epic theatre loses its ideological strictures without forsaking its dialectical basis, but how does this reconcile openness itself with Schleef's understanding of the tragic?

Tragedy as a genre was something of which Brecht was suspicious. He wrote that the tragic had no sense of inevitability but was the product of human action, not fatalistic forces, as many tragedies seemed to imply.[23] Tragedy suggests something unchanging through history; Brecht resisted that interpretation and sought to historicise the 'tragic' in order to bring out its specific manifestations and causes. This materialist exegesis does not, however, stand that far from Schleef's understanding of the term. In an interview, Schleef maintained: 'An individual may well bemoan his or her respective lot, but that's not tragic. Things get tragic only when the individual is confronted with the law of the masses.[24] Tragedy is therefore a social category to Schleef as well and it is clear from the production that the tragedy is contingent upon the dialectic and its operation in a society structured by class-based hierarchies. However, tragedy is neither deterministic nor logical, as Schleef stated elsewhere: tragedy cannot take place 'in this theatre of enlightenment [*Aufklärungstheater*] with all its trappings where everyone's so clever and knows everything.[25] The tragic for Schleef is overwhelming and cannot be controlled by the exercise of the rational mind. Puntila, the tragic centre of the production, is both the wielder of great power but also its victim. This dialectical bond of non-identity, to quote Adorno, may run counter to logical analysis but is nonetheless evident. The persistence of the dialectic suggests that tragedy in this production is an epiphenomenon of a particular type of society.

A postdramatic *Puntila* outside history

In many ways, Michael Thalheimer's production of *Puntila* exhibits a great similarity to Schleef's despite a distance of eleven years between the two premieres, and I shall consider the points of contact first, before proceeding to the crucial ways in which they diverge.[26] Thalheimer also edited the text, but here he followed his usual practice of cutting furiously to reduce the play to its bare bones. As Christine Dössel observed: 'concentration through condensation.

Figure 2.1 Brecht's *Herr Puntila und sein Knecht Matti*, directed by Michael Thalheimer. (Photo by Katrin Ribbe.)

Note: Isolated individuals set against a non-specific, open backdrop diminish the role of social relations in the production. Image shows Markus Graf, Norman Hacker, Katrin Wichmann and Andreas Döhler.

No-one gives dramas such short shrift.'[27] Thalheimer's focus was thus not on excavating a certain reading of *Puntila*, but heightening certain moments, something achieved by cutting extraneous speech and action. Consequently, while Schleef's production ran for a full five hours, including an interval, Thalheimer's did away with the interval entirely to retain a uniform intensity for around a hundred minutes.

As with Schleef, Puntila was without doubt the focus of the production, which opened in darkness to strains of Richard Strauss's *Alpensinfonie*. Puntila stood in front of the set, which revolved to reveal either two huge metal walls of a vast interior or, on their other side, two wooden walls of an exterior. Puntila, dressed in a white shirt and sweating profusely, pulled at his bow tie, which hung limp for the rest of the show. As the stage revolved, the only visible action was a figure in the interior bent double in the act of vomiting, an action repeated several times as the stage turned, before Puntila began his opening monologue. The extended non-verbal introduction, more operatic than dramatic, created an atmosphere of menace and despair which would not leave the stage for the duration of the performance.

Postdramatic theatre prefers to emphasise 'not action but *states*'.[28] Here, Thalheimer's treatment of Puntila left the dyad drunk/sober for a condition of an all-pervading world-weariness. As Hans-Dieter Schütt observed, Puntila 'knows no difference between a clear and a clouded mind'.[29] The same was true for Schleef in terms of Puntila's drunkenness: there was no attempt to differentiate between the two modes, something which would have diluted Schleef's notion of tragedy by suggesting that if Puntila could only enjoy his drunkenness or reform his views when sober all would have been well. For Thalheimer, however, the constant state of extreme despair was linked more to human weakness than social position. Although the director conceded that Puntila was in part thus because of his wealth and property, he continued: 'It would be banal to ascribe Puntila's behaviour exclusively to his social status. [. . .] For Puntila there are very personal things that lead to this behaviour. The proof is in the many quotations from the Bible that Brecht built into the play.[30] One can certainly agree with Thalheimer's reservations about deriving human behaviour exclusively from social position; society would be considerably more manageable if that were the case, and there is no sense in this play or indeed any other by Brecht that the playwright was a social determinist. However, rather than regarding the social as a major contributory factor, Thalheimer preferred to tap into an essentialism in human behaviour, derived from the Bible. Yet Brecht preferred to historicise the Bible in his works; Thalheimer views Brecht's Bible references unironically as a source of information about 'the human condition'.

In the same interview, Thalheimer revealed what interested him most about the character of Puntila: 'he's a mess. The fact that he's a human being who can't stand the world and himself, and thus tries to make himself bearable to others by getting drunk.'[31] The crucial term here is 'human being'. Brecht's dialectical understanding of people and society was based on a position that the 'human' itself did not exist as an essence but was produced in concert with society. Consequently, this 'humanness' was not an a priori condition but the product of class interest. Brecht had discovered from the Zurich production in 1948 that Puntila ran the risk of being perceived as a mainly sympathetic character 'with some nasty traits when sober' and set about keeping the character in check through the application of dialectical tension in the Berlin production.[32] Puntila's humanity when drunk could thus not be rendered in some way natural but as a particular behaviour which worked to his advantage. I am not trying to argue that Thalheimer was in some way 'wrong' to naturalise his Puntila, just that the practice was undialectical.

As is often the case in postdramatic theatre, conflict, a central category of drama, is downplayed or eliminated in favour of the evocation of the 'states' mentioned earlier. Eva, for example, offered little resistance to the flow of the production. In the scene in which Matti examines her suitability as a future wife, she is not even permitted to answer his questions. Instead, Matti continually cut her off with the text's own 'wrong!' ('Fehler!'). Writing about Thalheimer's 2001 production of *Emilia Galotti*, Peter Boenisch notes:

> Over the course of the eighty minutes it took the five-act tragedy to unfold [. . .], the space of emptiness did not make the faintest attempt at realistic or illustrative representation. It was filled only with bodies that entered and exited, yet remained in statuesque figurations for most of the time; with a rhythmic text meticulously defined as the performers shouted, whispered, and rushed through Lessing's lines, and by eternally looped musical fragments.[33]

The same could equally apply to the production of *Puntila*. There was no attempt to make the action on stage credible and the director preferred to offer the audience an experience which was 'quite atmospheric and associative'.[34] Again, we note that Thalheimer's use of signs left much open, like Schleef. The ambivalence was to be found in the production as a whole. The behaviours on stage remained elusive, articulated by lonely individuals rather than as the result of social interaction.

Thalheimer's was another tragic production, in that the catastrophe on stage was rooted in the notion of an immutable human condition. Puntila as a person could not live in his own skin, yet there was no suggestion that this was at all changeable. Thalheimer said: 'The Puntila character is a despot who acts in an arbitrary manner. But you love this Puntila, too! He's likeable, too! And that what you love, you don't want to do away with [*will man doch nicht überwinden*].'[35] Again, I am not arguing that one *should* direct *Puntila* as Brecht did, but note that this postdramatic rendition of the play as an extended, depoliticised character study of a fascinating figure is at odds with Schleef's post-Brechtian version.[36] It shared Schleef's desire not to be

restricted by pre-given political positioning but preferred to explore
the void that Puntila presents, which picks up the postdramatic desire
to go beyond illusion to reach a state of 'fascination' ('Faszination').[37]
This can be seen in one reviewer's summation: 'and all the same,
Thalheimer's nihilism has a certain magic, it's not that easy to drag
yourself away from this black hole of a production'.[38]

The post-Brechtian is not the postdramatic

Both Schleef's and Thalheimer's productions clearly deploy strategies
to frustrate a simple mapping of text and action referentially onto a
recognisable reality. Indeed, if one did not know the play beforehand,
neither production would have helped the spectator to piece together
the plot, let alone the *Fabel*. Both stagings seek to open up a play
which, in its original form, can be considered heavily loaded in
favour of an ideological explication. The directors wrenched their
productions out of milieu and dramatic characterisation as a way
of presenting the text to the spectators for their intellectual *and*
sensual experience of the material. On the face of it, this sounds
very much like postdramatic practice. Performance engages in a
'de-dramatization'[39] in which traditional tensions are banished for a
variety of reasons. These include the relativisation of values encoded
in the text, the dethronement of the text as the central constitutive
element of a production, and the promotion of space, rhythm and
bodies as equals in the theatrical event.

It is worth noting, however, that both directors very much believed
that they were not involved in directorial arbitrariness. Schleef derived
his production from an earlier version of the play that defined the
figure of Puntila against the backdrop of revolutionary conflict in the
wake of the First World War. Thalheimer's approach was also taken
directly from his reading of the text rather than from the imposition

of an alien aesthetic onto an unwilling or indifferent object. In this sense, both directors could argue that they were being 'faithful to the text'. That this faithfulness manifested itself in two radically open approaches to performance does no damage to the directors' textual points of departure; it is nonetheless clear that the means through which they realised their ideas displayed many features associated with postdramatic theatre. However, while the two productions apparently share a postdramatic veneer, they differ in one fundamental way. Put very crudely, a postdramatic theatre seeks to go beyond the limitations of representation. We can understand representation as a synecdochic process of embodying the particular from the general: the one stands for the many. Such an understanding of character and/or plot in dramatic theatre is based on representation's quality of referentiality: one is able to connect the particular back to the general because the former refers to the latter. However, referentiality starts to break down in postdramatic theatre; the link between the world of the stage and the world around us becomes strained and, on occasion, snaps completely. Both Thalheimer's and Schleef's casts live in a world cut off from a recognisable reality and refer only metaphorically to our experience of it. However, Schleef's post-Brechtian production had its point of reference not in its relationship to the empirical world of surfaces but to that world's construction, the dialectical organisation of reality. The persistence of the dialectic in its unfettered complexity marks the persistence of a concrete referentiality to historical reality while Thalheimer's production deliberately eschews dialectics in the name of the experience of human tragedy as an unchanging condition. Here one should emphasise that a dialectical text does not necessarily lead to dialectical performance. Schleef's is *also* a theatre of states, but the states suggest a series of complex permutations, of alternatives, which develop, however inexplicably, over time.

Post-Brechtian performance, as I have defined it here, is wholly different from the postdramatic in terms of its referentiality to historical reality. The former acknowledges that reality is organised dialectically, with all the implications that has for the possibility of social change. The latter does not ostensibly engage with such questions in such concrete terms and explores a different complex of issues. Lehmann's annexation of the post-Brechtian into the broader category of postdramatic theatre fails to acknowledge this distinction. The two may be aesthetically similar in that they seek to shift interpretation from the stage to the auditorium and thus leave the performed material more open and less referential but they are philosophically discrete. While I am not arguing that Thalheimer's *Puntila* was in some way unpolitical – its very challenge to the way we perceive reality militates against that – Schleef's production actively pursued a dialectical articulation of reality that implicitly allowed for the *possibility* of individual and social change to take place. The post-Brechtian, which could superficially be confused with the postdramatic, has at its core both a dissatisfaction with the narrowness of the Brechtian dialectic and a desire to expand its remit to address concrete social problems. Yet the dialectic is represented in forms that are qualitatively distinct from Brecht's. Postmodern uncertainty pervades both the post-Brechtian and the postdramatic, but in the former, it does not extend to the mechanism by which change occurs, only to the means by which it is articulated and expressed.

Political Fictions and Fictionalisations: History as Material for Postdramatic Theatre

Mateusz Borowski and Małgorzata Sugiera

It is only in the epilogue to his *Postdramatic Theatre*[1] that Hans-Thies Lehmann asks a number of significant questions about the relationship between the postdramatic aesthetic and its potential political reverberations. He makes his point very clearly when he writes that the fact that the politically oppressed are put on stage does not entail that this stage becomes political. Theatre, as he argues, becomes political not by dint of a direct thematisation of the political, but through specific means of representation.[2] It is difficult not to agree with him, about this as well as with his claim that in our current information society the notion of political theatre has gained an entirely different meaning. Lehmann adds that it makes no sense to expect that theatre will represent political conflicts in the globalised world, because the notion of conflict entails clear-cut, binary divisions into friends and foes, the social malady and the recommended cure. In the contemporary world it is no longer possible to easily determine what organisations or individuals wield control over global economic and social processes. Because these processes run on a global scale and the contemporary conflicts and tensions are so variously motivated they cannot be grasped in their entirety, let alone be represented in theatre.

This problem has existed for theatre practitioners at least since the first decades of the twentieth century, when Brecht tried to work out a new form of politically engaged theatre that would depart from the melodramatic conventions of the latter part of the nineteenth century. Showing the public and political dimension of individual and private experiences – the typical aim of the socially oriented artistic activity of André Antoine at the Théâtre Libre or Otto Brahm at the Freie Bühne – required foregoing a traditional conflict of individuals, endowed with free will and fully responsible for their deeds. Bertolt Brecht, in the late 1920s, immediately before laying the foundations for the epic theatre, encountered a similar problem posed by the traditional, conflict-based dramatic form. By that time he was trying to present in drama the workings of the economic system, particularly the principles of the functioning of the stock exchange. But ultimately he surrendered, claiming that the conflict of individuals cannot be used to present abstract economic principles; a new epic form was his response to this aesthetic crisis.[3] No wonder that a number of committed artists working around the turn of the 1970s (e.g. Joan Littlewood in Britain, Michel Vinaver in France or Peter Weiss, Heinar Kipphardt and Rolf Hochhuth in Germany) shared Brecht's conviction that classic dramatic conflict inadvertently made the spectator focus on the fate of individual characters, eliciting emotional engagement and identification. This, in turn, prevented the audience from looking at the stage events from the distance necessary to undertake a dispassionate analysis of the functioning of the social, political and economic system. Due to its parabolic form and manifestly anti-illusionist meta-theatricality, epic performance explained and laid bare the principles of the capitalist market economy. Thus, the far-reaching dismantling of the traditional form of a represented reality enclosed behind the fourth wall allowed Brecht to put individual fate and conflicts in a perspective which sought to position the spectator as a detached analyst. Through the atomisation of action with clear causal interconnection, accompanied by overt commentary and the introduction of alienation effects on all levels of a text's structure, the audience could see through the workings of the system and its impact on their individual actions, with this analysis unclouded by emotion. Thus the epic form seemed, for the politically committed theatre of the late 1960s, the most effective embodiment of the project of bringing out the public dimension of private experiences, in accordance with the watchword: 'the personal is political'. The strategies of typically Brechtian *Verfremdungseffekte* were adopted not only in the documentary theatre of Peter Weiss, Heinar Kipphardt and Rolf Hochhuth in Germany, but also by feminist or gay theatre groups in Britain (e.g. Monstrous Regiment, Gay Sweatshop) and the Theatre of the Everyday in France.

At the same time, in the closing discussion of his Epilogue Lehmann brings out another significant aspect of political theatre in the latter half of the twentieth century. Brecht conceives of theatre as having fairly 'direct' political effectiveness, inasmuch as it is thought to precipitate greater awareness of the contradictions inherent in the political and economic system and of the need to protect the rights of those oppressed and marginalised by that system. Contrary to that, Lehmann firmly states that theatre is political only in so far as it subverts and does away with the categories of the political, insofar as it does not seek to encourage politicised action beyond the theatre but rather elicits reflection on the dominant notion of 'political involvement'. Obviously, this change of expectations towards the outcome of the strategies of engaging audiences in a dialogue resulted from a significant change in the status of the theatre throughout the twentieth century. We could go in the direction that Lehmann indicates and ask if political theatre had to change its objectives because in the latter half of the twentieth century it ceased to be a mass medium. After all, not only Brecht, but also such politically minded theatre makers such as Erwin Piscator or Vsevolod Meyerhold believed that theatre was to function as a means of enlightening the mass audience, mainly workers. The theatre that they dreamt of and practised could exist only within a political system based on clear divisions between social classes, within the early capitalist economic system. After the Second World War the growing democratisation of Western societies together with profound economic and social changes shifted the old divisions between classes. Moreover, the advancement of television and other mass media of communication contributed to the change of the social status of experimental, political theatre. In fact it strengthened its position as an old medium and a bastion of high art. As an elitist phenomenon it set a different goal for itself. More and more often, instead of directly criticising the current political situation or commenting on topical affairs, as if from the outside of the political system, it rather started to question the underlying assumptions of political discourse, such as the division between culture and nature, for instance in the context of sexual politics or mass media.

This change in the status of theatre as a political institution has gained particular pertinence since theatre and drama in Europe had to face new political realities after the fall of communism and geopolitical changes in the last decade of the twentieth century. The growing tension and the long impasse in peace talks created a situation in which observers from around the world could not retain a neutral stance. Suffice it to recall Sarah Kane's *Blasted*,[4] one of the most celebrated and notorious plays of that era, which premiered in 1995. In the second half of the play, in a series of dream images, the stage is invaded by recollections of a war which clearly echo the conflict between Serbia and Croatia. An even more pertinent example is Peter Handke's play *Die Fahrt im Einbaum oder das Stück zum Film vom Krieg* (*Voyage by Dugout, or the Play on the Film about the War*, 1999),[5] which was written on the back of his earlier text *Journey to the Rivers*,[6] published first in the German paper *Süddeutsche Zeitung*, and soon after as a book. Against the general conviction that it was

Serbia that was to be held responsible for the atrocities of the war, Handke analysed the language of media reports to bring out the silently accepted assumptions on which journalists worked, eager to provide their readers with moralistic messages. They usually focused on the victims of war, which often determined the final conclusions that they reached in their articles. Therefore the political dimension of Handke's essay *Journey to the Rivers* lay in the critique of the media and the position of journalists as unquestionable experts. His play *Die Fahrt im Einbaum oder das Stück zum Film vom Krieg* takes place on the set of a documentary about the Balkan war. This meta-theatrical situation allows him to show the mechanisms of selection of facts and the montage strategies used to produce messages laden with ideological content. Both Kane's and Handke's texts testify to a very strong tendency in political playwriting in the 1990s, that took up political issues by taking a critical stance towards the language used by the media in everyday communication. However, the crux of the matter lies elsewhere.

It is difficult to escape the impression that Lehmann in his book, published in the middle of this newly political era, was not primarily interested in political questions. Most of the artists and theatre groups discussed in *Postdramatic Theatre*, such as Richard Foreman, Richard Schechner, Societas Raffaello Sanzio, the Wooster Group, La Fura del Baus, Forced Entertainment or Gob Squad, to name only the most obvious examples, either overtly embarked on a political mission or this function was ascribed to them by critics in the mid-1990s. However, Lehmann's entire book was written overtly as a guide through the theatre of the last few decades, in order to demonstrate how contemporary theatre uses theatrical signs in performance. His description of the new paradigm took the shape of a panorama, which represents phenomena synchronically, and not as a diachronic succession that could possibly show causal connections between them. However, in the context of the issues that we are addressing in this chapter, it must be stressed that the political character of theatre has to be regarded as a historical phenomenon. After all theatre is an institution deeply embedded in a given historical context and subject to historical change, but also to a large extent dependent on the audience, their current interests, frame of mind, cognitive capacities and dominant convictions. This aspect of theatre is easily overlooked in such panoramic works as Lehmann's book, which deals with those theatrical forms which may still be classified as high, autonomous art.

At the threshold of the twentieth century art gained the autonomy that it had fought for throughout the previous century and a half. The concept of aesthetic experience as superior to experiences in other domains of life has been in play at least since Friedrich Schiller's *On the Aesthetic Education of Man in a series of Letters* (1794).[7] Schiller defined the characteristics of an aesthetic experience as a suspension of the cognitive power of the intellect and categories of rational thinking, tapping into the power of sensuality which awakens human desires. Consequently, Schiller prepared the field on which he investigated the autonomy of art as a domain separate from anthropological and political activity. Until the mid-twentieth century the idea of aesthetic autonomy enjoyed immense popularity. However, in the latter part of the century the concept was put in question and increasingly regarded as a dangerous trap into which independent artists could easily fall. By that time two opposing attitudes manifested themselves as possible ways out of this impasse. On the one hand, art could give up its autonomy and instead of creating artefacts it could create local communities and within them reactivate long-forgotten forms of human coexistence. On the other hand, it could separate itself from the social domain through the resistance of form and the refusal to communicate with recipients.

The falsity of this binary opposition was laid bare by, among others, the French philosopher Jacques Rancière in his *The Politics of Aesthetics*.[8]

He does not follow in the footsteps of Schiller and his acolytes, who advocated the autonomy of art and aesthetic experience. He addresses the issue at the more fundamental level of the cognitive mechanisms which determine our understanding of aesthetic experience as unique and fundamentally different from other life experiences. As such, he goes back to the moment in European culture when the opposition between art and politics was established by the philosophers of the Enlightenment. As he reminds us, they constructed the notion of autonomous aesthetic experience as devoid of any direct significance for and influence on the spheres of politics and everyday life. Rancière asserts that politics is not restricted to the exercise and struggle for power. Also, art does not become political only when it takes up current political issues and reflects a particular social structure, a set of social conflicts and the identity of social groups or social strata. Both art and politics are forms of 'the distribution of the sensible', in the sense that they entail historically contingent conventions of social ordering and communication. As Rancière claims, art becomes political the moment it confirms the existing order or introduces a new pattern of distribution of the material and symbolic space, and shifts the borderline between that which in the public domain is either visible or invisible, excluded, and deprived of representation and autonomous voice. He redefines politics as the power to reconfigure the distribution of the sensible that is shared by the entire community; the ability to introduce new speaking subjects into the public view and making them visible as active political agents. In this sense politics lies at the core of establishing communities based on a set of shared values, beliefs and principles of conduct. Therefore art in order to be political does not have to take up topical political issues. Even when it retains its autonomy, it takes an active part in the current distribution of the sensible, in the sense that it provides or relies on conventionally grounded means of giving commonly intelligible form to individual and collective experience. Such an approach makes it possible to see better the political and ideological function even of those types of theatre which are generally considered to be apolitical and to belong to the realm of high art.

The problem is, however, that Rancière is a philosopher who uses examples from various arts in order to exemplify or corroborate his theoretical meditations. No wonder that in the context of the historically and culturally changeable definitions of art and artistic practices he chooses examples that are primarily from the field of visual arts, such as painting, sculpture and film, as well as pictorial representation in literature. With reference to these examples he can prove that images *as such* do not mean anything, and that their meanings are a result of the discourses surrounding them in a given place and time. Rancière mentions theatre only in the context of his discussion of the concept of theatricality as formulated by Michael Fried.[9] He argues that theatre is a space in which speech gains visibility, because it always appears on stage with an accompanying gesture, in the context of a specific situation or interaction. For him theatre is a space in which speech manifests its performative character and can be perceived by the audience as a social act. In this context he suggests that political theatre should work to produce within itself a position for an 'emancipated spectator', by subverting the order imposed by the proscenium-arch stage. Central to this order are the passive reception by the spectator and the notion of a theatrical production as an artefact with a clear message. The emancipation of the spectator should lead to a fundamental change in the theatre which should generate *dissensus* instead of clear messages, and is at odds with the existing consensus. Rancière posits that, in the place of the traditional conflict of views and emotions, a clash of sensibilities should be introduced, and that this clash should be effected both on stage and in the minds of the audience. The resulting shock opens up a space in which it becomes possible to verify the existing hierarchies of values and naturalised world views.

The most significant aspect of Rancière's argument for our concerns is his discussion of Brecht's theatre as an archetype of political theatre, which he juxtaposes with that of Antonin Artaud. Rancière describes epic theatre as a form of 'politicised' art, and as a very skilful fusion of political pedagogy and artistic modernity.[10] But according to Rancière Brecht's theatre did not subvert the practices of visibility that were dominant in the first half of the twentieth century. Rather it used prevailing theatrical solutions to formulate a political message and to seek to change the social structure. But Rancière's assessment of Brecht is only possible because he focuses on a conception of the stage production as a ready-made artefact, and on the strategies of adapting classical texts by Brecht. His claim would not hold true for the theory of the *Lehrstück*, a type of epic theatre that seeks to eliminate the division between the actors and the spectators. Instead of a typical theatre performance, the *Lehrstück* seeks to offer the participants a communal experience that would introduce them to the principles of dialectical thinking and everyday-life practices within a specific ideological context. As such, a *Lehrstück* is not to be conceived of as creating a stage production and should not be mistaken for an artefact.

However, Rancière's argument can be taken to another level, when the political function of theatre is considered from the point of view of its status as 'event' and its performative character. Traditional aesthetics, with its focus on the analysis of a discrete 'work of art', struggles to do justice to the 'event' quality of theatre, especially in the case of the deliberately open-ended and unfinished character of contemporary theatre productions. Such forms of theatre are more convincingly described with reference to the aesthetics of performativity put forward by Erika Fischer-Lichte in *Transformative Power of Performance*.[11] Here Fischer-Lichte introduces the notion of the 'autopoetic feedback loop',[12] which denotes the mechanism of drawing the audience into cooperation in the creation of a theatrical event, which is only partly predetermined as a repetitive artistic phenomenon. Significantly, Fischer-Lichte works on similar assumptions to Rancière, insofar as she does away with the clear separation between art and other forms of social interaction. In place of this dichotomy she introduces the individual's subjective recognition of the artistic character of an event, which is however not determined by any particular aesthetic structure. This recognition lies at the basis of an individual spectator's decision whether s/he should look upon the event from an aesthetic or ethical perspective and take upon him-/herself all the consequences of this decision. Combining insights from Rancière's and Fischer-Lichte's arguments, we would like to examine what political force can be ascribed to theatre that does not seek to produce artefacts but rather initiates events in which performers and spectators or, as we shall see, *witnesses*, collaborate.

In order to restrict the scope of the investigation we focus on those performances which define their political aim with reference to collective memory. Such a perspective allows us to demonstrate the ways in which the prior knowledge and memories of the audience are used to create a political event by aesthetic, artistic means. Such a concept of collective performative memory has already been discussed within the field of theatre studies. In *The Haunted Stage* Marvin Carlson has delineated the most significant aspects of theatre understood as a memory machine.[13] He argues that the performative arts engage the memory of the audience in a different way than, for example, novels appeal to the memory of their readers, mainly due to the specific, multi-medial and non-verbal character of theatrical communication. It always takes place 'here and now', with the consequence that the spectator cannot return to overlooked details and analyse their meaning indefinitely. As Carlson argues, in the theatre the spectators have to rely on their memory on many levels, which enables them to establish referential connections with the external reality, to recognise the stage-world and its inhabitants in their own terms and as copies of external reality.[14] They also have to possess the memory of specific theatrical and dramatic conventions, which lie at the core of the communication between the stage and the audience.[15] However, Carlson claims that the reception of a theatrical production can also be influenced by the memory of previous stagings that the audience watched in the same theatre, the costumes that are sometimes reused in another performance, or the stage set that can function in numerous productions shown simultaneously in the same theatre.[16] Thus the meanings of productions can also be enriched or even determined by the specific stage and its history, the very building of the theatre and its surroundings. Carlson also cites examples of theatre companies such as the Wooster Group, who deliberately use their own history as the material for their productions. Each performance not only produces its own meanings but also sets these meanings in a rich context of other performances that have been 'inherited' or remembered by the audience. One need not point out that any political theatre that deals with a collective past has to take into account the memory of the spectators involved in the creation of the theatrical event.

It is perhaps easier to grasp the political force of this collaborative performance if we examine the same theatrical signs which begin to fulfil different functions in different contexts, depending not only on the current political situation, but also on that which Stephen Greenblatt calls the circulation of social energies.[17] He used this term to describe the nexus of that which is artistically and institutionally theatrical with that which is political and social. This nexus actually determines whether, in a given context, some solutions and conventions are deemed political, while others are not. We will investigate this idea of a nexus with reference to two examples that take up historical themes, presenting events that had a fundamental significance for the nation. The first is the well-known production *1789* by Théâtre du Soleil (director Arianne Mnouchkine) from 1970, the second, the Polish production *Transfer!* (director Jan Klata), which was put on stage thirty-six years later, in 2006, and took up the theme of the compulsory migration of Germans and Poles after the Second World War. This performance was prepared as a Polish-German co-production and premiered in Wrocław, a city inhabited by many descendants of people from Lwów, a town currently located in the Ukraine, near the Polish border.

Although these productions refer to different historical events, they are linked by the same overtly political concern to present an alternative to the official versions of history. Their producers chose a number of strategies of theatrical presentation that seemed to diverge from the conventional institutional and artistic practices in the respective theatre of their time. Both *1789* and *Transfer!* presented epoch-making events from the perspective of direct participants in those historical events, which is set against that of those who at the time of the event made crucial political decisions. And this perspective is crucial to the political force of the piece in both cases. In Mnouchkine's production this point of view is concomitant with the chosen framework of a popular theatre which fulfils the function of a 'living newspaper' that both presents and comments on the consecutive stages of the French Revolution. In Klata's staging the historical perspective is introduced through the division of the stage into two areas. Up above, on a large platform, Stalin, Churchill and Roosevelt are presented during the conference in Yalta, deciding upon the fate of their nations. Below, a group of contemporary Germans and Poles speak on behalf of the ordinary people who were affected by the decisions of the politicians. Although both directors present the clash of opposing points of view, they make it obvious which one the spectators should identify or at least sympathise with most. In *1789* the spectators were assigned the role of the revolutionary crowd and identified with the masses. In *Transfer!* the audience is addressed directly by their contemporaries below the platform, while the politicians do not engage in direct contact with the spectators and remain behind the invisible fourth wall throughout, as in traditional theatre. In both cases the strategies employed were intended to make the audience more intensely engaged in the action and take a political stance towards the represented events. This concern about engagement is also reflected in the collective working method that was adopted by both producers, which served both as a clearly political statement and as a means to develop the productions over time and adjust them to changing circumstances. Moreover, both companies use the aesthetic format of a chronicle as well as storytelling techniques, which may be contrasted with the narrative schemata of the standard discursive approach to history, based for instance on causal logic. This is clearly visible in *1789*, in which the action begins with a story about the failed escape of the king and queen from Paris. The commentator then announced: 'Ladies and gentlemen, this was just one way of telling this story. However, we have chosen yet another one.' This was followed by a presentation of images of the poverty of the lower classes, with clearly contemporary undertones. But these similarities between the two performances should not lead us to overlook their significant differences. The two productions were prepared in different historical and cultural contexts, but also for different types of theatre. Mnouchkine's *1789* was situated on the margins of mainstream theatre, whereas Klata's *Transfer!* was staged on an institutional stage in one of the most renowned Polish theatres. Consequently, the two productions used different means of theatrical expression and in a different way elicited the audience's response. It is the existence of these differences that makes problematic the tendency to judge political performances of this kind from one's own perspective and in the context of the dominant means of artistic expression. This was the mistake that Freddie Rokem made in his widely cited book *Performing History*, when he set his interpretation of *1789* in the context of various other performances seen on Israeli stages that represented the trauma of the Holocaust.[18] Consequently the conclusions he reached were clearly a result of his assumptions of commonalities, but had less to do with the actual performance by Théâtre du Soleil and its reception by the audience.

Rokem analyses performances that were constructed as a testimony to past events. As he argues, in this format the actors become flesh and blood witnesses who testify to the credibility of the stage events enacted by historical figures.[19] However, this was not the case in *1789*, which becomes clear when one analyses Rokem's description of a selection of scenes from the performance. For example, he mentions the well-known scene of the storming of the Bastille from Mnouchkine's production.[20] First the actors scattered in the auditorium, summoning small groups of spectators in order to tell them about the event that they have just taken part in. Their voices intermingle, grow louder and louder, and when the lights come up again both the actors and the spectators become the people of Paris who celebrate their victory. It is clear that in this case the actors wanted merely to enact fictional characters; they could not give a testimony based on their own personal experiences. This precludes them from becoming the 'actors-historians'.[21] In Théâtre du Soleil the spectators became the people of Paris celebrating the successful storming of the Bastille because the borderline between stage and auditorium was done away with. The shared space was arranged in such a way that the physical contact between performers and audience, uncommon in the theatre of the 1970s and still regarded as a novelty, became a force that imposed fictional roles on the spectators. This incorporated them into the stage fiction, sending them on a journey into the two-hundred-year-old past. It is for this reason among others that Rokem writes that Mnouchkine merely staged the past, filtering the carnivalesque atmosphere of 1789 through the prism of the revolutionary theses of 1968.[22] In the context of his argument this statement becomes a reproach only because he judged this performance against the backdrop of the Israeli political theatre of the 1980s, which referred directly to the nation's painful past, the atrocities of the Second World War and the Holocaust, showing their impact on the current life in Israel. However, the deliberately theatrical treatment of the past in *1789* made it possible to refer to the events in 1968 from a clearly political perspective. The production invited the audience to make connections and comparisons between the two revolutionary moments. After all Mnouchkine did not end the whole performance with a scene of celebrating crowds, but showed that the revolution did not bring about any significant changes in the social structure and social practices. By the same token, *1789* fulfilled the same subversive function that Lehmann described in the section of his *Postdramatic Theatre* devoted to the new forms of political theatre that we mentioned above.[23] Instead of clearly formulating a political message, Mnouchkine indirectly drew parallels between 'now' and 'then', and treated historical events as a prism through which the current situation in France was to be re-examined. Clearly *1789* can be treated as a forerunner of the strategies of eliciting the spectators' engagement by stressing their inadvertent involvement in the political life of their times and thus encouraging them to adopt an independent stance.

At first sight the striking similarities between *1789* and *Transfer!* that we have referred to could be used as a basis for a harsh judgment of the Polish production, insofar as the latter, on a purely formal level, might seem far more conservative than Mnouchkine's production. The play was produced in an institutional theatre, in a space that excludes the kind of physical contact between performers and audience members that the effectiveness of the solutions in *1789* relied on. What is more, even by comparison with Jan Klata's previous theatrical works, *Transfer!* might be interpreted as a return to the traditional model of theatre, with political impact exerted on the audience mainly through clearly articulated messages. The Polish national past and the relationship between the new and the old social order has been the main topic of Klata's works since the premiere of *The Government Inspector* (2003), based on Gogol's novel, which served as a blueprint for settling the accounts with the communist era. His most famous production, entitled *H.* (2004), based on *Hamlet*, was played in the shipyard in Gdańsk, which turned Shakespeare's masterpiece into a story about the relationship between contemporary Poland and its past, mostly in the Solidarity period. The relationship between today and the past was also the topic of *Transfer!*, which was staged in 2006 in the Współczesny Theatre in Wrocław. Again, as in the case of *H.*, the political character of the production did not stem from the use of particular aesthetic techniques and solutions, but rather from the direct relationship between the problems taken up by the stage production and the local community for which it was produced.

The production tackled an issue which since the mid-twentieth century has remained very significant for the inhabitants of the south-western region of Poland, namely the displacement of populations for political reasons as a result of the Yalta conference after the Second World War. The place where *Transfer!* was staged in large part determined the difference between this production and the previous production of *H.* The shipyard in Gdańsk functioned as a place which consolidated the national memory of the Polish nation, while the south-western regions of Poland are a land of a variety of national identities that coexist there because of the tumultuous historical past. For this reason many competing versions of the past coexist there. Therefore the very geographic place in which *Transfer!* was staged problematised the relationship between the dominant historical narrative and various versions of collective memory. This discrepancy between history and memory was underlined by the spatial arrangement on the stage. As noted, in the middle of the stage, on a high platform Stalin, Churchill and Roosevelt convened in Yalta, taking decisions significant for the shape of post-war Europe. But Klata makes it obvious that he presents a theatricalised history that makes no claim to objectivity. So for instance the politicians every now and again grab musical instruments and play songs by the British band Joy Division. What is more, their highly rhetorical, anachronous acting clearly manifests itself as pretence when confronted with the voice of non-actors who were actual witnesses of past events. They stand under the platform, on the stage and each of them tells his or her own story from the time of the massive displacements of populations. This very clear structure allows Klata to confront historical theatre through the form of storytelling, but also to subordinate one to the other. Theatricalised history is merely a background for the theatre of individual memory that is enacted in the foreground. The speakers tell their private and often incongruous narratives about how they became toys in the hands of the Great Trio and cogs in the great mechanism of history.

Undoubtedly *Transfer!* does not show an alternative or a more reliable version of history, in order to subvert the dominant image of that era. It does not provide an analysis of certain historical rules and regularities. There is no framework that would encompass the voices of the speakers, no narrator whose voice would dominate, and no documents are shown on stage to verify the stories provided by the witnesses. On the contrary, Klata focuses on that which is hardly ever included in historical narratives and deemed inconsequential, too individual, unbelievable or impossible to be verbalised. What is more, he clearly stresses that among those who speak there are witnesses whose recollections are a form of post-memory, gathered from reading their parents' letters, their stories or their experiences after the war. Very often the storytellers illustrate significant passages in their story with a gesture, which in an empty space delineates the shape of objects or a landscape. The past becomes an absent reality that cannot be reconstructed. The presence of the witnesses, even more than their stories, functions as indexes that refer to that absent past. No wonder that Klata does not evaluate the testimonies and puts a tale about the functioning of a guerrilla unit on a par with old German jokes about the leaders of the Third Reich. All those heterogeneous testimonies equally testify to the past. Also the past becomes material, not only because a few of the witnesses are German and speak in their mother tongue. The witnesses come to the stage with authentic objects and perform gestures that are linked with a key moment from the past. Some of them sing songs *a capella*, with their untrained voices. In this way Klata may be said to try to grasp memories before they became part of an imposed, official history. He shows memory as a material remnant of the past that is no different from other objects that testify to the past in the 'here and now'.

Klata uses storytelling strategies in order to emphasise the individual dimension of memory which always registers events from a particular point of view. Therefore he manages to subvert the dominant account of the past without showing a better or truer version of historical facts guaranteed by the presence of witnesses and their testimonies on stage. He uses theatre in order to present the past in its multidimensionality, to let many voices speak, so that the listeners can try to re-read the past in the theatre. For this reason he uses a spatial arrangement which stresses the binary opposition between an objectified history of a nation and memory as a domain of individual, private and – above all – exceptional experiences. And it is the disclosure of this binary opposition that provides an ultimate political aim for Klata's production. Everything else has been subordinated to it. For this reason Klata and his collaborators so painstakingly hid the fact that some of the testimonies were prepared and edited for the speakers by the production team so that they could tell exactly the same story every night. Also, consciously or not, the production team did not include representatives of other nationalities and ethnic groups that inhabited south-western Poland before the Second World War in the performance, a decision for which they were heavily criticised. However, irrespective of those critical judgments, the strategy used by Klata proved to have another political layer. By including only Poles and Germans the performance played a part in the process of reconciliation between the two countries and the two largest groups that inhabited the region and whose presence there is still prominent today. Seen in this light, the political scope of *Transfer!* turns out to be very wide. Overtly the production addresses the problems of the local community, but due to its construction, the meta-theatrical structure and the participation of witnesses, it surreptitiously serves the current politics of national reconciliation by overcoming the division of cultural differences.

The comparison of Mnouchkine's and Klata's productions provides ample evidence that the political character of postdramatic solutions lies not only in the very fact that they serve to disclose the means of representation involved in the production of history that sanctions the current social and political order. In both performances the impact was dictated at least in part by the place occupied by each production within a specific context of institutional practices, dominant aesthetics and current political situation. It is only in this wider context that self-reflexive strategies typical of postdramatic theatre can be regarded as political, and accordingly their impact can be measured. Undoubtedly the synchronic panorama of aesthetic forms presented in *Postdramatic Theatre* cannot (and was not meant to) do justice to the diachronic development of forms of political theatre in specific, local contexts. However, a return to the good old Hegelian scheme of development, which proceeds progressively and irrevocably towards its finale, will not do either.[24] Perhaps Greenblatt's theory of the circulation of social energies, which was reformulated in 2010 as the theory of cultural mobility, provides a way out of the traditional way of ordering the aesthetic tendencies, artistic strategies and performative genres. This Hegelian, teleological scheme of development of artistic forms can lead all too easily to hasty generalisations and judgments that assume the same pace and direction of development of political forms as theatre in the Western context. This becomes especially significant in the context of the theatrical strategies of staging post-traumatic memory. Very often these depart from the concept of theatre as a space of remembering the past towards the idea of a theatre as a realm of collective rewriting, reconstructing and partially forgetting, understood as the conscious and active rupture or modification of the links with tradition and the accepted narratives about the past. Such strategies can be encountered, for example in Tadeusz Kantor's performances, especially from his *Wielopole, Wielopole* (1980) onwards, in Eugène Ionesco's late works or in the play *Seefahrerstück* by the German author Oliver Schmaering (2005).[25] This rupture may also be a basis for a new collective identity when it paves the way for a new narrative about the past, a past yet to be found or discovered. However in our paper we have focused on the problematisation of the traditional pattern of subverting the one-dimensional view of the past. At the same time we analysed some typical strategies of socially and politically committed theatre in the past few decades. The examples that we have chosen demonstrate that the salient feature of political and postdramatic theatre has been its performative character. In each of the analysed performances the aim of the various staging solutions is to engage the audience in an act of participation, whether physical or mental. These performances engage the audience by making them draw upon the stock of their own individual and collective memory to go beyond the domain of pure fiction towards an experience that has a public, and therefore political character. In this sense the performances under scrutiny can be treated as examples of such a reformulation of the traditional stage-audience contract which lead to the emergence of Rancière's 'emancipated spectator'.

A Future for Tragedy? Remarks on the Political and the Postdramatic

Hans-Thies Lehmann

The problem of the 'political' in contemporary postdramatic theatre practice is brought to the fore again by the fact that we are witnessing more and more attempts at making use of theatrical practice with the aim of realising some direct intervention in the political sphere. New social and political mass movements in different parts of the world put the question on the agenda of the ways in which a development of new 'creative practices' (this was the title of a conference in London in May 2012 at the ICA) takes place in the context of these movements. It becomes hard to tell the difference between political and aesthetic gestures when, for instance, photographers make use of their craftsmanship to create a new visibility of the unemployed by introducing a 'blow up' of individual portraits of protesters, which are then carried as posters during demonstrations; when activists gather the countless daily 'narratives' about people's encounters with the police and other experiences in Cairo during the upheaval and transform them into documentary art; when street art in different versions creates a new aesthetics of political statements. Let me give an example from performance which in many ways is telling about the curious twilight zone between political activism and aesthetic practice. In her project – or performance/lecture? – *No Time for Art*, Egyptian artist Laila Soliman invites the audience to enter a lecture hall. At the door I am handed an envelope with an address on it, handwritten: it is to the International Court of Human Rights in Brussels. I take a seat and open the envelope. It contains two sheets of paper, one showing a written text in a black frame: 'I demand a trial for those responsible for the killing of Mina Daniel Ibrahim, age 19, died at Maspero, Cairo, on October 9th 2011 by an army bullet to the right corner of his chest which shattered his right lung and liver and caused intense bleeding . . .'. The content of all of these letters is similar: a name of one of the victims of police violence during the mass demonstrations in Cairo, as well as some brief details and a precise date and place. On the other piece of paper is an instruction to me, the audience member:

> Dear audience member, we would like to ask you for your help. We want to give as many martyrs as possible a face and a voice. If you are willing to help, please read the following instructions: 1. Somewhere in the theatre, someone will begin to read the name, age, circumstances, and place of death of a martyr into the microphone. 2. The microphone will be passed on and at one point the microphone will reach you. 3. If you want to, please read the statement, name and details of the martyr whom you have been given with this letter. 4. After you finish, please pass the microphone on to the audience member next to you; if you happen to be at the end of the row, please pass it on to the person in the row in front of you. Thank you, No Time for Art – Team.

I sit and wait, then indeed hear a voice calling for a trial for another person, then another voice, and so on. When the microphone is handed to me, I read and pass it on. When everybody has had his/her turn, the artist comments that she will now show some unpublished film documents of the events in Cairo. It is tough material. I find it at times difficult to watch the scenes of the bloody, brutal violence of the police against demonstrators. Then it is over. 'Questions, please!'

It was an intense moment. But what exactly happened here? The first answer which comes to mind: we passed a certain amount of time honouring the memory of these 'martyrs' of the democracy movement who, heroically, sacrificed their life for freedom, for democracy, for the attempt to change Egypt's society for the better. Just reading and hearing the names became an act of awareness and engagement. Second thought: we did *not* engage in a political or even a juridical act in any pragmatic way. An accusation without concrete name has no legal status. And it remains up to me what I 'do' with the letter with the handwritten address in front of me. Shall I post it? We are instead experiencing a moment, very strictly, of *theatre*. It is about voices, individual voices, in a space where I see and hear. I am engaged and there is emotion. The process remains without propaganda, or even political statement. Instead, I have the chance of an experience with myself: suddenly I feel the demand which this envelope is addressing to me. And I feel uneasily confronted with my not doing anything about this reality. The event is a very strong version of what we may call a 'dramaturgy of the spectator'. There is no performance, no theatre, no acting out of a dramatic story. But there is the audience – our voices in a public space, our silence, our listening, our common moment of '*Eingedenken*' (remembrance). It is postdramatic theatre practiced as a theatre of situation.

Although in this event, *No Time for Art*, there is no performance of a drama, we may speak here of tragedy. Not because the event in itself will be called 'tragic' by many. But because – anticipating my argument – tragedy in our time no longer has to take the shape of a dramatic process but may with equal – and I add: superior – legitimacy appear in moments of performance, in postdramatic theatre. And it is not by chance that such a presence of the tragic is closely related to the issue in what ways the relation of theatre and the political may be thought and practised today.

Let us take a big step back. The question whether there is still (or again) room in our contemporary culture for something which may be called tragic and/or tragedy at all can be answered neither easily nor quickly. Much important theory (from Hegel to Lukács and Benjamin) historicised and relegated tragedy to antiquity, spoke of the 'death of tragedy' in many tunes, saw tragedy as dissolved and as of yesterday. Adorno saw tragedy as something of the past and spoke of catharsis as a piece of art mythology.[1] Since someone's suffering calls for help, not for aesthetic appreciation, Brecht objected to any pity or empathy that is without consequence and held the view that the talk of tragedy was substituting an ideological notion of fate for concrete analysis of society. There is indeed much reason to detest the ideological transformation of man-made sufferings into fate, as well as the inflation of the media's talk of 'tragedy' when terrible events happen on a grand scale. And if some advocates of 'modern tragedy' commit the error of consciously and seriously proposing that 'tragedy' is a reality of life, instead of a specific way of presenting it, everything gets mixed up completely. Events in themselves are neither tragic nor not-tragic, rather tragedy is a certain *perspective* on the event. You may give a narrative of tragic events which does not create a 'tragic feeling' at all. (This insight does, of course, by no means imply a criticism of the use of the name 'tragic' in order to give expression to the complex mixture of emotions and admiration that these events arouse in the observer.) From the beginning the articulation of the tragic was closely connected to basic questions of the political, the *polis*, to history, power and conflict. Today is no exception to this rule. There can be no private tragedy. Where we find the tragic, we hit upon the political.

I will try to bring a modest amount of light into this debate. Let me first of all distinguish between two main theoretical approaches to the problem of the tragic. In one view, and especially in *philosophical ethics*, the central problem is the nature of certain conflicts – basic political, moral, social conflicts (roughly speaking between the individual and the community, the personal and the social), which traditionally have been labelled tragic and which form the stock repertoire of the great European theatre tradition from Aeschylus to Shakespeare, Racine and Schiller. Here the essential question today is whether conflicts of this particular kind still exist in modernity or postmodernity, or whether they are, strictly speaking, a phenomenon of earlier states of society, history, civilisation, of the 'Hegelian Geist'.

Hegel situated tragedy historically in the development of the *Geist* (the Spirit). Tragedy belongs strictly to the ancient Greek world of the *polis* state. His model case is *Antigone* by Sophocles. The ancient Greek *polis* is representative of what Hegel calls the world of '*Sittlichkeit*' – a term that is difficult to translate but which encompasses something like generally accepted morality, binding ethical rules that govern the way of thinking and acting of a community and thus constitute it as a practically working and concretely articulated but – most importantly – specific culture. This culture cannot be generalised, let alone globalised. *Sittlichkeit* constitutes a world of specifically determined 'dos and don'ts', values and styles of behaviour, rules, interdictions and obligations, which, although not (or only partially) fixed in the modern way as written laws, function as an unquestioned order and orientation for everyone within the boundaries of this given culture. Thus, 'ethical order' is a rather inadequate translation of '*Sittlichkeit*' because it carries the suggestion of a kind of logically structured ethical system. Because of the double existence of the spirit of *Sittlichkeit* as, first, publicly known rules and, secondly, individual consciousness, there is a systematic possibility and thus a necessity of conflict – where both sides, individual and state, are in a way right, justified, but must be destroyed because of their very one-sidedness. For the onlooking consciousness the result of experiencing the tragic conflict is, according to Hegel, that we are deeply moved (*erschüttert*) by the fate of the hero, but at the same time satisfied (*befriedigt*) in the recognition of the deeper unity of the colliding opposites.[2] Should this not be so, the poet has failed and written something which perhaps can only induce 'mere sadness' (*bloße Trauer*).[3]

As is well known, Hegel views the process of thought as well as of history as a kind of (spiral) staircase, leading step by step to ever more encompassing abstraction, rationality and finally absolute (self-)presence of mind – no longer shadowed by relicts of materiality, unrestricted by ingrained and 'un-thought' unconscious cultural values. The ultimate truth of the Spirit is therefore beyond any graspable concrete *Gestalt*. Hegel views the tragic type of conflict just sketched as grounded in an as yet insufficiently clear degree of rationality and abstraction. At the same time – just as with ancient sculpture and ancient art in general – it is exactly this very limit or lack of abstraction that allows tragedy to be so beautiful – *Antigone* is for him the most satisfying work of art ever – and ancient sculpture the most beautiful art forever. Interestingly, it is its very limitation in terms of spiritualisation which allows it to be concrete to such a degree that it can assume a beautiful *Gestalt* and can be considered the most beautiful sensuous appearance of the Spirit ever. 'Nothing is or could be more beautiful' ('*Schöneres kann nicht sein und werden*').[4] Tragedy in this reading is basically a representation of intense 'collision', which logically begs for a representation as dramatic opposition.

A second line of thought – that extends from Nietzsche to Karl Heinz Bohrer – insists on the *autonomy of the aesthetic experience* as such, as opposed to all ethico-political perception. There are in this view, to cut a long story short, certain artistic productions or practices which articulate (or lead us to recognise) human existence as essentially transgressive, thus risky, inherently disastrous and potentially self-destructive. Such a tragic view exists and keeps returning in different versions throughout European theatre history. It catches those moments and structures of life where the human goes to the limits and crosses them. A tragic dimension in this sense characterises human existence as such in its internal rift and drift into the unknown, creating collision and transgression, such that terror, sacrifice, downfall, are unavoidably at the core of human life. However, the transgression of limits is at the same time possibly an 'enthusiastic' uplifting, a revolutionary spirit of revolt and 'self affirmation'. The tragic transgression leads us to a recognition of the radical possibilities of the human being to transcend itself and its world and at the same time to choose the path where self-destruction awaits.

The tragic articulates the sense of a disruptive and destructive force working within the self and also a sense of the elusiveness in the last instance of its goals. The provocative aspect of this analysis is this: even if it may assume the form of a political fight, tragic experience as such takes place beyond any moral, ethical or political – and even any rational – consideration. Martin Heidegger in his reading of the famous stasimon about man in *Antigone* insists that the ancient hubris (the tendency to overstep given limits) is by no means a mistake (the tragic *hamartia*) which could or should be avoided in favour of rational self-conservation. On the contrary, venturing into the unknown, overstepping given limits, defiance of disaster defines the human being as such, and constitutes its very humanity.[5] Thus, the tendency towards disaster comes close to being not only one particular but the essential feature of human nature.

There was always protest and resistance from the point of view of rational political analysis (and enlightenment in general) against tragedy, on the grounds that it presents suffering as unavoidable. Indeed it is exactly this notion of a certain unavoidability of catastrophe which constitutes the tragic dimension – as opposed to all kinds of saddening, terrible, horrible realities in general. This view of tragedy does, however, by no means imply a general statement or theory about life. Art is not philosophy. Rather tragedy focuses on this particular possible way of viewing life. It by no means implies that this must be the only way to think of it. There has been much talk of an ultimate tragic truth, a 'tragische Weltanschauung'.[6] If something of the sort existed, Shakespeare for example would have had to switch his world view like his shirts from comedy to tragedy and back, likewise Racine, Corneille or Hofmannsthal who all wrote tragedies or *Trauerspiele* as well as comedies. No, tragedy is not necessarily the expression of a tragic outlook on life but a matter of a certain artistic approach to and rendering of it. It no more expresses the one and only ultimate truth about our world than, say, – and I refer here to Clifford Geertz[7] – the *corrida* encapsulates the ultimate truth about the Spanish way of thinking or the cock fight the truth about Balinese culture in general.

If tragedy is a matter of a certain perspective on human life, it is however turning up again and again with impressive insistence, and particularly in certain periods of European history. We find it especially in the hubris of the hero of ancient Greek tragedy who appears to be the rival of the Gods, and in Elizabethan heroes who impress by their desire and passion beyond measure, rationality and morality – in the last instance without sense, auto-destructive. Life becomes then a 'tale told by an idiot, full of sound and fury, signifying nothing' (Macbeth, V, 5). Richard III will refuse the horse to save himself in withdrawal from the battle with these words: 'Slave I have set my life upon a cast and I will stand the hazard of the die' (V, 4). Thus, after a long drama of seeking and preserving the magic crown, he is transforming all his doings in one moment into: a game. We find in these gestures a transgression of all sense, morals or even goals. The tragic is not about a telos, an aim, at all. Not even the aim of self-realisation. Or we may say that, in the tragic perspective, realisation of the 'self' would paradoxically imply the drift towards a transgression of the limits of the self, so that constitution and loss of the self are experienced as inseparable.

Tragic transgression can take very different forms. From one point of view it may appear as the irresistible charm of crime: the transgressive act happens not – as ethical consideration would have it – in spite of but because of the violation of the ethical norm. This is the way Lacan reads *Antigone*.[8] Alternatively, transgression articulates the craving for complete union with the other which turns out to be aggressive and self-destructive. Transgression may be a dangerous erotic adventure, putting personal honour, recognition by others and even life at radical risk. In this sense Georges Bataille, Michel Leiris and others held that only taking such a risk is capable of giving real value to human existence. Bataille states that 'Eros is the tragic god',[9] and speaks of the complicity of the tragic – which is grounded in death – with *jouissance* and laughter. And for Nietzsche tragic experience is not definable as an artistic representation of ethical or political conflicts but the experience of the unconditional affirmation and the acceptance of life, even and particularly in pain, suffering and death. He therefore arrives at an identification of the tragic with the Dionysiac.[10] Tragedy makes us aware of the cruel truth of Dionysus, which inheres in the ecstasy and the dangerous pleasure of the loss of the self, of overcoming individuation as such. Along these lines, Georges Bataille developed his notions of 'dépense' and 'transgression'. This way of reading the tragic as an experience of transgression differs essentially from the first in that it does not necessarily suggest a factual or theoretical connection to a certain artistic form. While the concept of conflict is obviously closely associated with some kind of dramatic representation, the tragic as transgression is a phenomenon of a sphere where bodily awareness, sentiment, mental shock and thinking may find articulation without dramatic structure.

I will now address the question if and in what ways the tragic gesture may be related to the dimension of the political. However beautiful, the lack of abstraction in the tragedy of *Sittlichkeit* must lead in Hegel's implicit and explicit logic and historic development to a next step of comprehension: to the world of general, formalised, abstract law in which all individuals get their fair share, insofar as each individual enjoys the abstract recognition as a person – just like everyone else.

Therefore Hegel places tragedy historically at the borderline between the Greek *polis* and the more modern world of the Roman Empire and the Roman idea of law, of a legal system. Here already, it's over with tragedy. The new formalism and the higher degree of abstraction are the emblems of modernity, and they overcome the traditionalist world of the unquestionable values of *Sittlichkeit*. They constitute a progress in themselves of rationality and spirit (*Geist*), but they carry with them a number of grave problems. As we have come to realise, the modern principle of legal abstraction can turn into the most dreadful barbarism. 'Infinite justice' as well as the pure and graceless execution of formal equality can turn into sheer despotism (military 'human rights' interventions). Rationalism without wisdom can be auto-destructive.

And furthermore, in reality the process of formal equality of the person remains bound to certain assumptions or values of a cultural and hence relative nature – even if the Western mind tends to think of them as unquestionable, universally valid values. In other words, the old *Sittlichkeit* which bred tragic conflict will survive somehow and not disappear altogether as foreseen. Even if we assumed optimistically today that the normative value of abstract justice is spreading worldwide, that it is more and more widely accepted and practised, we have no sufficient reason to affirm a dissolution of tragic conflict altogether. Even if lawful procedure increasingly reduces the limitations of specific ingrained cultural norms and values of this or that culture, this process does not automatically bring to an end conflicts between the principle of justice as a rational political guiding norm and the uncompromising desire of individuals to live in a way that they deem to be authentic to their culture. Also, today we find individuals who cling to their specific cultural behaviour as stubbornly as a Sophoclean hero, because to give up on it would mean nothing less than giving up themselves. Thus, with Hegel, and *against* his view of the one and only logic of the process of history, we are led to acknowledge the space for tragic conflict in the field of the kind of sociopolitical conflict that becomes especially intense in the multicultural world of today. There is space for tragedy even organised along the patterns of traditional conflict dramaturgy, and these conflicts may be representable as dramatic conflicts to a certain degree, in certain fields and under certain conditions. But these conditions allow only for a small path of such dramatic tragedy. The habit of spectating is so strong in a 'society of the spectacle'[11] that even the most burning political issues instantly lose their edge by being transformed into an element of spectacle. Although there are exceptions in today's institutionalised theatrical practice, I doubt that the necessary shock to our cultural habits can be achieved within the limits of a theatre of representation. Since tragedy is essentially the experience of reaching and overstepping for a moment the limits of a given 'cultural intelligibility', a presentation of tragedy within a theatrical convention that does not put basic cultural presuppositions at risk cannot be a legitimate heir to the tragic today. Instead I have the strong impression that nowadays the field of what we may term the tragic is rarely found any longer in the realm of the theatre where ancient, classical, modern and contemporary tragedies continue to be staged. On the contrary, we have good reason for seeking an experience of tragic transgression mainly in the seemingly marginal, dispersed, creative as well as problematic field of performance, 'live art' and postdramatic theatre practices.

The fact that *dramatic* form and dramatic theatre of representation are becoming problematic as a support for tragic experience does not prevent the closest relation between the tragic and *theatre*, which has a much wider scope than drama. Systematically, the articulation of tragic experience is not bound to dramatic procedure – but to theatre. It is not by chance that in the nineteenth century the great conceptions of the tragic, which had the idealist systems as a point of departure or of demarcation (Hölderlin, Kierkegaard, Schopenhauer,

Nietzsche, Hebbel), coincided with the factual decline and becoming problematic of the genre of tragedy.

If ancient tragedy obviously had the specific feature that the tragic was closely bound to the theatre, then, I would argue, this undoubtedly intimate connection between the tragic and the theatre was due to the fact not that theatre is drama but that theatre was still closely related to ritual: ritual was the prehistory of the newly invented art of theatre, and there existed a large number of ritual activities in the *polis* which theatre performances constantly alluded to (punishments, ritual death penalties, sacrifices of bulls and goats, ritual ceremonies of all kinds, and of course the ritual of the Dionysian festivities themselves, of which tragedy was a part). All this is hardly taken into account by Aristotle, who famously claimed that tragedy (and its catharsis) worked very well even without any real theatre. 'Opsis', the theatrical representation proper, he considered to be the least artful part of tragedy, even superfluous.[12] The key point here is that the emancipation of the *aesthetic* sphere or the theatrical play and game from ritual was not yet complete in the classical age, even if it had begun and was advancing. And it was exactly this *in*complete distinction between art and ritual, thus between the aesthetic sphere and the seriousness of religious reality which was responsible for the fact that in ancient Athens the tragic experience could take place in and remained closely bound to theatre. Much recent research[13] has confirmed that the classical tragedy remained very much in touch with ritual and was in no way considered a purely aesthetic/artistic phenomenon.

Today this insight serves to enhance our understanding that in fact tragic experience can take place only if (and to the degree that) the aesthetic articulation is crossed out by an *interruption* and caesura of the sphere of aesthetic representation. Then and only then is it possible to experience a shaking or destabilising of the basic grounds of our cultural existence, even a blurring of the boundaries of the self, of conceptual understanding as such.

Therefore, if we ask where and how tragic experience may take place in our society, we have to look not for aesthetically faultless tragic representation along the lines or conventions of drama, but exactly for those practices which to some degree blur the distinction between the spheres of the aesthetic and the real, between the sphere of irresponsible artistic pleasure (which all art, including tragic theatre, must still give) and the sphere of ethical and political consideration and responsibility (which all art, including tragic theatre must refer us back to). It is just because of the awareness how completely we have achieved the separation of the aesthetic sphere from the rest of our experience (ethical, moral, political, religious) that we must insist that aesthetic practice as such cannot be grounded in the conviction that it constitutes in and of itself a 'promise', a foreshadowing of a utopia of a different human reality. Art must posit itself in this other place of non-artistic reality where seemingly there is no place for art.

Tragic experience is bound to a process where we are taken to the edge of normative and conceptual self-assurance, and this process cannot be achieved by purely theoretical subversion but by the uncanny mental and physical experience of entering the twilight zone, where the sustainability of cultural norms which we adhere to is put into doubt. This, however, can also be said about the dimension of the political where the latter is understood in the sense of questioning the fundamental structures of our being together in a *polis*, rather than taking positions on concrete political issues. In theatre this condition can easily be translated into one formula: one precondition of the tragic – and as we may add now: of the political in theatre – is the momentous undermining of key certainties: about whether we are spectators or participants; whether we perceive or are confronted with perceptions that function 'as if' or for real; whether we dwell in the field of aesthetic make-belief or in real actuality.

The creation of this grey zone of overlapping experiences and perceptions can happen in extremely different ways. One result of such a practice of shuttling between states is the necessity for the participants to make a decision about the nature of what they live through or witness. They find themselves in a double bind, calling for an aesthetic appreciation and at the same time for a reaction of responsibility which would be to some degree 'real'. There remain 'grey' zones of indistinction between art and the political which can be explored, opened, enlarged by theatre practice. Tragedy may come about in such artistic practices which, on the one hand, imply a clear consciousness of the autonomy of the aesthetic sphere, but on the other hand find it difficult to remain within it, and seek ways not to dissolve but to *interrupt* this autonomy. What then happens is this: it becomes possible to *re-invest* the sphere of the real into the aesthetic domain which systematically is defined precisely by the exclusion of the real. Ethico-political responsibility re-enters into the aesthetic experience.

I hope it has become clear at this point why I started with the example of Laila Soliman's *No Time for Art*. The example is also helpful in demarcating the argument put forward here about the political in theatre from the position of Jacques Rancière who is – with good reason – impatient with activist ideas, teaching concepts in theatre, and utopian notions of community in theatre. While I endorse Rancière's refutation of simplified models of the political in theatre which tend to think of it as a 'teaching', and while he is certainly right in criticising the illusion of an anticipated community or collectivity in theatre, I must quarrel with the alternative he proposes and which tends very much to revitalise the notion of the autonomous aesthetic sphere as such. Reading Schiller, Rousseau and Kant in a reductive way, Rancière wants to convince us that his notion of artistic practice as a contribution to the 'redistribution of the sensible field' of perception, 'le partage du sensible', is best served by a new version of the old idea that art best remains non-political in order to be political. This in turn may amount to the position that all art as such is political.

Reading Schiller's *Aesthetic Letters*, Rancière defines the aesthetic experience as an experience of 'zero', of neutrality.[14] This is indeed what Schiller, in the spirit of unification which profoundly marked the project of idealism, explicitly claims: 'In the aesthetic state the human is zero.'[15] Here Schiller means that man is not determined, either by conceptual or by sensuous constraints. The beautiful is characterised by indeterminacy ('Bestimmungslosigkeit'). With a little 'trick', however, Rancière transforms this 'neither-nor' into a purely neutral state. From this small misinterpretation grave consequences follow. For Schiller, in contrast to Rancière's reading, the aesthetic state is a state of bliss: no sorrow, no desire, no fear. Hence, no will is needed. While in Schiller the intermediate sphere of art is neither dominated by sensuality nor conceptuality, in Rancière it is only the latter non-determination which counts. Art appears in Schiller (as presented by Rancière) as a sphere beyond and free of conceptuality. Thus, the genuinely idealistic approach of Schiller disappears. The subject in the aesthetic state, Rancière points out, is not in the Schillerian-Kantian state of bliss when experiencing the beautiful, but in a 'state of war'.[16] But it is evident that the Kantian project on which Schiller largely relies defines beauty as something that puts the human subject in harmony. Kant's argument runs like this: we find a phenomenon beautiful if and insofar as our experience of it causes in us the pleasurable impression (regardless of whether this impression is correct, grounded or not) that the world for the subject is a home: what is presented by the senses to the imagination (*Einbildungskraft*) puts our two basic capacities in harmonious exchange and cooperation. The reason for this pleasure is not at all a liberation from a dominating conceptuality but, on the contrary, precisely the feeling that what the senses present is open to a conceptual understanding – even if we do not grasp this understanding concretely. Like the 'aesthetic idea', which is defined by Kant as a representation that gives much to think about without being subsumable under a certain concept, the beautiful achieves the impression in the subject of being, so to say, 'at home in the world'. Here there is no conflict, but rather joyful unity between what the senses present and the capacity of understanding. Kant states that the 'Einhelligkeit' or harmony of imagination and mind in itself produces pleasure – and because there is no external reason for this, because this pleasure is completely self-referential, related only to the subject's experience itself, it is obvious that it produces a purely subjective feeling of 'being right'. Aesthetic pleasure is the feeling that the mind can relate logically (as a being of thought) to the world presented to the senses. Kant relates this experience concretely to the (political) idea of a unity of all humans in the sense that they cannot be at odds about the pleasure of the understandability of the world: 'The excitement of both faculties (imagination and understanding) to indeterminate but yet, through the stimulus of the given sensation, harmonious activity, viz. that which belongs to cognition in general, is the sensation whose universal communicability is postulated by the judgement of taste.'[17]

We may say: the subject has a 'one-world-feeling' – it is at home in the world and this pleasurable feeling must be generally human exactly because (this kind of) rationality is general for humankind. This is the essence of aesthetic pleasure, not the liberation from the dominance of the concept but the affirmation of the potential to grasp reality conceptually. This is the idealist notion to which Schiller refers, even if he goes beyond Kant in postulating not only this sensory experience (*Empfindung*) but the experience of 'freedom in the appearance' (*Freiheit in der Erscheinung*) as the nucleus of the beautiful, in a way that Kant never would have accepted, since freedom remains for him a pure 'concept of reason' (*Vernunftbegriff*) for which no reality can be found, since our categories of understanding (*Verstand*) necessarily structure all perceptions along the lines of causality.

Rancière's simplification/falsification of the concept of artistic autonomy is followed by a strong statement: drawing a direct analogy to politics he sees the rulers in the position of the Schillerian form (*Form*) and the masses in the position of the Schillerian material (*Stoff*): 'The power of the form over the material is the power of the universal of the state over the anarchy of the individual and the masses.'[18] For Rancière, this symbolises the power of culture over nature, of the classes of leisure over the classes of work: 'The true revolution would be to bring about a change in the distribution of the sensible that separates two humanities, one of which is dedicated to the autonomy of action, the other to the heteronomy of passive materiality.'[19] But whence this desire to save the Schillerian gesture by cleaning it of its idealist drive? The answer seems simple enough: this is done in order to promote a version of the relation/tension between art and politics in such a way that the slightly dated idea of art as a 'promise' of a different human reality can be sustained. If, as Rancière affirms not once but three times in the text on Schiller, there is in fact no opposition between the autonomy of art and political heteronomy, then we may indeed forget about any concrete attempts not to uphold the autonomy of artistic work but to realise an *interruption* of the aesthetic stance. 'Politics revolves around what is seen and what can be said about it, around who has the ability to see and the talent to speak, around the properties of spaces and the possibilities of time.'[20] This very just remark by Rancière, indeed the whole line of his argument is most useful as a refutation of all concepts of the 'political' that reduce it to a play of distribution of political power within a given system. The other side of his argument is less convincing. On the basis of a more than superficial insight into the questions which haunt theatre practice today, Rancière seems to massively under-define the problems posed nowadays for theatre and performance in terms of their relation to the political – even taking the term as Rancière's fruitfully uses it above to denote a practice which brings the voice of equality to attention. In some of his writings we find an almost unqualified revival of the aesthetic sphere as it appears in Schiller, whose ideas he repeatedly calls 'unsurpassable' or 'unsurpassed'. But in view of contemporary theatre practice it is highly questionable that art, in order to maintain a genuine relation with the political, should be in need of the 'purity of its theatre, i.e. the radical separation of art work and life'.[21] I will not go into the background of Rancière's saving the beautiful against the sublime, as read by Lyotard. It is important in our context to make clear that the re-invention of the classical notion of the aesthetic as an autonomous sphere, the purity of which is a promise for an existence beyond bad reality, is – besides being a long-established trope of art theory – simply too abstract to cope with the difficulties that have to be dealt with in contemporary artistic life and especially theatre. Rather, Rancière's position tends to lead straight back to the idea that all art as such is political. The problem is to be situated in the idea of the model or 'promise' given in art of a different reality. Rancière states clearly: 'Again and again it [the theatre HTL] has to play a lost power of the body and anticipate a future communion.'[22] The impulse (which one cannot but share) to liberate theatre theory from the idea of either a teaching process or a hasty affirmation of anticipated communal being tends in Ranciére's conception to fall back on the aim 'to restore [the theatrical stage HTL] to an equal footing with the telling of a story, the reading of a book, the gaze focused on an image'.[23] This phrase simply passes by the concrete questions which theatre and performance practice, as specifically different situations from reading, viewing, telling, have to tackle. It discourages any necessary attempts to develop forms and theatrical settings that overcome the private, individualistic mode of perception that surfaces here.

Epilogue

From the dawn of European theatre until Beckett, the human being has been staging the theatricalised tragic experience. But in our times this experience has taken place in forms beyond drama and even beyond the traditional dramatic idea of theatre in general: for example in the Brechtian *Lehrstück* (even if this view of Brecht might be surprising); in Beckettian standstill; in a wide range of postdramatic theatre and performance practices. In his later texts, Heiner Müller was seeking articulations, combinations, compromise between, on the one hand, the dramatic mode (in which to demonstrate political conflict and paradox) and, on the other hand, ways of opening up the closure of the tragic and dramatic mode: by means of chorus and monologue, montage and discontinuity, seeking for example in *Wolokolamsker Chaussee* to bring the historical narrative close to a solo performance. This does not happen by chance. Müller's texts have at their innermost heart a specific artistic and at the same time political experience: the loss of a visible enemy. The subject of the text is an 'Ego without adversary'. The subject as political agent is thus threatened with losing the very ground on which alone it could be constituted. The other, as an adversary with whom strife, argument, war, political decision is possible – this other is missing. Hence, no more drama. At the heart of its contemplation of the political sphere, the political agent finds a reality – the empty space where it looked out for the enemy to fight against – that de-constitutes its very being. This uncanny and uneasy inner catastrophe is the dimension which carries Müller's texts far above being simply the reflection of the breakdown of a certain state socialism. It articulates a tragic experience beyond the structure and form of tragic drama, approaching the practice of poetic or scenic performance.

Or take Sarah Kane. Even in her very first play, *Blasted*, the dramatic representation broke down in the middle of the play and gave way to a scenic and literary phantasmagoria very different from the still conceivably realistic mode of the first part of the play. And if I should have to mention a postdramatic text in the tragic mode, that is: a tragic text which corresponds to the aesthetics of postdramatic theatre, I would certainly point to the later texts of Kane, culminating in '4.48 Psychosis'. Here a genuine tragic experience is communicated: it is the radical uncompromising drive for a completely authentic meeting and contact with the other (which alone could constitute an authentic self), which at the same time seems to destroy the possibility of the self to exist. On the last page of Kane's text the gap is wide open. One sentence at the top of the page: 'It is myself I have never met, whose face is pasted on the underside of my mind.' – then the blankness of the white paper – and at the bottom: 'please open the curtains'.[24] This is the last phrase of '4.48 Psychosis'. Since we feel it is us in the theatre who (metaphorically speaking) should open or who should have opened these curtains a long time ago, a tragic experience takes place.

I might also mention *The Crying Body* by Jan Fabre, a disturbing, sometimes shocking experience, torturing at times, with moments of repulsion and anxiety that are awe-inspiring. Fabre's theatre is a theatre of physicality which makes manifest the body in pain and humiliation, it is a tragic theatre in that it realises a risky transgression on the edge of what is culturally acceptable. It evokes repulsion and melancholy, it forces the spectator to choose between opening to a radically obscene, but at the same time deeply touching experience – or to reject this presentation of the tears of the body – including, for example, also pissing in public on the stage. The emotion is centred on the physical tragedy of the body. Artaud's tragic 'emotional athlete' is back (recalling the ancient sacrificial hero and the athletic combat which had deep religious and cultic significance). By taking the spectators as well as the performers to the edge of culturally coded acceptability, it leads us to experience the tragic shock, for a moment exposing our civilised psyche to a different kind of experience.

We may label as 'tragic' the inner breakdown of the subject as a political agent (Müller); the breakdown of the subject as nameless and thereby the evaporation of authentic love and desire (Kane); the subject of a physicality which calls for humiliating transgression in the search for an ultimate sovereignty (Fabre). And in a radical way we see the possibility of a tragic process beyond representation when the borderline between the (overlapping) ethico-political dimension and aesthetic experience is crossed and we enter the twilight zone or border area between play and seriousness. There are performance practices today which leave behind the frame of presenting a tragic process at all and generate theatre without staged theatre, and it has become essential to realise that theatre of tragedy as well as political theatre practice work with this option. I do not wish to simply recommend *No Time for Art* as a model to be copied. There are certainly other ways to make use of the theatrical situation to engage with the political. But it brings to light the essential dimension of the tragic process: that it cannot remain confined to an experience which remains in the framework of consuming an aesthetic reality. The same is true for the 'political' dimension of theatre, which does not develop without a radical rethinking of the act of spectating as such.

We have to maintain the *interruption*, the caesura of the aesthetic-contemplative mode in theatre. Not that there is something intrinsically wrong with the latter. But in many ways it is worn out. But worn out are also the hopes connected to the activating, inter-active mode as a solution. The omnipresence of passively consumed narratives in pictures and words as well as the activist inter-active gameplay in computer games and participatory shows have ruined both models for any critical purpose. The aesthetic opportunity for intervention in the political lies elsewhere – notably, in variants of an interrupted aesthetic experience. The historical phase of the autonomy of 'Art' is drawing to its end, therefore the notion of an autonomous art which emphasises the sphere of non-will, non-action cannot be the answer.

At the same time it has become clear that theatre is not a place and a means to distribute an ideology, to teach an insight. It works only *modo obliquo*, for example by laying bare ideological structures in our everyday way of seeing the world. I still consider Althusser's notion useful that our mindset is defined by a kind of 'melodramatic consciousness' which constantly seduces us to misread and to re-humanise social processes, to personalise them. Ideology is essentially self-misunderstanding. In this respect theatre must necessarily find ways to confront this habit of perception with the utterly non-personal economic, financial, social, political processes. At the same time we have learnt that the Brechtian answer of presenting the political problem in epic distance to an audience is no longer sufficient, even if it presents the insight into our lack of insight rather than a didactic message.

Is *No Time for Art* a theatre of 'participation'? Not at all. Participation, a notion very fashionable these days, can mean very different things. And simply the demand to be asked about political decisions and even the demand to take part in these decisions makes clear the failure of a society which does not live up to its democratic claim. But theatre practice tends toward modes of participation also for genuinely aesthetic reasons. Much postdramatic theatre is in fact a theatre of *situation*. A correct appreciation of these practices depends on the recognition that they are not necessarily claiming an ideology of participation and equality between spectators and performers, but rather that they seek ways of creating a meeting point and conflict between aesthetic contemplation and its caesura by the intervention of social reality. In *No Time for Art* the participant is drawn into a 'warm' process of sharing admiration, pity and terror (classical notions associated with the effect of tragedy). At the same time he/she feels a lack in the face of the absence of action. The aesthetic appreciation is broken by a concrete questioning of the self.

Here as in other works (and with other techniques) theatre or performance dismisses the scheme of separating reception and presentation. In this situation, which is indicative of the state of art of theatre, a call to arms in favour of a Schillerian 'aesthetic regime' seems to be misplaced. At the same time we must, with Rancière, safeguard against a new ideology of the unified theatre community. Theatre presents an exceptional possibility of communication, it is by nature 'relational art'. In a sense, in theatre the ways and possibilities of communication can become a direct object for artistic research and working through on all levels – communication by the body, by the voice, by the gesture, and also, among other things, by meaning; communication between performer and audience, among audience members and so forth. This does not mean that the art work of mise en scène simply vanishes – in many cases it will continue to constitute a part or even the heart of the performance and theatre event. But a future of genuine tragedy – not a museum of tragedy – will in each case be found only in such performance practices which undermine our melodramatic way of perception within or without the frame of classical theatre. In this way the future of tragedy will be political or it will not be. It remains true that the task of art is, as defined by Heiner Müller: to make reality impossible.[25]

Spectres of Subjectivity: On the Fetish of Identity in (Post-)Postdramatic Choreography

Peter M. Boenisch

Postdramatic theatre has, as Hans-Thies Lehmann suggested, dissolved the absoluteness of the 'fictive cosmos' of the dramatic regime;[1] meanwhile, dance has in the course of the past decades dissolved the frontiers of its entire discipline. In *Tales of the Bodiless* (2011), a dance performance by Hungarian dancer-choreographer Eszter Salamon, there were not even any dancing bodies. Only for a brief scene, two immobile figures appeared on stage, bathed in colourful atmospheric lighting in the midst of a dark and sombre empty stage, and even here one was never quite sure whether these were real bodies or merely projections. Spatial sculptures formed of fog, smoke and light, along some projected texts and images, constituted the actual site of choreography. A soundtrack of mesmerising electronic music (by Cédric Dambrain and Terre Thaemlitz) accompanied the narration of, initially, a sonorous male voice, later a dialogue, then a multitude of sampled voices (sound design Peter Böhm). They told a science fiction story in four acts, about future worlds where humans have become bodiless, while only dogs retain their corporeal presence. The complex audio-scape was relayed through an assortment of loudspeakers meticulously arranged throughout the theatre, enveloping the audience, who for once actually mostly listened to this bodiless dance piece. Salamon's piece provides a salient example of a recent challenge to the now-established postdramatic discourse in theatre and performance studies. While, following an era of playful deconstruction, dance performance has arrived at its most extreme of becoming 'bodiless', an emerging 'post-postdramatic' generation of artists now puts emphasis precisely on the 'tales' again: as in Salamon's choreography, not only authorial voices of storytellers and narrators re-enter the performance space, but also characters and dialogic speech reappear as spectres of the dramatic legacy. At the same time, we witness a new engagement with the historical past, of the genre itself, but also beyond. 'Re-enactments' have become the mode of the day, for example of Alan Kaprow's *18 Happenings* and Yvonne Rainer's *Trio A*, both by dance scholar André Lepecki (created in 2007 and 2009 respectively), or Lucinda Childs' and Robert Wilson's own restagings of their signature pieces *Dance* (2009) and *Einstein on the Beach* (2012). This perspective of the former avant-garde as historic event of the past is accompanied, elsewhere, by an interest in popular and national folk dance traditions.

The return of these notions shifts not least of all the issue of subjectivity once more into the centre of dramaturgic concern. This chapter explores these concurring recent developments in both dance and theatre as important further 'turns of the (postdramatic) screw'. These productions disclose horizons of subjectivity which no longer support subjectivity as an expression of an authentic self, nor as purely ideological misrecognition. Instead, they assert a subjective position of formal self-reflexivity that always maintains a distance from itself and thereby can never become identical with itself. I suggest that this 'empty' core of subjectivity, which resonates with the Lacanian-Žižekian perspective on subjective (political) agency, becomes the ground for what French philosopher Jacques Rancière cautiously termed 'politicity' in contemporary performance-making.

To start with, however, we first need to clarify the not altogether straightforward position of dance within the postdramatic paradigm. After all, the influx of *dramatic* ingredients into dance generated many aesthetic innovations in the genre during the twentieth century: most notably in the *Tanztheater* of Pina Bausch and Johann Kresnik, but already from the 1920s, when Mary Wigman, Kurt Jooss and other pioneers of German Expressionist Dance coined the term *Tanzdrama* to articulate their unconventional, progressive impulses. It would thus be entirely misguided to simply equate a 'dramatic' dance with the narrative ballet of the Romantic French and Classical Russian traditions of the nineteenth century alone. To trace the 'postdramatic moment' or its equivalent in dance more precisely, one should instead consider the far more important simultaneous birth of the classical ballet regime and of French neoclassical tragedy. Both ballet and the 'absolute drama' of French classicism[2] were rooted in what Rancière calls the 'representational regime of art':[3] this is his term for the political-aesthetic order which, up until the nineteenth century, governed both the sense of meaningful discourses and our sensory perception, thereby instituting what Rancière famously terms a 'partition of the sensible'. In drama, it manifested itself through the very 'fictive cosmos' Lehmann evokes, with its logics of linearity, causality and finality. As the term 'cosmos' aptly suggests, it was also conceived of in terms of spatial organisation and representation, pointing us directly to the very category that ruled and regulated classical (French) ballet, too. Spatial calculations remain the absolute category for ballet, where they absorb and integrate the individual human body into the choreographic design. Individual movement and body-spaces fade into the singular focus of the organised perspective of the stage space within its strict demarcations vis-à-vis the spectators.

When Lehmann therefore asserts for contemporary performance that 'in dance we find most radically expressed what is true for postdramatic theatre in general',[4] we can make the same claim about the dynamics connecting classical ballet and classical 'absolute' drama. At the same time, we should be careful not to be too hasty in identifying either 'ballet' or 'drama' *as such* with a conservative, traditional approach to performance. Even the most rooted tradition may generate the most experimental innovations, as another generation of radical dance-makers demonstrated throughout the 1980s: choreographers and companies such as Anne Teresa De Keersmaeker's Rosas, Lloyd Newson's DV8, William Forsythe's Ballet Frankfurt and Édouard Lock's LaLaLa Human Steps all departed from within ballet. Similarly, the earlier German *Tanztheater* pioneers emerged from modern or classical traditions: Bausch had trained with Kurt Jooss and José Limon, Kresnik came from ballet. Meanwhile, the emergence of postdramatic forms on (mostly Continental European) stages during the 1980s and 1990s was largely orchestrated by corporeal and visceral work that more often referenced visual arts contexts than dance, as in the work of, above all, Jan Fabre's Troubleyn, Jan Lauwers' Needcompany, Wim Vandekeybus' Ultima Vez and the Castelluccis' Soc̀ıetas Raffaello Sanzio. Their genre-bending choreographic transgressions, while in no way following, referring to, or even rejecting any rule book of established dance forms, still found a home at the many European dance festivals, often side by side with those other innovators from within the dance lineage itself. The common momentum is precisely what reveals the 'postdramatic moment' (or its equivalent) in dance. Certainly, a main accent of the postdramatic focus on moving bodies and choreography was put on elements of visceral sensuality and corporeal experience, so perfectly exemplified by the non-traditional choreographic work mentioned above. This tendency is usually discussed with reference to concepts such as Kristeva's 'semiotic' and Agamben's 'gesture':[5] 'it articulates not meaning but energy, it represents not illustrations but actions'.[6]

Does this perceived shift from meaning to energy, from illustration to action, however, truly exhaust the full meaning of postdramatic innovation in dance and choreography? Has not, already within the strict classical coordinates of ballet, even the moving body of the ballerina promised precisely such a dip into a Deleuzian field of energy *beyond* realistic representation? Similarly, one may argue that the peculiar supernatural and exotic narrative fairytale frameworks that underpinned Romantic and Classical ballet – the swans, medieval country virgins or Oriental temple maids – were only peripherally concerned with 'meaning' and 'illustration', and hence with drama: did they not equally (and perhaps primarily) serve as a phantasmatic trigger of corporeal 'action' and 'energy' in the fullest sense of its libidinal investment? In an odd way, classical ballet seems therefore to offer an outline of prototypical postdramatic qualities *avant la lettre*. As a consequence, from the early modern dance of Isadora Duncan and Rudolf Laban, to Martha Graham and the 1960s Judson movement, and most recently again with the 1990s privileging of somatics over semantics, both dance scholarship and dance practice almost habitually pitched their genre against the logic of the word and the textual regime of drama.

But, what is now truly at stake when Lehmann defines postdramatic choreography as 'writing of bodies' where 'the body becomes the centre of attention, not as a carrier of meaning but in its physicality and gesticulation' and where '[t]he central theatrical sign, the actor's body, refuses to serve signification'?[7] Once we leave a traditional focus on styles, schools and terminology behind and again concentrate on the underlying *dispositif* behind the concept of the 'postdramatic', some common principles that frame moving bodies in both postdramatic theatre and contemporary dance emerge: dramaturgies which propose new relations between actions, bodies and narration beyond causality, linearity and absolute closure. They introduce vigorously different coordinates of space and time that notably depart from the representational order of art. Three hundred years after Louis XIV and his court culture spawned ballet, which would eventually become the dominant paradigm in Western stage dance, similar to the dominant mode of 'the dramatic' in theatre, the epochal experiments of John Cage, Merce Cunningham and others at Black Mountain College in 1953 provided another pivotal node in the history of Western dance, from which various developments in performance art, postdramatic drama, visual arts, music and postmodern dance cropped out. Much of this performance work can be analysed following the prominent critical paradigms of discourse analysis, deconstruction, gender studies and other branches of 'postmodern theory'. From a wider transdisciplinary perspective, both postdramatic theatre and recent dance performance from Cunningham onwards links seamlessly into a wider cultural context. Following that all defining crisis of the Second World War, the spirit of assertive, enlightened exploration and explanation was no longer perceived a source of progress; instead its negative, even destructive force was acknowledged as well. Similar to critical theory, performance aesthetics in postdramatic theatre and dance also made attempts to escape logic by becoming anti-referential, to leave metaphysics behind by turning anti-foundational, and to blur its cultural anchoring by being explicitly anti-representational.[8] This resulted in a dominantly *reflexive* approach to the materiality of the artwork, to the form of dance, and also in a reflexivity of the performance event and performance situation, which challenged not least of all the assumption of presence and present of performance as its privileged site or foundational moment. Rather than 'authenticating' dancing bodies, their presence was now perceived as an effect in itself, the result of a specific construction of the sensible which was always overshadowed by absence as its ultimate horizon.[9] These developments culminated in the 'concept dance' of 1990s European dance performance, associated with prominent protagonists such as Xavier Le Roy, Vera Mantero, Boris Charmatz and Jérôme Bel.[10] Their dance works escaped any effortless consumability of 'beautifully moving bodies', which still continued to underpin the genre elsewhere.

Here, however, choreographic 'strategies of avoidance'[11] interrupted our consumerist gaze, while the very fabric of choreography was re-patched by new 'movements of embodied thought'.[12]

As a result, contemporary dance has transgressed former boundaries. Terms such as 'choreography' have come to signify a diverse variety of strategies, taking dance far beyond the planned movement of bodies on stage in accordance with certain traditions and conventions of set steps and other spatial patterns that used to define dance composition.[13] New modes of (un-)writing bodies and movements clearly converged with the concurrent shift beyond dramatic theatre, as outlined by Hans-Thies Lehmann: '[T]he dramatic process occurred between the bodies, the postdramatic process occurs with/on/to the body.'[14] Helmut Ploebst described this body of work, which today is itself at the cusp of becoming another episode in dance history just as the now historic postmodern experiments of 1960s New York did, as 'new choreography in the society of the spectacle':[15] it was not least a response to the omnipresence of the imaginary and symbolic order circulated by global media, even before our daily routines became immersed in the augmented realities and social networks of today. Boris Groys described the characteristic attitude towards the globally streamed media economy as a constant 'suspicion' that behind the surface of reality and representation some 'real', actual truth is hidden.[16] The choreographies in question interrogated precisely such remnants of 'truth'. Following Slavoj Žižek's foray into Lacanian psychoanalysis, we can describe their key structural principle as a 'dramaturgy of the symptom': it was based on assuming a certain difference between the phenomena and their representation, or – in Lacanian terms – a gap between the core of the Real and the representation of reality within imaginary and symbolic orders. A 'symptomal dramaturgy' (which similarly underwrites most concurring critical approaches as well) asserts that the seamless surface of our ideologically grounded perception got cracked through the 'return of the repressed', and that the 'true Real' would eventually shine through the false face of representation.

Precisely these ideas of 'reflexivity' of artistic materiality, and of symptomal dramaturgy find themselves challenged and complicated in more recent performance work, such as the choreographies of Eszter Salamon. In another one of her works, a solo piece titled *Dance for Nothing* (2010), she 'interpreted' (as the programme notes described it) John Cage's famous *Lecture on Nothing* from 1949. Via headphones, Salamon heard the original lecture as recorded by Cage, played back at a slightly slowed down speed. Wearing sneakers, a tracksuit and T-shirt, thus a dancer's 'unmarked' everyday outfit, she repeated the words, while accompanying her speaking with what seemed like a Cageian chance-like sequence of movements and physical actions. Salamon travelled through the intimate performance space, frequently establishing eye contact with the spectators who sat around the performance space on all four sides. At times, she appeared to address individual spectators directly, standing right in front of them. A concluding discussion with the audience was then indeed not merely a 'post-performance talk', but formed an integral part of the production itself. There are many other examples that point to the issues of interest here. In *Monument G2* (2009), for instance, Slovenian artist and performance scholar Janez Janša re-staged *Monument G*, a 1972 production by Dušan Jovanović, which at its time was the 'Black Mountain' moment for a new Yugoslavian theatre avant-garde. Jovanović had staged a play by author Bojan Štih in collaboration with the dance performer Jožica Avbelj; they did not *speak* the text, but embodied it, recreating and representing the play purely through breathing, the tonal qualities of Avbelj's voice, and movement. More than 35 years later, Janša sought to bring this production back to the stage, with Jovanović and Avbelj themselves. As their legendary work had only partly been photographed or documented otherwise, even its original creators were unable to remember and reconstruct more than fragments of their own 'original'. In *Monument G2,* young dancer Teja Reba and Janša himself were also on stage with them, while quotes from academic essays and other documents and testimonials about this eminently important, yet ultimately absent historical performance, its origins, effects and receptions, were projected.[17] Elsewhere again, the five dancers (and one musician) from the Slovakian-Belgian collective Les SlovaKs (2009) presented in their piece *Journey Home* (2009) what they describe as 'new traditional dance', invoking traditions of folklore as well as popular elements such as storytelling and slapstick comedy: again with a certain twist that shifted the perception, starting from their all too cliché costumes that signified the former communist 'East'. This somewhat random selection of recent dance works still maps out a representative phenomenology of that core issue in twenty-first-century choreography: the 'post-postdramatic' return of history and subjectivity. Or, with Les SlovaKs, precisely the 'journey home'.

Salamon's work is particularly pertinent to an interrogation of this phenomenon. From her early work, her choreographies engaged with aspects of 're-enacting', hence notably re-appropriating rather than neutrally reconstructing history. This trend of referencing seminal 'avant-garde' works has become very prominent in recent dance and theatre performances (from the Wooster Group to Gob Squad) and seems omnipresent in the popular media imaginary of the early twenty-first century, from cinema to TV-series such as *The Tudors* or *Mad Men*. Salamon first came to attention in *Giszelle* (2001), choreographed by Xavier Le Roy for the Festival d'Avignon and subsequently touring widely, including to New York. To the well-known score of the nineteenth-century ballet classic *Giselle*, the spectators were presented with a gallery of movement images and physical tableaus: a montage of iconic, easily recognisable corporeal actions and behaviours. Salamon's body performed Rodin's thinker pose, the crucified Jesus, the actions of a football player, some folk dance steps or the inevitable Michael Jackson moonwalk. These poses and gestures were all properly 'sampled': again not only repeated and represented, but also edited, changed, defamiliarised, for instance by manipulating physical dynamics and slowing actions down, or speeding them up frantically. In 2005, Salamon's *Hungarian Dances* presented us not just with popular folk dances of her native country that she had learnt in her childhood, but also with some members of her family whom she brought on stage. In *And Then . . .* (2007), another production that bears a reference to narratives and storytelling in its title, she told the stories of Eszter Salamons – in the plural: with her now regular dramaturg Bojana Cvejić she had researched the biographies of other women of the same name, past and present, some of whom appeared either live on stage with the dancer or through excerpts from sound or video interviews conducted with them; others were purely remembered, such as the Eszter Salamon killed in a Nazi concentration camp.[18]

Throughout this body of work, we encounter the concern with the passing on and representation of history, of a legacy, of an identity and of memory, underpinned with questions about its status, accessibility, the limits of its availability and even its validity, its translation, translatability and inevitable transformation. Karen Jürs-Munby suggests that a 'palimpsestuous intertextuality and intratextuality' that writes over both 'personal micro-histories and public macro-histories' has become 'a significant quality of much postdramatic theatre.'[19] I suggest, however, that contemporary (dance and other) work such as Salamon's points to a different 'post-postdramatic' spin on this peculiar historical 'self-reflexivity' when compared to the reflexive postdramatic strategies employed by the companies Jürs-Munby refers to, such as Forced Entertainment, Stan's Café and the Wooster Group. To start with, it seems noticeable that Salamon, Janša and Les SlovaKs all come from the 'new Europe', and that they all, to various degrees, articulate in their productions the gap still remaining between Eastern Europe and the West. Nevertheless, the geographic provenance neither fully explains nor determines the core of the artistic manifestations under scrutiny here. It does point us, however, to the relevance of the wider geopolitical situation after 1989 in East and West; it has shifted frames of references and experience on both sides of the former iron curtain. The same issues have emerged in recent Western European choreography, from Jérôme Bel's much noted series of dancers' biographies (including *Véronique Doisneau* [2004] on the Paris Opera *corps de ballet* dancer, and *Cedric Andrieux* [2010] on the former Cunningham dancer) to Le Roy's mentioned *Giszelle* and his more recent *Le Sacre du Printemps* (2007), to Boris Charmatz' Cunningham re-take *Flip Book* (2009) and the engagement with dance history in the work of other choreographers such as Martin Nachbar and Thomas Lehmen.[20] Spectres of history are evoked, and they point us to the heart of those 'spectres of subjectivity' that re-emerge in contemporary performance.

This return of history, of narratives, of subjects and subjectivity challenges not least the established analytic apparatus informed by postmodern critical approaches. We are pointed to the very aporia of some contemporary critical thought which, taken to its extreme, may all but nullify any position of sociopolitical agency. Trained in postmodern critical theory, we have come to experience any positive content of 'subjectivity' as an effect of language, of the symbolic order, of imaginary misrecognition or as another ideological, phallogocentric fabrication and suppression – and hence as an ultimately arbitrary, contingent, and optionally assumed 'pathological' (in Kant's sense) position. Yet, where the 'subject' has thus been shown as an entirely externally posited construct, how do we negotiate between such 'subjectivity' and our very being as 'actually existing individuals'? Where any notion of a definable standpoint dissolves into contingency, academic thought loses any political force, becomes rhetorical language itself, while ultimately playing into the hands of the ideology of globalised capitalism with its endless demands for infinitely malleable 'flexible personalities'.[21]

Across the field of theatre and performance studies, this same deadlock resulted from an exclusive analytic focus on theatre semiotics which had become the 'master discourse' in the 1970s and 1980s, suggesting its readings of everything as a sign, and nothing but a sign. Even in artistic practice a stalemate was reached, as in choreography movement, music and other theatrical means had been granted their full autonomy in the works of Cage, Cunningham and the postmodern choreographers after them. As a result, we found ourselves 'up against a brick wall', as composer Thierry De Mey, a regular collaborator of Anne Teresa De Keersmaeker, William Forsythe and other contemporary dance artists, remarked:

> Once you are working 'non-synchronously', you cannot work even more 'non-synchronously'. You can allow chance to play its part, but there is no superlative of 'chance'. So even in art one has to recognise the dead ends. The separation of music and dance entailed a danger: to lose the ability to communicate with what allows music and dance to mutually enrich each other. If these two arts no longer communicate, they run the risk of impoverishment.[22]

This encompassing deadlock has not only artistic and aesthetic, but also political and ethical consequences, and the recent revival of ethical discourses (equally emphasising communication, commonality, mutual enrichment) is testimony to the uncomfortable effects not least of all of our own academic critique. If dance performance provides us, as Lehmann suggested in the earlier quote, with an even more radical and concentrated manifestation of the true stakes of the matter, we should be able to read the current wave of 'post-postdramatic' dance work precisely as a possible response to this dilemma of subjective agency *after* its critical deconstruction. At the same time, we may find here, likewise, a critical assessment of earlier attempts to respond to this impasse, such as the boom of phenomenology that was distinguishable in much 1990s critical writing, which tended to replace one end of a binary with its other end, shifting from ultimate contingency to unfettered subjectivity and 'felt experience' that at times reject any intersubjective basis. I suggest that our own academic analysis can indeed learn from the dramaturgic structures embodied in the works discussed here: above all, we find these very binaries – of 'semiotic objectivity' and 'lived individuality', and of similar antagonisms – challenged from a dialectic perspective. Such a move reflects the project at the heart of contemporary Neo-Lacanian cultural-political criticism (Slavoj Žižek and others).[23] It resorts to a Hegelian re-reading of the Lacanian ethics of psychoanalysis, adding complexity through the challenge of both dialectic and materialist positions – a complexity I consider very much needed in order to respond to the challenges of our present-day global situation. Lacan's dense approach to subjectivity suggests that one should not do away with foundations altogether as a result of their inevitable contingency, but precisely assert and insist on the position that contingency is that very foundation – that the subject is, so to speak, 'essentially contingent'. The Lacanian position is thus, in Oliver Marchart's term 'post-foundational': in asserting the contingency of this founding position it also acknowledges the inevitability of any such founding moment in order to render subjectivity as (political) agency (still/again) a possibility.[24]

Let us return to Salamon's *Dance for Nothing*: the term to be noted here is, of course, the elusive 'nothing' of the title. In a dance performance staged in the early twenty-first century, this 'nothing' is precisely no longer an emptying gesture, calling for a *tabula rasa* in the spirit of the reflexive challenge to dance performance represented by works from Cage and Cunningham to the early Bel. What was 'nothing' in 1949, is no longer 'nothing' today. Rather than emptying, it has become a gesture of *insistence* on an empty position. This is then what we find in productions by Salamon, Janša, the SlovaKs and elsewhere: the histories, traditions and identities evoked here are always already deconstructed, seen in a dialectic vision that no longer suggests their origins and foundations but asserts their 'essential contingency'. In contrast to the 'foundational' perspective (on history, origins . . .) that characterised the dramatic or representational regime, we are here presented with (in one of Žižek's key terms) a 'parallax' perspective.[25] From this unstable position, a new dialectics emerges that goes categorically beyond a tension between form and content, or the distance between the present individual of today and the (past) background of a tradition. Instead, the parallactic relation creates a multiple exposure that blurs conventional dual delineations of represented and representation, of original and interpretation, of fixed mise en scène and emergent co-presence of the singular performance event. As an essentially relational dialectics, it points us towards a central third term that 'goes beyond' and sublates established dichotomies.

Such a triangular formal relation in an important way also integrates us – the audience – within its ultimately open dramaturgic system. The reflexive dramaturgy of previous decades has therefore made way to a relational dramaturgic network, where the spot is always also put on the spectators – very literally so in Salamon's *Dance for Nothing*: during the production, in the small theatre studio space, we were always just slightly blinded by the lights from all four sides, and hence as an audience pushed beyond the usual transparency of our spectatorial gaze. The light even induced a quite tangible sleepiness which again facilitated our relation to Cage's text as we listened to it: at some point, it actually talks about the 'slumber' of the audience. Elsewhere, Salamon stops voicing the lecture text she hears in her earphones for about four minutes. When thereby the third term in the relational network momentarily falls away, we can fully grasp the 'parallax effect': exactly in the moment where we should be able to see the performance purely as dance, we can no longer do so precisely because by now we know that the Cage lecture *continues* in the dancer's earphones. Our own complicity and involvement as spectators in the relational dramaturgy is here pointed out in all its contingency – as precisely an empty spot of spectating, and it is here where a Rancièrian 'emancipation of the spectator' is realised:[26] instead of finding ourselves trotting around performance spaces, pushed and guided into the 'proper place' where we are meant to stand at any given time – *nothing* happens. The true moment of emancipation is, somewhat paradoxically again, grounded in the very 'nothingness' of the structural position of self-relation. Here, my outline of a negative 'relational dramaturgy' departs far from the affirmative concept of 'relational aesthetics'.[27] It presents us, instead, with spectres of subjectivity that emerge from asserting and assuming the contingency, the gaps, the void, the 'absent centre'.[28] I here build on Žižek's Hegelian re-reading of Lacanian psychoanalysis which outlines contours of subjectivity that assert the subject not as filled by any positive content, but precisely as an abyss, a void of negativity – and thereby turns the very contingency into a critical, radical force.

The implications for our analytic approach becomes particularly clear in the contrast with the Althusserian subject of interpellation as paradigmatic instance of postmodern and, by extension, also postdramatic subjectivity. Rather than understanding, as with the latter, subjectivity as ultimately reducible to a (linguistic, discursive, ideological or other) structure, we can assert that the subject is precisely what remains *after* the deconstruction of these structures has been completed. With Kant, Hegel, Lacan and Žižek, behind the symbolic and imaginary representation of the subject, we won't arrive at a 'real' subject, but only ever at this empty position. Or, with Žižek: '"subject" is that very X, the empty form of a "container," which remains after all its content was "subjectivized".'[29] Subject is rather the name, as Mladen Dolar has shown, for the ultimate failure to *fully* become an

Althusserian subject – subject to and of the Ideological State Apparatus that summons it – and it is precisely this failure which bestows agency in the contemporary context.[30] The task of analysis is therefore not to address ideological illusion, attempting to 'rectify' and instil 'proper' consciousness – this is precisely the Rancièrian 'stultifying' dramaturgy that precludes the very emancipation of the spectator it claims: the dialectic illusion of the subject is an outright existential illusion which 'does not involve a deception in which something is falsely represented; it involves deception by the simple fact that it is.'[31] In making as well as analysing contemporary performance, we should therefore draw the conclusions from the key Lacanian distinction between the subject of the enounced (the subject *in* language, in the symbolic order – the ideological constructs of 'subjectivity'), and the subject of enunciation – the 'I' who is speaking (or, for that matter: watching, spectating, performing) – which is precisely that empty point of self-relating: rather than assuming a fixed, positive position within the symbolic order and structure of the Other, it emerges only in the very act of enunciation. The kernel of my being as 'empirical' individual thus asserts itself in a performative act of self-relating: not as presence, but at retrospective position that 'will have been', in the future-perfect, this principal tense for both Lacanian psychoanalysis and Žižek's materialist cultural analysis. It is no longer the presence and present of representation, but the future-perfect – where, above all, the agency of an act cannot be 'willed' into being, but only ever 'will have been' retrospectively.

This is the very parallax relational position we find in the performance setups conceived by Eszter Salamon and others: they deal, in the triangle of performers, texts (the histories, traditions, etc.) *and* spectators, with the sites of subjectivity in the empty space that is left after all the work of deconstruction has been done. This then no longer employs a reflexive 'dramaturgy of the symptom'. Instead, the relational dramaturgy of post-postdramatic performance suggests what we can describe as a 'dramaturgy of the fetish', activating a term that is crucial for Freud and Marx, and certainly also for Lacan and Žižek.[32] In the binary (somewhat Freudian) structure of reflexive dramaturgy the repressed 'actual' thing was assumed to show its symptoms and to perforate the surface. Žižek highlights a specific, contrasting aspect in Marx's theory of the commodity fetish: It describes the mystifying transformation (into commodities) of ordinary objects with – and not against – our better knowledge. We know perfectly well the true and trivial nature of these fetishised things, but we then ignore or reject this insight. Marx's position therefore contrasts with the traditional stance of enlightenment criticism, which assumes that it needs to expose and explain the 'real' triviality and 'actual' material reality of the fetishised commodity in the first place. According to this psychoanalytic take at the Marxian view, fetishisation, instead of obscuring real knowledge, 'can play a very constructive role by allowing us to cope with the harsh reality'.[33] The fetishists of the present are thus, for Žižek, not daydreaming escapists, but on the contrary realists who fully grasp the reality and see through the lie – but only this knowing lie of clinging to the fetish (e.g. to 'perform' subjective acts), and of rejecting the truth (that the subject is an empty, negative void) makes it possible to maintain agency.

This is what is at stake with the shift from a reflexive to the relational dramaturgy in the post-postdramatic productions discussed here: the re-enacted highlights of performance history in Janša's production, folk-references in the SlovaKs's piece, Cage in Salamon's performance all provide fetishistic points of reference. They no longer serve as ground for dramatic causality and finality (the well-known postdramatic gesture), but are still asserted as necessary, as vital contingent element in a relational network, as the third element that sublates unproductive binaries: as neither purely 'nothing' *nor* fixating a ground, but as structural function of occupying this 'transcendental' position through the very emptiness of a placeholder (constituted by the post-postdramatic parallax). This dramaturgic dynamism of contingency and agency strategically insists on the fetish of identity, history, etc. thereby allowing both performers and spectators to momentarily position themselves within a relation that is neither entirely within (the fiction, representation, mediation) nor without, but oscillates in the parallax in-between. As Eszter Salamon expressed it in one of the part-of-the-performance talks with the audience: it allows both a greater detachment and distance, while at the same time generating an even greater degree of involvement.[34] Grappling with empty signifiers as fetish, contemporary dance performance (as well as other 'post-postdramatic' theatre forms of the twenty-first century) tackles existential illusions from a dialectic perspective. Rather than *reacting* to the given (i.e. re-presenting) as in the symptomal mode of reflexive dramaturgy, these performances actively carve out new relations. The parallax perspective that frames the fetishistic insistence thereby tests alternative 'partitions of the sensible', which go beyond binaries and hierarchies, as well as beyond the relativism and the disciplining dissolution of foundations of agency that used the mask of critical intervention. Positions are instantiated performatively. The relational, no longer purely reflexive dramaturgy generates a parallax perspective that requires our self-relating in the very act of negotiating the 'spectral appearances', negotiating our own, different, new, alternative, perhaps radical relation to our histories, subjectivities and identities, too. The resurfacing of local and national traditions, of histories and subjectivities hence must not be dismissed straight away as simple conservative and reactionary reflexes. This would mean interpreting (post-)postdramatic performance as no more than another symptom of the global ideology of digital market economies.

Christoph Schlingensief's *Rocky Dutschke, '68*: A Reassessment of Activism in Theatre

Antje Dietze

The arts in the 1990s were marked by a debate regarding the meaning and potential of leftist politics and politically engaged artistic practice in a period in which they seemed to have lost social relevance. This problem was linked not only to the disintegration and fall of the Eastern bloc, but also to the crisis of Western leftist art and politics since the decline of the movements of 1968. There was both a widespread perception of the exhaustion of the protest movement and a sense that political and artistic activism had much lower social impact as compared to the past. Thus, in the 1990s, anti-capitalist, leftist, and socially engaged activists and artists made various attempts at reorientation in searching for new modes of action and intervention and in re-evaluating their political and cultural repertoire.[1]

In this chapter I will discuss Christoph Schlingensief's stage production, *Rocky Dutschke, '68* at the Volksbühne am Rosa-Luxemburg-Platz in Berlin in 1996, which I view as a significant and thought-provoking contribution to the ongoing debate. Schlingensief typically worked with techniques of appropriation as an aesthetic means of addressing social and political issues. In *Rocky Dutschke, '68*, he used these strategies to tackle directly the question of leftist traditions and socially engaged theatre practice in post-socialist and post-unification Germany. *Rocky Dutschke, '68* was an appropriation and reassessment of political activism, performance art and forms of audience activation from the 1960s and 1970s. The production focused on Rudi Dutschke, an activist in the West German student movement and one of the icons of 1968.

After briefly outlining Schlingensief's appropriation practice in general, I will focus on two central aspects of *Rocky Dutschke, '68*. First, I will analyse the position the performers took towards their activist role models of 1968 – Dutschke in particular – and how they appropriated and reflected on them. Secondly, I will examine the attitude the performers took towards the audience. Just like the activists of 1968, they engaged in attempts to activate the audience in order to emancipate them. They did this by means of education, direct action and participatory performances. In conclusion, I will ask what contribution Schlingensief's use of these techniques made to the cause of activism in theatre in the post-1989 period. His production can be seen as a reassessment not only of traditions of leftist activism in arts and politics, but also of some basic features of postdramatic theatre. As described by Hans-Thies Lehmann, postdramatic theatre emphasises the theatre situation itself. The interaction and shared experience of performers and audience is the basic given and central field of interest of this form of theatre.[2] Lehmann sees the political dimension of postdramatic theatre in the way it lays bare this '*mutual implication of actors and spectators in the theatrical production of images*'.[3] In view of this definition, Schlingensief's *Rocky Dutschke, '68* makes an interesting case as the production explicitly and provocatively explores the political potential of the theatre situation.

Christoph Schlingensief (1960–2010) was one of the most prolific and original German artists of recent decades. He started his career as a film director in the 1980s with wildly eccentric and widely discussed works, drawing on the traditions of avant-garde film on the one hand, and popular genre films (such as trash, splatter and exploitation) on the other. But he was also heavily influenced by the auteur-centred and socially critical New German Cinema which began in the 1960s. It was only in the early 1990s that Schlingensief also ventured into stage directing, after having been invited to do so by the Volksbühne theatre in Berlin. The topics of his projects included the after-effects of Germany's National Socialist past – especially with the problem of neo-Nazism and xenophobia that became prominent after 1989, leftist activism, and marginalised social groups (such as the unemployed and people with illnesses or disabilities). While working in film and theatre on a regular basis, Schlingensief also started to engage with social issues more directly. To that end, he experimented with different formats, including TV shows and interventions in public space. He founded the political party, *Chance 2000*, which took part in the 1998 German federal elections and openly criticised the conservative chancellor, Helmut Kohl. After 9/11, he founded the *Church of Fear*, a combination of sect and self-help group that satirised the instrumentalisation of fear for political or religious purposes. His final (and still ongoing) project, the *African Opera Village* in Burkina Faso, is both a socially engaged development project and an attempt to overcome aspects of development politics by 'learning from Africa'.[4]

Schlingensief constantly addressed the question of how to produce socially critical art, and often in provocative and at times scandalous ways that attracted public attention. His work was based on strategies of appropriating existing narratives, role models and social and artistic practices in order to reassess them. He usually did not judge these appropriated elements from a safe distance, but instead opted for a trial-and-error approach by engaging in a practical evaluation of the models he used, often distorting them in the process. For example, he criticised xenophobia by staging the deportation of asylum seekers in his infamous *Please Love Austria* project in Vienna. *Chance 2000* was a party without a party programme, based on the slogans 'Vote for yourself!' and 'Failure as Chance!' The *Church of Fear* was a community of non-believers. His projects were both a revival and a parody, but at times also strongly critical or subversive. Additionally, he created bewilderment and confusion as to what positions he himself took towards the questions he raised, as he refused to deliver ready-made answers or conclusions, forcing the audience to confront their own positions towards the issues at stake. Schlingensief never promoted any specific political agenda or ideology. Instead, his work had a highly ironic side to it, leading to his public image as a kind of modern jester or political prankster. But his constant efforts to transgress the status quo also had a very earnest and at times obsessive dimension, ultimately revolving around questions of transience and salvation as part of both his Catholic upbringing and his interest in the heritage of political and artistic avant-gardes.

The ambivalent inheritance of 1968

In *Rocky Dutschke, '68*, Schlingensief worked with the appropriation of given models and their transformation. In this case, he used the symbolic and performative repertoire of the activist movements of 1968. The production took Rudi Dutschke as a starting point and role model. Dutschke (1940–79) was a Marxist intellectual and leader of the West Berlin student movement. He was shot in 1968 and suffered severe head wounds, but survived the assassination attempt. Schlingensief's production focused not so much on the 'real' Dutschke or his ideas, but on the iconic images of Dutschke as part of collective memory. Like a revue, *Rocky Dutschke, '68* presented different scenes from the protagonist's life, such as his departure from his East German hometown, his studies in West Berlin, his involvement in theoretical discussions, speeches and agitations, the assassination attempt and Dutschke's death from its after-effects eleven years later. Some scenes also dealt with other aspects of the protest movement, such as left-wing artists and intellectuals (e.g. Wolf Biermann and Heiner Müller), sexual liberation and coming to terms with Germany's National Socialist past. The production also consisted of re-enactments of avant-garde art performances from the 1960s and 1970s.

From the outset, however, the performers were ambivalent towards these historical figures and events. After nearly thirty years, the protest movements of the 1960s were dead, their activities having declined during the 1970s. Its activists had brought about many changes in society and culture, but had failed to achieve most of their main goals, such as radically changing the existing political system. Some had abandoned their ideals and tactics and had successfully conformed to society, some had turned to violence. But their legacy remained alive, as it was an important point of reference for efforts to revive political and artistic activism in times of ideological disorientation. In 1996, there were student protests in Berlin against education cutbacks, in part based on forms of protest from 1968, such as sit-ins, naked protests, student strikes and political happenings, but these demonstrations did not have a comparable impact. However, the earlier movement still fascinated younger generations. As an eventful and mythical era of revolt, it was an unattainable role model for political and artistic activism.

In an interview, Schlingensief, who was born in West Germany in 1960, also expressed mixed feelings towards the generation preceding his own. For him, the activists of the 1960s were teachers and mentors. He expressed his fascination with their work, and his frustration about not having had the chance to participate in what was regarded as a golden era. But at the same time, he complained that this inheritance was a burden that stifled attempts to create something new.[5] The generation of 1968, it seemed, had already accomplished all possible political and artistic experimentation. But now it was time to overcome the 'intimidation by the classics'. *Rocky*

Dutschke, '68 articulated and addressed this ambivalent relationship with the activist tradition. He described it as both an 'evocation and a disposal' of the German protest movement.[6]

The production of *Rocky Dutschke, '68* was based on two main concepts. The first was learning by doing. The performers appropriated forms of political activism and avant-garde art from the 1960s and 1970s in order to explore them, thereby learning from direct experience of these approaches rather than judging them from an external perspective. The second concept was that of overcoming role models. The performers engaged in a practical evaluation of their activist inheritance, transforming it and making it their own. They subjected these role models and forms of action to an endurance test so as to liberate themselves from their predecessors in order to create something new.

Revival and remembrance

The performance began with a prelude on the street in front of the theatre building.[7] Schlingensief, dressed as Dutschke, shouted into a megaphone, leading a staged street demonstration against cuts in social welfare. Then the performers set out to storm the nearby headquarters of the PDS, the Party of Democratic Socialism and successor to the East German ruling Socialist party, the SED, encouraging the audience to participate. The actress Sophie Rois, who was also dressed as Dutschke, was shot in a re-enactment of the assassination attempt. The scene was confusing, with performers overacting and the audience positioned to function as both observers and extras. After staging some of the central scenes from the Dutschke myth, both audience and performers entered the theatre, passing naked commune members who were occupying the lobby. In the auditorium, the seats had been removed, and the audience gathered on the floor. Then the teach-in began.

While the introductory part of the production clearly focused on reviving the heated atmosphere and the activist dimension of protest, revolt and violence of the events of 1968, its main part started with an act of remembrance. Schlingensief and the other performers gathered in the auditorium, formally greeting the audience and holding speeches. They were re-enacting the opening of a commemorative exhibition for Rudi Dutschke in the public school of his hometown of Luckenwalde, East Germany. But in the stage version of the event, the speeches were made awkwardly and often bordered on nonsense, in effect failing to convey the contemporary relevance of a long gone West German protest movement for students in a small East German town. The speakers spluttered, heckled each other and started to quarrel. It remained unclear whether this reflected problems at the original event, whether it was being mocked and deliberately distorted by the actors, or whether they were just unable or unwilling to perform well. Adding to this confusion was the fact that some of the speakers were not trained actors from the Volksbühne theatre, but instead belonged to Schlingensief's team of performers, some of whom were disabled or mentally ill. The entire scene was not only bewildering and funny, it also raised reasonable doubt as to whether this attempt of reviving and evoking the movement of 1968 should be read as a parody, a critique, a subversion or a failure.

Activists as role models: The melodrama

The production was not a literal reconstruction of the past, but invoked the power of myth. The central questions were: what position could the actors and audience take towards the myth of 1968 and the idea of activism, and how could they use it for their own purposes? The performers appropriated the activist role models of the past in order to explore these questions. In one scene, the actress Sophie

Rois played a mixture of Rudi Dutschke and the fictional character Norma Desmond. Desmond is the protagonist of Billy Wilder's 1950 film, *Sunset Boulevard*, which presents the melodrama of an ageing Hollywood diva and faded silent movie star, whose career had ended with the advent of films with sound. Desmond cannot deal with this; her attempts to revive her career fail, but she does not acknowledge this failure. Rather she withdraws into a fantasy world where she is still a big star. Her delusion has fatal consequences, in that she shoots her younger lover who had tried to free himself from her fantasy world.

Rois merged Dutschke with Desmond, performing slightly altered scenes from the film while parts of the film were simultaneously projected on stage. She used the character of Norma Desmond to play the revolutionary as an ageing diva desperately trying to return to the golden era of revolt, and who is clinging to the fantasy of still being relevant. The nostalgia for the revolt was cross-faded with Desmond's bouts of delusion, a fame junkie suffering from withdrawal symptoms. Rois as Dutschke/Desmond then tried to ease her craving for these lost times with images from the past, including one of industrialist Hanns-Martin Schleyer, one of the most iconic pictures from the so-called German Autumn. The German Autumn of 1977 had followed the emancipatory spring of 1968, when some of its activists had chosen the path of violence. Schleyer, taken hostage by the Red Army Faction, the most notorious West German terrorist group, was eventually killed by his kidnappers. Rois pointed at the photograph of Schleyer in captivity, exclaiming: 'I want you to look at this image, isn't it still wonderful? I don't know of any comparable image today. Look at this image, when did we last see such an image? Such things don't exist anymore – these times are over!'[8]

The meaning of this scene remains ambiguous: does it express nostalgia for terrorism? Or does the scene criticise nostalgia for the revolt of 1968 because some of its activists eventually turned to violence? Does it mock the audience that had come to see a revival of the golden era of activism? Or does this scene just state the obvious: that the past cannot be revived? It can be seen as an ironic self-reflection on the performance itself: just like Norma Desmond cannot return to the golden era of silent pictures, and just like the generation of 1968 cannot return to their revolutionary youth, the actors also could not revive the protest movement, which itself retained a difficult and deeply ambiguous legacy.

Like Norma Desmond, who at the peak of her delusion promised to make another film, and another and another, Rois then excitedly proclaimed that she would start another revolution, and another and another. As she used a megaphone to shout 'Ho, Ho, Ho Chi Minh', the other actors shouted along, trying to engage the audience to participate. But if spectators chose to participate, they could only do so at a certain risk. They could not be sure what it would mean to take part in a deeply ambiguous situation that they were not able to fully assess or control. This is one of the defining features of the entire performance: the performers created a strategic ambiguity about the position they took towards that which was being appropriated. They provided neither a clear rejection nor a simple affirmation of their activist role models, emphasising instead their own conflicted relationship to the activists of 1968. The actors denied the spectators any secure external perspective from which to judge, and as a consequence the latter were thrown back on themselves, forced to assess their own involvement with the activist inheritance as well as their own desire for revolt.

Activating the audience: The boxing match

The stage production not only built upon the images and icons of 1968, but also consisted of re-enactments of the direct actions and participatory performances from the 1960s and 1970s that had aimed at educating and activating people. Activists, including Dutschke, tried to create situations that involved people in the concrete experience of and made them aware of the inherent violence of the ruling social and political conditions. The aim of these direct actions had been to transform people's consciousness to allow them to become liberated individuals and revolutionary subjects. But to reach that goal, political and artistic activists had often used provocation, shock and sometimes violence to make people think and feel differently and to involve them in their emancipatory project.

Schlingensief's production took up these principles, as the performers used methods of direct action and participatory performance on the audience. Here as well, they wanted to explore these forms of activism by appropriating and testing them, and by allowing the audience to experience them. The performers made it their task to draw the audience into the performance – to invite them to participate, but also to compel them to take part or to attack them in order to provoke reactions. For example, spectators were asked to perform a collective re-enactment of Dutschke's departure to West Berlin from his East German hometown. They were also invited to participate in what was presented as an African fertility rite consisting of bathing one's bare bottom in a bowl of milk. Sometimes audience members were also attacked or drawn into fights with the performers staged in the auditorium. It was mainly the role of actor Bernhard Schütz to provoke confrontations and clashes. He was Rocky, the boxer, searching for a fight, whether with the other actors or with members of the audience. Schütz playing 'Rocky Dutschke' referred both to the *Rocky* films by Sylvester Stallone and to Graciano 'Rocky' Rocchigiani, a popular German professional boxer at the time. This provocative behaviour brought up the question of violence that had been so prominent in 1968, and subjected spectators to a concrete experience of it.

In *Rocky Dutschke, '68*, the performers wanted to destroy the possibility of retreating to a distant and neutral point of observation. According to a description of the stage production on Schlingensief's website, their aim was to create a sense of crisis and a climate of uncertainty, to fuel conflict among the actors and with the audience, and ultimately even to risk a breakdown of the performance. They wanted to create an experience that resembled that of insurgence, revolt and subversion.[9] The performance made the audience lose their safe distance and feelings of autonomy and security – whether they wanted to or not. But while constantly and at times forcibly activating the audience, the performers denied any clear frame of reference or action. They tried to involve the spectators in both a learning experience and a process of emancipation.

The lesson

As they repeatedly stated during the performance, the performers' aim was to set in motion what might be called an open process, and to activate the audience to take part in it. The production itself was framed as a lesson, with the performers in the role of teachers and the audience as students. It replicated the aim of the protest movement (and of Dutschke in particular) to enlighten people and to help them find the capacity to emancipate themselves and create a better society. The performance highlighted the problems in this agenda and its asymmetrical relations, as the performers tried to impose liberation by assailing the audience members' minds and senses, exposing and at times overemphasising the self-contradictions in their predecessors' struggle for the cause of emancipation.

Schlingensief himself repeatedly interrupted the performance to explicitly comment on its aims. Like a teacher, or a reincarnation of

Joseph Beuys, he drew diagrams on a blackboard, summing up what the actors and audience together had just experienced and learned. But he never formulated the precise lesson to be drawn; instead he asked the audience not to make connections, draw conclusions or judge. This marks an important difference to other forms of didactic theatre, even to participatory and communal formats like Bertolt Brecht's *Lehrstücke*. Schlingensief invited the audience to take part in a mutual-learning process which did not aim at imparting political or social lessons, but at blowing up the didactic framework altogether. He claimed that the goal of the performance – for the performers as well as for the audience – was to liberate themselves from any pre-given rules, from historical role models, and from any lesson taught. On the one hand, this meant transgressing the achievements, guidelines and dictates of previous generations, and of their ideologies and policy models. But on the other hand, Schlingensief urged the audience to liberate themselves not only from historical role models, but also from the emancipatory goal of the performer-teachers, and ultimately to break out of the prescribed process of the performance itself. So, paradoxically, the performers and audience were supposed to emancipate themselves from the inherited project of emancipation, thus both overcoming and continuing it. The entire staging was both a citation and an affirmation of the basic concerns of the protest movement, and the attempt of a new generation to redirect these concepts against their originators.

Of course, this was not only an ironic *mise-en-abîme* of the emancipatory project that was being reassessed, and a comic articulation of the dilemma of the second generation of protesters vis-à-vis their predecessors. It also brought the conflict of agitation and liberation to breaking point. The paradoxical lesson was *not* to learn a lesson and *not* to be guided by the teachers in order to learn the lesson and gain liberation. Schlingensief exposed the internal contradictions of any form of activism aimed at emancipating others by imposing liberation on them. But here again, he did not judge from a superior external position, but re-enacted the contradictions of his activist role models, emphasising his own involvement in them *and* his desire to free himself and the audience from any pre-given impulses and models. Still, self-liberation and participation could not go very far here. Within the performance, the spectators were only given limited agency. All they could participate in was a self-reflection that stayed within the limits of theatre, but there was no movement towards something else. In his later projects, Schlingensief experimented with other formats that gave the participants more room for manoeuvre. But in order to do so, he had to leave the theatre space.[10]

Schlingensief's *Rocky Dutschke, '68* was an attempt to address the problem of socially engaged artistic practice by means of a critical appropriation of the leftist political and artistic heritage of the movements in the West in 1968. It served as a way to reassess political and artistic traditions and to evaluate their pitfalls and contradictions, but also to examine the fascination they still hold and desires they still trigger. Schlingensief's practice of appropriation was a form of subversive affirmation, an aesthetic strategy that became increasingly important in efforts to revive left-wing activism in the 1990s. It consists of imitating persons, actions, objects or ideologies in such an exaggerated and revealing way that ultimately, it can be used to critically assess or even attack the imitated. Subversive affirmation has a long tradition in Eastern and Western art and cultural activism: from Dadaist political performances to the *détournement* of political and economic symbolical structures in Situationism, culture jamming and communication guerrillas. It also at times bears striking similarities to the work of artist groups such as Neue Slowenische Kunst and Laibach, with their 'overidentification' with (meaning subversive mimicry of) totalitarian art and political performances, or to various forms of political pranks and parodies, called *stiob*, in the former Soviet Union.[11] In these traditions, appropriation and subversive affirmation were mostly used to critically undermine totalitarian or capitalist symbolic structures. But in *Rocky Dutschke, '68*, Schlingensief used them to tackle leftist activism itself.

His stage production responded to a widespread desire for renewed political and artistic activism, but also to uncertainties about political objectives and effective forms of action that characterised the reorientation of left-wing activists, intellectuals and artists after 1989. Schlingensief navigated between an uncritical imitation of past activism on the one hand, and fatalist claims that activism was dead on the other. Instead of searching for external causes for the crisis of the Left in the 1990s, the performers in *Rocky Dutschke, '68* polemically focused on left-wing activist practices themselves, starting in their own backyard. Schlingensief called this strategy self-provocation. In its first form, the performers did not take a critical distance towards the traditions they reassessed, but rather emphasised their own ambivalent relationship with and implication in their activist inheritance. They evaluated practically their own desire for activism, their activist role models, and the dead ends and inconsistencies produced in this process.

In the second form of self-provocation, performers tried not to provide the audience with conclusions, but tried instead to irritate them, polemically overemphasising contradictions and ambivalences. With this strategy, they wanted to provoke spectators to reassess their own relationships with political activism. To achieve this, the performers drew on the leftist activist practices of consciousness-raising and direct action. In 1968, these were used to protest, to unmask social hierarchies and oppression, and to undermine and change existing routines and ruling conditions. But here the performers directed those subversive practices back towards leftist activism itself. They tried to subvert their own frame of reference in order to bring down the 'system' – not the political system this time, but the burden of leftist role models and traditions – and to liberate themselves and the audience from any pre-given models.

But the question remained: if such a state of liberation and inconclusiveness can eventually be reached, what happens once it is achieved? The theatre staging created an experimental space in which audience members could evaluate by their own experience how they felt about and how they could deal with the project of social and political liberation. Judging from the video and accounts of people who have seen the production live, for many it was a deeply bewildering, incomprehensible, and at times paralysing and uncomfortable experience. But there were others who enjoyed the production's humour, suspense and absurdities.[12]

Schlingensief's production can be seen as an instance of postdramatic theatre precisely because it provided a space for reflecting on the concrete theatrical situation itself. Postdramatic theatre emphasises the performative dimension of a theatre event, offering spectators the chance to actively engage in a sensory and communal experience. It is often charged with expectation that this process can help liberate the audience and be a model for alternative forms of social and political life. In this sense, the artistic neo-avant-garde, postdramatic theatre, and the direct actions of 1968 share similar historical roots, forms of performance and sociopolitical concerns. Schlingensief's production addressed this tangled inheritance. It reassessed not only leftist activism, but also the political potentials of postdramatic theatre. He subjected the notion of the transformative and liberating power of the communal experience to an endurance test, exposing some of its basic problems – namely, the asymmetrical relation between activists and those being activated, and the fact that participatory impulses do not easily lead to the emancipation of participants or to the creation of a new form of community.

Rocky Dutschke, '68 emphasised the complexity of the postdramatic theatre experience and the difficulties that attend attempts to achieve political liberation. With his approach of strategically breaching the inherited repertoire, Schlingensief ultimately remained in tune with Dutschke's objective to overcome given structures and rules and to create an open process of emancipation. But at the same time, Schlingensief's performances highlighted the ambivalent dimension of liberation as well. Not only is it often imposed on audiences and, more generally, on groups in society, but these emancipatory strategies may also meet with opposition, as given values, traditions and expectations are neglected or wilfully destroyed in the process. For this reason, Schlingensief was criticised not only by those who disapproved of his strategic distortions of cultural and moral frames of reference; he also faced objections by leftist activists and critics, precisely because his forms of self-provocation laid bare some of the contradictions of politically engaged artistic practice, thereby highlighting the ambiguities of emancipation, be it through art or politics.

Schlingensief's work created strategic ambivalences towards historical role models and forms of activism, potentially forcing audience members to take active positions themselves in this evaluation process. The performers also distorted, transformed and recharged the models they used with different meanings and potentials. These techniques created a space for dealing with these issues on different levels and in various ways, by means of trial and error, leading to new forms of socially critical artistic practice. Schlingensief's performances always had a dilettantish, raw, and sometimes clownish character, and it often remained unclear whether certain parts of the performance actually failed, got lost in chaos and improvisation, or were planned that way. His mode of appropriation was not an attempt to fulfil or surpass his role models, but instead to underline the fact that their example can never be fully attained in the first place, and – as the example of Sophie Rois as Norma Desmond/ Rudi Dutschke showed – any attempt to do so might lead to delusion and failure. But role models can serve as an inspiration and starting point to discover new modes of thinking and action. Distorting them might be a necessary strategy to break out of the exhaustion and crisis of inherited forms of political and artistic activism in order to experiment and ultimately create something new.

Schlingensief's stage production *Rocky Dutschke, '68* was a thought-provoking contribution to the debate on the inheritance of 1968. It can be seen as a younger generation's attempt to come to terms with its legacy by searching for ways to affirm and continue the activist tradition and to reassess it critically in order to overcome its impasses. Schlingensief did not provide his audience with answers, but instead articulated unsolved problems that needed to be addressed. He emphasised the prevailing question of both the limits and the potential of political activism in the 1990s. At the same time, in this and his numerous subsequent projects, Schlingensief and his production team developed new performance forms that allowed for an immediate experience and assessment of the effects and implications of activist practices. In my view, one of Schlingensief's most important achievements was to lay bare the desires that drive artistic activism and the possibilities it creates, but also the risks both performers and audience take when engaging in it.

Postdramatic Reality Theatre and Productive Insecurity: Destabilising Encounters with the Unfamiliar in Theatre from Sydney and Berlin

Ulrike Garde and Meg Mumford

Since the early 1990s, Western theatre has witnessed a marked rise in cultural prominence of what we refer to as 'Reality Theatre'. Such performance engages overtly with the 'facts' of social reality, and presents 'real' contemporary people and their lives on stage, either in person or in a carefully scripted text based on real-life interviews and documents.[1] While the staging of contemporary reality has informed Western performance since its inception, interest in drama devoted to the literal words and actions of people has particularly come to the fore in the last two centuries. Since the proto-documentary Enlightenment drama of playwrights such as Georg Büchner, significant waves of interest have included: Erwin Piscator's epic documentary theatre of the 1920s; the continuation of this tradition in the documentary performance of the 1960s and 1970s (Peter Weiss, Rolf Hochhuth, Joan Littlewood's Theatre Workshop, John McGrath's 7:84, etc.); and the recent proliferation of Reality Theatre genres as diverse as audio-verbatim theatre, autobiographical performance and theatre of experts.[2]

This chapter focuses on Reality Theatre productions that can be designated 'postdramatic'. We argue that this designation is appropriate because they create porous and ambivalent worlds where real-life people, stories and places invade and are invaded by the frame of the stage. In these worlds fiction and reality meet or even become indistinguishable, and fiction can seem to put us more in contact with truth than facts do. Through an analysis of two very different types of performance event we demonstrate that what makes both of them a thoroughgoing challenge to the dramatic cosmos is their destabilisation of a sense of authentic and graspable subjects, texts and communicative situations. We also outline how this destabilisation can generate a 'productive insecurity',[3] one that invites fresh ways of engaging with people and related phenomena that are unfamiliar.

The contemporary surge in the presenting and watching of 'real' people on stage can be interpreted, in part, as a manifestation of a general 'reality hunger' linked to the perception, described by David Shields, that we live in 'a manufactured and artificial world' wherein 'we yearn for the "real", semblances of the real'.[4] Much recent Reality Theatre has been driven also by the desire to explore the implications of the culture of the artificial, of spectacle and event generated by media technologies, and of an increased importance of virtual worlds and identities. These implications include a heightened interest in the perception that everyday life itself is performative. According to such perception, humans perform their social roles and identities, and their actions and interactions are practiced, framed and displayed just like staged events.[5] Reality Theatre's approach to these issues has ranged from an assertion of facticity and unmediated access to original speech and bodies, to oscillations between *a sense of* the 'real' and 'authentic' (as defined below), and a creative interplay between fact and fiction. All of these responses have been marked by the use of 'authenticity effects', strategies for creating (and in some cases then unseating) *a sense of* direct contact with living people and truthful representations of their lives and social contexts. Here we use 'authentic' as a synonym for 'truthful', 'genuine' and 'immediate',[6] and refer to these strategies with the shorthand term 'A-effects'. Our use of this term is not to be confused with – and indeed contests – its use as shorthand for Brecht's *Verfremdungseffekte* (V-effects), a concept which we argue elsewhere has been misleadingly translated as 'Alienation-Effects', rather than, say, 'Defamiliarisation-Effects'.[7] Reality Theatre relies on and/or plays with the assumption, in line with a standard realist epistemology, that 'knowledge is available through sense perception and cognition linked to objects/documents' and that such aspects of a performance can put spectators in contact with 'the reality they are trying to experience or understand'.[8] When using the term 'reality' we draw on the pragmatic approach adopted by Pam Morris and define it as that which, in intersubjective communication, is agreed to exist.[9]

We argue that both our experiences of performance as Reality Theatre, and of performance segments as 'authentic', are constituted by a certain mode of (re)presentation and viewing that frames spectators' interactions with a performance. The 'authentic' is not a given and fixed entity, but rather the product of a contract between performers and spectators which has to be renewed for each 'authenticating act'. For example, a performance by Rimini Protokoll which uses 'experts of the everyday' (people who are specialists in a particular field of life) rather than professional actors might be watched by audiences under the premise that it offers an 'authentic' glimpse of the social realities that mark these peoples' lives. During the performance each instance revealing the experts' genuine vulnerability or uncertainty in a theatre context can initiate a renewal of the 'authenticity contract', while another performance segment, such as the elaborate enumeration of numbers, could challenge this contract because it might appear rehearsed. A distinguishing feature of the postdramatic productions under discussion is the way they introduce the *volatile* and *constructed* nature of the authentic. It is our contention that such destabilisations of the authentic can be used to unfix stable and possibly oppressive perceptions of strangers and the unfamiliar.

Reality theatre and the postdramatic use of theatrical signifiers

The productions analysed here both use theatrical signifiers in ways that are by no means unequivocally postdramatic. In fact, their usage is often more typical of dramatic theatre, or at least an impure form of this tradition. For example, each case study *seems* to foreground easily comprehensible linguistic processes of signification, particularly by means of sequentially arranged and pre-planned texts, most of which are presented through memorised utterances, readings, recordings and projections. Emphasis is put on the meaning-making qualities of language, and the smooth comprehension of written and spoken texts is rarely impeded by either the density or simultaneity of signs. The majority of performing bodies seem to function as carriers of meaning, and the landscape is dominated by the language, diction and gestures of the unfamiliar (or insufficiently familiar) human personae they embody.[10]

In the tribunal and testimonial performance *CMI (A Certain Maritime Incident)* (2004) by Sydney-based company version 1.0, the personae and texts come directly from the transcripts of the Australian 2002 Senate Select Committee inquiry into the so-called 'children overboard' affair. This inquiry investigated claims that the Federal government had participated in the dissemination of the false story that asylum seekers on the Suspected Illegal Entry Vehicle (SIEV) 4 had undertaken the barbaric act of throwing their own children into the water in order to force an Australian maritime rescue. The story was released during an election campaign that emphasised the strength of the incumbent government's border protection policy. Created by an ensemble of professional performers dedicated to 'investigating and also enacting' democracy,[11] *CMI* focuses on the under-investigated responses of Australian government personnel to so-called boat people, thereby turning attention to the unfamiliar within the host culture. In the biographical installation *Chambermaids*, an ongoing work curated by Lola Arias and Stefan Kaegi (of Berlin-based Rimini Protokoll) as part of the *Ciudades Paralelas/Parallel Cities Project*, the unfamiliar subjects are real-life cleaners in a metropolitan hotel. Audience members spend an hour walking through five hotel rooms, originally in the transnational space of the ibis Hotel in Berlin, where they experience portraits of the cleaning staff via films, voice recordings, letters and photographs. Most of these 'invisible spirits who clean up after others' are migrants who, through their stories and a guided hotel tour, address audience perceptions of and attitudes towards unfamiliar people.[12]

It is our contention that what makes these two case studies most clearly enter the realm of the postdramatic is their rupturing of a fictional cosmos and/or the sealed nature of the representation. That is, of a coherent self-contained reality. We argue that the case studies effect a rupturing particularly through making audiences uncertain about how the people and events they are experiencing are connected to representation, reality and fiction.[13] This fissure is achieved because they create ontologically unstable phenomena that appear to oscillate between or simultaneously inhabit the realm of the authentic (or as close to it as we will ever get) and the patently staged or manufactured. For example, autobiographical performers can appear both to be re-presenting rehearsed personae (versions of themselves) and to be being themselves, spontaneously living and in one sense 'off-script'. As our case studies demonstrate, '*indecidability* [*sic*] whether one is dealing with reality or fiction'[14] is caused not only by the creation of phenomena that do not sit clearly within one or the other of these problematically binarised categories, but also by representations whose very nature is uncertain. In the case of Rimini's theatre of experts performance in particular we may be left asking where on the reality-fiction continuum the representations sit. For example, are they everyday-life portrayals of self that have been put in a theatre frame, or are they heightened performances of self lifted from everyday life?

A further postdramatic feature of both performance events is their open-ended and polysemic nature, and concomitant invitation to spectators to create their own meanings and conclusions. In keeping with the invitation for personal meaning-making, the analyses below are based on the individual response of one author to one of the production events and associated materials. In the case of *CMI*, Meg Mumford addresses the use and destabilisation of A-effects, and the resulting uncertainty about the nature of the performed human subjects and texts. She also explores how certain types of 'inauthentic' performance can paradoxically create a sense of authentic contact with aspects of reality and social truth, but then, in a double move, undermine even that sense. In the case of *Chambermaids* the analysis is provided by Ulrike Garde, who focuses on how an aesthetics of undecidability, where audience impressions oscillate between having access to 'authentic' or to 'fictional' stories, can disrupt audiences' viewing habits. The case study illustrates how this aesthetics invites spectators to reflect on unfamiliar aspects of other and their own cultures. Both analyses consider the possible political implications of the experience of ungraspability generated by each performance event.

CMI: Destabilising subjects and texts

As is typical of documentary theatre, *CMI*'s A-effects include the use of advance signs that highlight the production's close connection to social reality. For example, the programme notes include a statement that '[a]lmost all of the spoken text for this performance comes from transcripts of the Senate Select Committee', as well as an assurance that the transcripts are quoted verbatim. Moreover, a short letter from the clerk of the Senate to producer-performer David Williams is included in which the clerk states: 'If you reproduce only extracts from the evidence, you are not protected by privilege unless the extracts are fair and accurate.' However, the promise of authentic contact with the 2002 inquiry is destabilised by signs such as the darkly comic flyer that depicts suited bodies, resembling government figures, who are struggling in the ocean with only children's beach equipment to keep them afloat. Moreover, the programme notes explain that while the performers will refer to one another 'by names such as "Senator Brandis"', and so on, 'This is a theatrical device. We are not implying that the Senators or witnesses so named performed any of the physical actions that we will perform tonight.'

In response to the mixed messages to be read from the entire production event, theatre critics designated the work a transgressive genre, one that 'breaks the mould of verbatim theatre's typically earnest style',[15] or produces a 'mock-verbatim' theatre which subverts 'the "authenticity" of [the] testimony'.[16] However, the mock-verbatim category sits uneasily with some aspects of the production, especially the final section with its collision of a real-time preparation of a naked male performer's body for the morgue with a chilling, highly mediated presentation of testimony from primary witnesses to another maritime incident addressed by the Committee, the horrific SIEV X, in which 353 lives were lost. Both the heralded disjuncture between 'authentic' text and 'inauthentic' performance in the programme notes, and the production's play with genre categories was one of the factors that contributed to my inability to fully grasp the nature of the representations and ontology of the performed subjects. To exemplify how *CMI* works with ungraspability I refer to the use of metatext, casting and modes of delivery, as well as the opening frame scene.

Some way into the first section of the show, a metatextual address to the audience is projected by means of an old-tech overhead projector (OHP) that announces the obvious inauthenticity of the performers:

WE KNOW THAT YOU KNOW WE ARE NOT REALLY THE
SENATORS/
WHO TOOK PART IN THE CMI SENATE INQUIRY/
STEPHEN IS A LOT SHORTER THAN SENATOR COOK AND
DEBORAH WHO PLAYS SENATOR FAULKNER IS ACTUALLY A/
WOMAN/
WE FOUND THAT OUT AFTER THE AUDITION.

On one level this humorous commentary gives a nod to one of Brecht's defamiliarisation or V-effect strategies, self-reflexively commenting on the constructed nature of the performance. This constructedness is heightened throughout the piece not only by means of cross- and anti-type casting, but also role doubling and a mixture of epic and post-structuralist delivery modes *à la* Forced Entertainment and The Wooster Group. The OHP projection also resembles a Brechtian V-effect in the way it embodies a socially critical attitude towards the testimony it interrupts, that of Vice Admiral Shackleton, chief of the Navy. The projection is inserted immediately after a poetic disquisition from the vice admiral on the subject of the 'fog of war', a text the female performer playing Shackleton reads in a very deep and slow voice off a beer coaster while turning the coaster in circles to decipher the tiny writing. Tone, content and delivery of the text may make it difficult for those spectators who are unfamiliar with the Senate transcripts to discern whether the text is cited verbatim (which it is!) or fabricated by version 1.0. The script suggests government personnel found themselves in a 'fog of war' when faced with Iraqi and Afghani asylum seekers on the SIEV 4, and that in this fog, where 'everything is real but it is not real', personnel have to 'build a puzzle from many disconnected pieces' that then sometimes 'disintegrates again as the events change'. As a result judgements are made that are 'never absolutely right', and 'never absolutely wrong'.[17] Placed as it is after this speech that thematises epistemological instability, the metatextual address seems to mock Shackleton's use of relativist thought to create a fog machine that removes blame from the relevant authorities, including himself.

The metatext also draws attention to his suggestion that the attempt of the HMAS *Adelaide* to force the small Indonesian fishing vessel out of Australian territorial waters was a war event. The positioning of the SIEV 4 as 'the enemy', even if only a metaphorical one, is particularly strange given that Australia had just, or would soon declare war on the very countries the asylum seekers were fleeing.[18] Thus one might read the metatext as also illuminating a 'real' misperception about encounters with strangers amid a period of border panic. As producer David Williams reveals in an article written after the show, one of the social insights he was interested in was anthropologist Ghassan Hage's ideas about a warring society. Such a society gives precedence to defending the good life over enjoying it, and to justifying bad actions as temporary necessities that should be publicly legitimated. In Brechtian fashion, the metatext helps the piece to connect the spectator with the company's political position, especially its interest in the idea, referred to by Williams, that 'the warring society marshals a phantasmic unreal war to justify a delimitation of reality'.[19]

Paradoxically, like the showing of the actor-character split in Brecht's theatre, the OHP declaration of the performers' inauthenticity – that they are not the real referents and that they are fabricators – has the potential to create a sense of contact with the authentic. This is partly because, as Caroline Wake points out in her analysis of false witnessing in *CMI*, the acknowledgement of the split and the imposter role can make the performers seem more 'truthful' than literally mimetic actors.[20] Furthermore, it seems to connect the spectator with the company's sceptical perspective towards the production of 'fog' within the inquiry. We are also put in contact with the company's legal reality: it is in their interests to declare their artifice in order to avoid being penalised for a misleading treatment of Senate Committee evidence.[21] As dramaturg Paul Dwyer points out, the aside betrays 'a quite genuine anxiety'.[22] Thus the projection V-effect also operates as an A-effect. However, the metatext's play with a speech about the difficulties of making judgments in a kaleidoscopic world is complex. For example, it seems also to acknowledge the performers' own inability to fully grasp the ever-changing objects of *their* inquiry. Like the Senators and witnesses, they too fail to arrive at truth in any absolute sense and present a partial grasp, in the sense of both partisan and incomplete. The spectator who experiences the difficulties of navigating a kaleidoscopic world created by both history and version 1.0 must similarly face up to the partiality of her grasp. In my case this has involved acknowledging that when I first experienced the 'fog of war' speech I was not fully sure why it was being problematised as it seemed in many ways an apt description of the complexity of border control encounters. In other words, during the first performance I suffered from a similar misperception to Shackleton.

A particularly vivid experience of the way 'inauthentic performance' can offer both a sense of close contact with social reality and truths, and an undermining of that sense, is offered in the opening frame scene. Here a dialogue unfolds between an unnamed male figure, played by Stephen Klinder, and an entity he refers to as 'Mr Reith', the name of the person who was defence minister in 2002. At the episode's beginning, the entity created by Klinder invites Mr Reith to talk into a lie-detector microphone, an unusual request from a figure who otherwise comes across as some sort of public presenter. The primary-school child tasked with representing Reith gives a non-mimetic reading of a statement on a laminated sheet with both exertion and excited self-consciousness at being in a theatre show. Klinder ends the scene by thanking Reith, saying: 'That was much better than last time', and explaining as the child waves goodbye and exits that 'unfortunately, Mr Reith wasn't able to stay with us for the inquiry, as he had to catch a flight to London'. During the scene Klinder at one moment seems to be citing a comment from a reporter who refers to 'this photo', and indeed one of the lines in the published play script is attributed to ABC radio presenter Virginia Trioli who interviewed Reith during the SIEV 4 storm. That Klinder is quoting is hard to decipher, thanks to both cross-casting, and the lack of clear character, time or place designations – although the reference to the strangely missing photo suggests he is.

At first glance the actor-character disjunctures and the merging of a historical interview with what seems to be a fictive lie-detector scene serve a straightforward satire that presents the defence minister's actions as perjury – rehearsed testimony with an intention to deceive.[23] The situation set up by the scene, whereby the audience find themselves warmly barracking for the Reith-child who 'offers an innocent smile in return, waves and exits, scot-free, home to bed'[24] also satirises the Australian public's positive response to the Liberal Party's Federal Election campaign, despite media expressions of doubt about the SIEV 4 story. However, the scene's disjunctures and lack of designations also makes the audience uncertain about how the scene connects with historical documents and hence whether they have grasped Reith's historical actions and the nature of the representation. For example, some may be left asking: does it contain material from an actual interview and statement and if so which one? Where does fiction start and stop? After the show, those who are not familiar with lie detectors may learn how partial their grasp of the scene was too. This is because it is not declared during the scene that the lie-detector technology used is real, and only specialists will know that its software invariably records a 'truth' reading for actors performing texts, because they are not lying, so much as telling a truth that is not their own.[25] This belated knowledge makes even clearer that the inauthentic performers in this scene both do and do not provide a connection with reality and the authentic.

To my mind the uncertainty *CMI* generates around this sort of connection has the potential to produce an inquisitive attitude towards both representations and the unfamiliar, in this case the disavowed lack of hospitality[26] within one's own self and culture that is symptomatic of border panic. That is, it has the potential to produce reflective citizens who cannot be conscripted into an unquestioning defence of the 'good' society against the inhumane stranger. This questioning participant resembles Brecht's ideal spectator, but is neither guided by a model of how social contradictions can be resolved nor the assumption that the ever-changing world is governed by deducible and constant social laws. *CMI*'s spectators must face phenomena that simultaneously inhabit seemingly authentic and overtly manufactured realms. Repeatedly they are put in contact with materials from historical and contemporary reality through authenticating strategies, and repeatedly that contact is troubled. One result is that spectators are encouraged to create their own navigation strategies for a mediated and kaleidoscopic world full of encounters with people and representations whose ontological status is hard to assess, and who bring spectators face-to-face with the culturally unfamiliar.

Hotel/*Chambermaids*: 'Authentic' or 'fictional' stories?

The Reality Theatre performance, *Chambermaids*, serves as an example of postdramatic theatre's general interest in processes of fictionalisation,[27] as it challenges common perceptions of authenticity and facts on the one hand, and fiction on the other. In *Chambermaids* it is significant that the fictionalisation process cannot always be detected by audiences, particularly in the final segment of the five biographical installations when audiences are unable to differentiate between the referential and poetic function of the language used. As in *CMI*, participants in *Chambermaids* are exposed to phenomena that simultaneously inhabit the realms of the seemingly authentic and of fiction. The resulting state of insecurity invites audiences to discover and reflect on unfamiliar aspects of other and their own culture(s).

To begin with, however, this performance presents an abundance of details that create A-effects. These are reinforced by the performance location and space, which, for the premiere 2010, was the ibis Hotel at the Potsdamer Platz, Berlin. Apart from having to present a ticket at the beginning of the performance, audience members are given no meta-signs that would identify the hotel environment as a performance space. They are handed a hotel key card that provides access to the five hotel rooms that constitute the performance spaces. These cards function as props as well as serving a practical use, in that they open the doors to the relevant hotel rooms. In the individual rooms, audiences have access to written texts, 'original voice recordings' and videos that tell the personal stories of five male and female 'chambermaids'. These autobiographical narratives contain detailed factual information about their occupation and the cleaning work in an international hotel chain. With one exception, Arias' and Kaegi's protagonists are not present in person during the performance. As 'invisible spirits who clean up after others',[28] they do not pursue a work life characterised by public performance as do many of the 'experts' of Rimini Protokoll's theatre. As a result of their absence, the authenticity contract between experts and audience is potentially challenged, and the audience cannot use live delivery as a possible indicator for the degree of artifice involved in a particular performance.

The mediated and edited character of the stories is counterbalanced by A-effects, such as the use of untrained voices and sociolects in the audio and audiovisual documents which suggest immediate access to unaltered statements. Documents, such as photos and the photocopy of an application for asylum, or – in the later production in Zurich – a letter, seem to provide 'evidence of [a particular chambermaid's] story'.[29] However, it remains unclear to what extent the stories presented to the audience have originally been told by 'real people', to what extent they are fiction, or whether they are both. The ambiguous status of the stories is replicated on another level by the performance spaces: the hotel rooms also oscillate between representing 'real' hotel rooms where participants walk around, sit on beds and watch a video on TV on the one hand, and more or less obvious performance spaces on the other hand, such as an exotic wedding suite, a room with a bed full of used towels, and one filled with plants and sounds evoking Palma de Mallorca. These ambiguities set the tone for *Chambermaids* as a performance that plays 'with the liminal space of reality and fiction'.[30] With audiences being deprived of live delivery as a possible indicator for the degree of artifice involved in a performance, they have to trust the experts when they present each individual story as their own 'authentic' narrative. This state of dependence is reinforced through the experts' advantage in knowledge: as audiences cannot verify the detailed information themselves, they have to rely on the experts' insider knowledge about hotels, as exemplified by a DVD recording in which a young woman seems to be able to describe the layout of the hotel rooms with her eyes closed. The audience are thus placed in a situation where they are unable to grasp fully either the authenticity or fictionality of documents, settings and narratives.

An explicit reference to processes of fictionalisation can be already found in the first room where a letter by a 'chamberboy' from Cameroon states: 'Perhaps refugees always tell the same story . . . I have told my life story so many times that it seems like fiction to me'.[31] It is unclear whether the repetition he refers to has been part of the process of applying for asylum, as suggested by a photocopy of the relevant paperwork hidden behind a painting, or whether the fictionalisation process has been triggered when his life was framed as an element of a biographical performance. In both cases any version of the story has probably been fictionalised through acts of selection, combination and aesthetic reframing.[32] In a similar way to *CMI*, the V-effect resulting from the open admission turns into an A-effect that paradoxically endows the voice which has created it with the authority of speaking the 'truth'.

Audience insecurity regarding the factual or fictional nature of expert statements is further reinforced in the last scene, where participants undergo a subtle shift in their social role from audience member to hotel guest, when they are invited to lie on the hotel bed for a video presentation by Jinrong Li, a Chinese university student. The participants themselves might not even become aware of this role change as it is simply related to the fact that they are lying down in order to watch the video, which is projected onto the ceiling rather than being shown on TV. This is unlike the situation in the previous rooms, where they were invited to sit down as in a conventional performance or to move about as might be the case in environmental theatre. At this point the hotel's original functions as a place offering accommodation and employment are partly reclaimed. Yet the transformation of audience members into hotel guests is neither stable nor complete because, even as 'hotel guests', participants continue to observe and engage with an audiovisual documentary about Li's work and his everyday life in Germany which is tailored to this segment of the performance. As a result, audience members lose their stable frame of reference for assessing the communicative situation which impacts on their ability to differentiate between the referential and poetic function of the language used in Li's narrative. Consequently it remains unclear whether the video is to be interpreted as fiction or as 'real' information provided by a hotel employee, or as an alternation between the two.

The loss of a stable frame of reference is illustrated by my own reaction to the moment in the video when Li reports that he had come to Germany to study automotive engineering, but that he had hardly any friends in Berlin. As he also states on video, Germans hardly have Chinese friends. Once this story had been told, Li himself knocked on the hotel room door, which compelled me to respond within the conventions that are part of a 'normal' hotel stay. As part of the performance, he was ready to take me on a guided tour through rooms that ordinary hotel guests do not have access to, such as the linen room. At this stage it was unclear whether Li acted as a Reality Theatre performer, or whether he performed his role as a 'real' hotel employee. There was insufficient time to clarify the situation as I had to spontaneously react to Li – his guided tour started immediately after I opened the hotel room door. This combination of having lost the frame of reference for assessing the function of language and the role he was playing, together with the altered cognitive frame of mind when lying down and the pressure to react quickly, created the temporary illusion that the story told in the last biographical installation was largely 'real' and 'authentic'.

At first Li's presence seemed to further authenticate his story and with it the other performance details, which appeared to be representative of the 'real hotel life' usually inaccessible to the 'normal' hotel guest. Yet my initial perception of his having shared an excerpt of his 'real' life with his audience was challenged when I asked him during the tour about his comment in the video on German-Chinese relationships. Instead of entering into a discussion he continued the guided tour into the next room, as though he had never made this remark. In a video available via the *Ciudades Paralelas* website, Li shows a similar reaction towards another spectator's question during the tour, again deflecting attention from a certain remark which he had made about marriage, and avoiding further questions.[33]

Chambermaids invites audiences to *experience*[34] encounters with the unfamiliar both between and within cultures in two ways in particular: first, as an encounter between the participant and the usually invisible and thus unknown person working in a hotel; and second, as a discovery of one's own desires with regard to intercultural encounter across national divides. In my example, the unsuccessful attempt to initiate a real intercultural discussion resulted in my astonishment, and a later musing on why I had asked my question in the first place. Was it because I wanted to experience the type of 'multicultural harmony' in the German context that I had experienced from time to time in the Australian context?

In the performance itself, like Brechtian defamiliarisation, audiences' astonishment also opens up fresh ways of looking at an issue because it interrupts our usual ways of viewing.[35] However, the interruption is initially neither a rational process nor is it guided by a stable understanding of social reality. To begin with, this disruption of underlying attitudes primarily confronts audience members with their own disorientation. As Peter Boenisch has stated, the 'situation of spectating is thus turned from the traditional aesthetic attitude of "reception" into an act of encounter.'[36] When spectators are invited to question their own attitudes and behaviour as active participants of a performance, the deceptive image of innocent spectatorship is destroyed.[37] In my case, *Chambermaids* compelled me to reflect on reasons for my interest in German-Chinese intercultural relations, particularly against the background of my Australian and German national identities, and prompted me to ask further questions about my attitude towards the underlying sociopolitical issues, such as the working and living conditions of hotel staff from various cultural backgrounds. While the programme notes already pointed to the fact that in the transcultural space of an international hotel chain, both the guests and the 'chambermaids' are usually foreigners, it was the personal *experience* that challenged me to explore this idea further. When notions of what is authentic and what is fictional have been destabilised, as in the last performance segment, the resulting insecurity potentially also puts into question participants' memories, perceptions and interpretations of their experiences of the previous performance segments and their overall interpretation of the unfamiliar experts. As Christine Regus has pointed out in her study of intercultural theatre, the failure to grasp the full meaning of a performance segment emulates the productive insecurity that also characterises processes of 'getting to know one another in an ongoing dialogue'.[38]

In conclusion, postdramatic Reality Theatre is distinguished by the use of authenticity effects in such a way that they open up liminal states of disorientation for the spectator. These states encourage new and unstable modes of perceiving self, other and representations. According to Erika Fischer-Lichte, 'irritation, the collision of frames and the destabilisation of perception and self' is a more appropriate performance strategy than 'detached and free pleasure' for a world characterised by 'on ongoing aestheticisation of everyday life based on an event-culture'.[39] The liminal experiences of the theatre we have analysed encourage: first, engagement with the act of trying to grasp social reality, in the sense of being in contact with it and reaching for understanding of it; secondly, the realisation of both the capacities and limitations of inauthentic performance for giving temporary and partial access to reality and the real; and thirdly, acknowledgment of the difficulties of grasping and inability to ever fully grasp strangers and the unfamiliar. As Regus points out this acknowledgement is highly critical within the realm of intercultural encounter, an arena of ongoing dialogue, as it opens up a possibility for intercultural communication beyond dispossession and appropriation. Such challenges to viewing the unfamiliar in intercultural contexts confirm that, as Lehmann contends, '[t]he politics of theatre is a *politics of perception*'.[40]

Postdramatic Labour in The Builders Association's *Alladeen*

Shannon Jackson

We have to start with the diagnosis that the question of a political theatre changes radically under the conditions of the contemporary information society.[1]

Hans-Thies Lehmann

Hi, I'm in Bangalore (but I can't say so.)

Quote in the *New York Times*[2]

As an intermedia performance group that works within a theatrical frame, The Builders Association (TBA) has figured prominently in contemporary discussions of postdramatic theatre. They are theatrical labourers who rely on professional theatrical networks to support their experimentation. At the same time, they question inherited conventions of acting, staging and storytelling in their technologically innovative stagings. While the specificities of their practice will unfold as I continue, TBA artists are productive interlocutors for a number of reasons. First, they embody one of the central arguments of Hans-Thies Lehmann's characterisation of the postdramatic in that they challenge conventions of theatrical presentation while simultaneously re-connecting us with the fundamental elements and fundamental capacities of the medium. While they make use of the proscenium stage, the Builders often use the techniques of other forms – site-specific installation, sculpture, architecture and video – to expand or redistribute the effects of theatrical engagement. Additionally, they respond in intriguing ways to the changing social landscape brought on by new technologies and 'the contemporary information society', whether by incorporating those technologies into the medium of enactment or by offering counter-spaces that anachronistically – and hence provocatively – return us to the low-tech space of personal encounter. Finally, this is an international company whose work thematises and formalises issues of globalisation. Their members navigate the politics and logistics of being international touring artists in their modes of address and in the ways that they organise their labour. And, in moves that trouble distinctions between form and content, they also incorporate issues of global politics into the structure of their work. Most intriguingly for me, TBA explore the position of workers within globalising networks driven by the affective labour of a service economy, asking what kinds of materials are still needed to motor this presumably 'immaterial' sphere. As such, their work provides a prime site for exploring the relation between postdramatic theatricality and the contemporary political landscape of our presumably post-Fordist moment.

My goal here is to use works by TBA, and in particular their 2003 piece, *Alladeen*, as indexes in a larger conversation about the varied role of 'the political' within a variety of postdramatic forms and postdramatic aspirations. As a US-based company with an international reputation, their work often explores how twenty-first-century humans imagine their relation to larger systems of support, labour and digital technology.[3] In Hans-Thies Lehmann's own characterisation of contemporary politics (and in political theory more generally), it often seems that a globalising world of digital connection has done away with terrestrial systems of labour and support. Rather than the under-mounted 'base' of industrial labour imagined in vertical Marxist (and often Brechtian) visions of social organisation, humans are now connected electronically and even wirelessly in laterally networked relationships. With the 'loose ties' of a network replacing hierarchical social systems, citizens are presumably freer to move; we can make connections and drop them; we can transfer money without ever seeing cash; we can initiate new collaborations without ever meeting our collaborators in real time. In such a changing context, theorists of globalisation also speculate that our concepts of work have changed as well. The hyper-material labour of a Marxist base has been replaced by the mobilisation of what Michael Hardt and Antonio Negri call 'immaterial labour', whether taking shape in the exchange of information or in the 'affective' offering of compassion, care, excitement and hospitality – in Hardt and Negri's terms, 'a feeling of ease, well-being, satisfaction, excitement, or passion' – in a growing service economy.[4] Overall, then, the digitally networked world of immaterial work presents itself as a kind of frictionless space, one where economic exchange seems to bypass the gravitational and referential pulls of economic power, one where labour seems no longer to leave any material trace of its enactment.

Importantly, such images of a friction-free world have been complicated and qualified by those who think precisely about how they actually work. Saskia Sassen argues that the global marketplace remains 'embedded' in the material infrastructures of cities and citizens who animate them. 'Emphasizing place in a complex global economy', she says, 'is one way to address what I see as the need to destabilize the accepted dominant narratives and explanations of globalization.'[5] For Sassen, global exchange, no matter how electronically 'diffused' and 'dispersed', will still always require its 'territorial moment'.[6] Similarly, Hardt and Negri argue that a so-called immaterial sphere is still dependent upon material labour whether or not we notice it:

> Immaterial labor almost always mixes with material forms
> of labor: health care workers, for example, perform affective,

cognitive and linguistic tasks together with material ones, such as cleaning bedpans and changing bandages. The labor involved in all immaterial production, we should emphasize, remains material – it involves our bodies and brains as all labor does. What is immaterial is *its product*.[7]

For those who study theatre history or work in the theatrical field, this kind of simultaneity has an intriguing ring. Indeed, long before we began to speak of globalisation, the labourers of the theatre could be found engaging in all kinds of material production to create an immaterial product. Mobilising the resources of bodies, space and the props of the object world, theatre artists have been in the business of creating affective spaces of 'ease, well-being, satisfaction, excitement, or passion' that have left little material trace. It is precisely because of this long-standing conjunction – one where performance can stand in both for the encumbering realm of material making as well as the ephemeral realm of motion and affect – that postdramatic theatre seems a prime place to investigate the paradoxes of globalised connection. Indeed, postdramatic theatre conventions have developed in part to stage the dramatic unities of time, place and character in a context that perpetually undoes them. It is thus no coincidence that Hans-Thies Lehmann invokes this media scene in his meditations on the politics of the postdramatic:

> The basic structure of perception mediated by media is such that there is no experience of connection among the individual images received but above all no connection between the receiving and sending of signs; there is no experience of a relation between address and answer. Theatre can respond to this only with a *politics of perception,* which could at the same time be called an *aesthetic of responsibility (or response-ability).* Instead of the deceptively comforting duality of here and there, inside and outside, it can move the *mutual implication of actors and spectators in the theatrical*

production of images into the centre and thus make visible the broken thread between personal experience and perception. Such an experience would not only be aesthetic but therein at the same time ethico-political.[8]

If an unfettered mediascape of electronic connection currently predominates in our social imagining, then perhaps the anachronistic materiality of theatre can be a reminder that such a world still needs a human body to change its bandages. And it is with such reminders that 'the broken thread between personal experience and perception' becomes visible. In TBA's use of a contingent postdramatic theatrical medium, we find them illuminating the contingencies of an immaterial global economy that still depends upon a material apparatus of time, place and people in '*mutual implication*'.[9]

While searching for a productive anachronism in theatrical responses to contemporary global themes, I simultaneously wish to explore how TBA, like other contemporary theatres referenced in this book, have 'modernised' their and our sense of what politically engaged theatre might mean. In part, this is a question of how far theatre's 'politics of perception' might go. In fact, explicitly political theatre has worked throughout the twentieth century to emphasise the material apparatus behind both aesthetic events and social subjects. For Bertolt Brecht and for generations of artists and critics who have interpreted him, political engagement came about in a context that announced theatre's formal dependence upon its material apparatus of production. As Brecht and his contemporaries puzzled over the exploitation of labour, the mystification of the commodity, and the equitable re-organisation of society, he felt that such critical reflection could only occur in a theatre that had relinquished its own illusory tricks. The construction of society could only be explored in a theatrical environment that avowed and exposed its own processes of artistic construction. Today, artists and critics think regularly about what if anything a Brechtian theatre offers our contemporary moment. Put another way, we think continually about what 'post-Brechtianism' means for a postdramatic theatre, one where – as Hans-Thies Lehmann writes – the 'post' never denotes complete rejection but always exists in productive tension with precedents and histories. While Barnett in this book makes a compelling argument for distinguishing post-Brechtian theatre from the postdramatic, I have found it more helpful to think of the former as a variant of the latter. While all of the Builders' work uses the conventions and perceptual techniques that we now associate with the postdramatic, some of their works maintain a kind of Brechtian dialectical engagement, addressing 'fables' of social asymmetry even as they question older reality principles with properly post-Brechtian suspicion.

One way of framing the political underpinnings of a globalising postdramatic theatre is to map them to changes in contemporary social discourse, perhaps asking to what degree the post-Brechtianism of postdramatic theatre can be analogised to the goals and reality principles of post-Marxism. What if, for example, we go back to the metaphors, truth values and central assumptions of a certain kind of Marxist imagining? What if we follow by thinking about how such terms have been redefined by generations of thinkers who sought to unsettle its determining vision? How have they questioned the hierarchies that would give an authenticating finality to the 'base' realm of labour and necessity, opposing it to the superstructural illusions of representation and ideology? For Ernesto Laclau and Chantal Mouffe – the thinkers whose work prompted the coining of the term 'post-Marxist' – such a task meant rejecting any social model that would give structural primacy to any single dimension of a socio-psychic system. Indeed, even in Louis Althusser's attempts to offer Marxism a complex theory of psychoanalytic subjectivity, Laclau and Mouffe find that he overly stabilises the nature of the exchange by invoking a final 'determination in the last instance by the economy'.

'If society has a last instance which determines its laws of motion,' they worry about Althusser's paradigm, 'then *the relations between the overdetermined instances and the last instance must be conceived in terms of simple, one-directional determination by the latter*.'[10] This 'last instance', whether imagined temporally in terms of finality or spatially as an under-mounted operation, thus short-circuits our ability to plot relational exchange and contradiction across multiple registers of the social. Laclau and Mouffe reject the notion that social formation is unidirectionally determined by a fixed realm of necessity or an immovable conception of the 'base'. They also use the concept of 'hegemony' to complicate Marxist visions of an ideological, superstructural realm of false consciousness, in order to dramatise the complex psychic enmeshment of selves within institutions that they seek to contest. Intriguingly, their language echoes that of an aesthetic discourse preoccupied also with unsettling divisions between art and apparatus, sculpture and base, foreground and background, inside and outside. Laclau and Mouffe continue:

> Here we arrive at a decisive point in our argument. The incomplete character of every totality necessarily leads us to abandon, as a terrain of analysis, the premise of 'society' as a sutured and self-defined totality. 'Society' is not a valid object of discourse. There is no single underlying principle fixing – and hence constituting – the whole field of differences. The irresoluble interiority/exteriority tension is the condition of any social practice: necessity only exists as a partial limitation of the field of contingency.[11]

While it could never be said that Brecht accepted a fixed vision of society's supporting apparatus, it can be said that his theatre laboured under a determining vision of labour. Theatre's 'exterior' processes backstage bore an analogy to the real, authenticating realm of necessity that theoretically was both hidden from and necessary to the operations of illusion. But if a post-Marxist vision is, in part, about antagonising the values and reality effects given to certain 'underlying principles', then a post-Brechtian postdramatic theatre might also ask what it means to imagine material necessity not as given, foundational, or determining 'in the last instance' but as a 'partial limitation on the field of contingency'. A twenty-first-century post-Brechtian postdramatic theatre would also be skeptical of any theatre that imagined itself outside or uncorrupted by the social structures it tried to question.

Such an orientation qualifies and complicates the weight that any critic might give to either material or immaterial registers that we find in contemporary society – and that we find indexed in its postdramatic theatre. Arguably, the structures of feeling that celebrate a friction-free digital world of immaterial connection need to be reminded of the material labour such a world requires. At the same time, a post-Brechtian theatre that takes seriously post-Marxist revisions will have to be careful of giving such material registers – whether imagined in bodies, in economies, in necessities, or in 'territorial moments' – a structurally determining place. I have found that such reflection is an important check on my own tendencies to give the material operations of support a certain kind of determining value. To engage in a post-Brechtian exposure of the apparatus of support is, in fact, not simply to show 'reality' behind 'representation', but also to find in that exposure evidence of their intimate and ever-shifting co-imbrication. It questions Marxist and Brechtian reality principles even as it remains dialectical. Much of TBA's works provide an opportunity to think about the materiality of immaterial labour at the same moment that they animate the material sphere with the contingent dynamics of theatrical representation. The networked worlds they dramatise have by no means done away with the claims of necessity, but they are not unidirectionally determined by them either. The backstage of labour and technology is not the 'exterior' real but in irresoluble tension with the interiority of the aesthetic event, an irresolution that is, to echo

Laclau and Mouffe above, 'the condition of any social practice'. In the analogue realm of theatrical analogy, we find stagings that show the limiting conditions of what we used to call the 'base'.

Seated in rows before a proscenium stage, it suddenly seems as if we are here to watch a video . . . or maybe a video game. A panoply of kaleidoscopic squares move in and around a video screen, forming grids that constantly change, their internal patterns lining up to form new symmetrical decorations. The images dance to the steady beat of techno-music, and more shapes zoom and unravel to form new arrangements of luminous, multicoloured eye candy. Columns of rectangles slide in from the side with the sound of a whoosh, changing pattern sequentially as if opening a series of doors. Large digitised squares descend from the sky and land with a synthesised plop on top of each other, eventually forming the blocked landscape of what seems to be a city street. As the techno beat continues, the iconography of LED advertising appears inside of the blocks that form stores, signs and billboards; digitised buses and taxis pass through the screened proscenium. In their pixilated luster, the digitised screens of global consumer culture advertise international clothing chains, telecommunication conglomerates and athletic equipment. Under the banner of Virgin Atlantic, a small grid of squares appears in rows that would be 'thumbnail' if this was a computer screen; the rows form shelf after shelf of CDs for sale. The synthesised whooshes, plops and kerchunks continue, mimicking the soundscape of a search on a high-end website. Suddenly, a mailbox, a phone booth and a fire hydrant slide onto the set together; they get there not by means of a gurney, a trap, a sliding stage, or a run crew, but as electronically mediated objects riding the transit systems of a video software program. Human characters begin to appear throughout this opening sequence, although we realise that they are – like the fire hydrant – digitally rendered figures moving through the mise-en-scène. By the same means, a vendor's food cart drops from the sky with a synthesised crash.

One human character, however, walks onto the stage supported by the embodied medium of a live actor; in so doing, she also clears a three-dimensional set space in front of the video-screen's two-dimensionality. She is speaking into a cell phone headset in a not fully locatable cosmopolitan accent. 'I love karaoke', she says to a friend on the wireless line. 'It's like magic. You can be anything you want. You just have to find the right song.' She goes on to confirm a rendezvous with her friend in Las Vegas at the newly refurbished 'Aladdin Hotel' when she switches off to make another call. Her solicitous tone changes to a demanding one as she speaks with a car-rental operator named 'Monica'. She bristles at what she decides is a slow and unclear response to her request for a rental reservation: 'Don't you speak English?' she asks of the unseen Monica. 'Where are you from?', she berates Monica, who – we will learn later – is trying to avoid the lilting tones of a South Asian accent, blaming her for the fact that a car cannot be found quickly enough. 'Well, this is obviously going to take longer than I thought. I'll have to call you back.' She immediately takes another call from a friend in Hong Kong, speaking in Mandarin about their travel plans, with Anglophone references to 'Las Vegas' and 'package deal' interspersed. And then another call comes in from a boyfriend. She tells him that she is in a 'permanent state of jet lag', and then apologises for being interrupted by the noise of a bus that has just stopped next to her. The digitised bus 'leaves', and the conversation continues.

This opening scene from *Alladeen* represents in miniature the unfettered space of possibility afforded by global travel and global technologies. Its imagery and its soundscape mimics that of the web, the sense of 'choice', 'presence', 'movement', 'possibility' that Tara McPherson argues 'structure a sense of causality [. . .] structuring a mobilized liveness which we come to feel we invoke and impact, in the instant, in the click, reload.'[12] We seem to have complete freedom of movement in an uploadable world. If we have come to feel that this 'volitional mobility'[13] is a condition of contemporary existence, this scene from *Alladeen* also suggests the fragile frictions of wires, cables, broadband, planes, cars, buses and labourers on which that apparently friction-free world relies.

The 2003 production of *Alladeen* was the seventh project created by the loose network of actors, designers, writers and technical and assistant directors called TBA, incorporated in 1994 by Marianne Weems, who has directed all of their productions. They named themselves while creating their first production of Henrik Ibsen's *The Master Builder* (1993) in an illegal New York loft above what was then a dilapidated Chelsea food market, and the anachronistic associations connected with the labour of 'building' continue to inform their interventions into mediascapes where, it would seem, material labour is no longer required.

The standard way of framing TBA is as a company that combines 'new media' and 'theatrical' forms. Many forms of theatre use new media and screen technologies, including Disney musicals. The Builders' is a brand of new media theatre, however, that more directly announces an interest in grappling with the effects of new technology by staging those new technologies themselves. 'I'm not interested in the stage apart from the screen', says Weems. 'We all spend a good portion of our day in front of one whether it's a computer, TV, or movie and this affects the way we see the world.'[14] The Builders' work thus walks a line walked by many twenty-first-century artists who find themselves enmeshed within the social and technological forces that they simultaneously critique. On the face of it these two different domains, 'new media' and 'theatre', also index a difference between 'new' and 'old' aesthetic domains, in which the new is not a surprise so much as it is a brand.

Such a state of affairs threatens both to excite and to foreclose an analysis of TBA, replicating a mode of argument that both excites and forecloses the political possibilities of postdramatic theatre more generally. In the last decade, dozens of reviews have celebrated them as 'the future of theatre', an appeal to futurity whose calibrations of old and new made TBA artists extremely uncomfortable. Interestingly, reviews that are negative about their work criticise them in almost exactly the same terms, lamenting their collusion with a 'future' of new technology that leaves the tradition of theatre and live performance behind.

These anti-technological impulses are of course at risk of ignoring theatre's long history of technological incorporation and cross-medium redefinition. Theatre and technology have always been in a constant state of mutual transformation, whether one imagines that cross-media relation in bodily systems for blocking a scene, in mechanical systems for transforming a scene, or in incandescent systems for lighting it.

In *Alladeen*, those bodily, mechanical and incandescent systems re-appeared in new form, under the glowing lights of an LED billboard connected wirelessly to the fluorescent-lit space of a call centre in India. After the opening scene of the multitasking global citizen on her cell phone, the stage switches to a call centre company in Bangalore where 'Monica' and her colleagues are being trained. Weems, working in collaboration with Keith Khan and Ali Zaidi of the UK-based arts group, *motiroti,* travelled to Bangalore to conduct interviews with trainers and trainees at several call centre operations, including 24/7 Customer.com, whose 'multi-channel, outsourced solutions deliver twice the quality of other alternatives at a lower cost'.[15] In videotaped interviews, a trainer spoke directly into the camera about her attempts to 'hire people without any mother tongue influences . . . [I]f there are any dialectical or mother tongue influences, we do our best to neutralise it [*sic*]'. The scene then switches to documentation of a vocal training session in Bangalore that is simultaneously re-enacted by actors on the stage. A white American-accented male trainer stands next to a trainee who is trying to pronounce American capitals; in the video and onstage, the trainer and trainer-actor stop the student and student-actor as they refine syllables and consonants for 'Santa Fe, New Mexico . . . Santa Fe . . . Albany, New York, Albany, New York . . . try this: Albany . . . Albany, New York'. As they move down the list in American geography, the trainer and trainer-actor both tell the student not to rush, and offer encouragement by saying there was 'great energy . . . a lot of juices there . . . a lot of juice.'

As with so much of their work, *Alladeen* shows TBA using the tropes of acting ('great energy') – and the long-standing anxieties about authenticity that acting provokes – to trouble conventional assumptions about the reality effects of performance. With the live actors taking on the personae of those who take on a persona, juxtaposed with the videotaped documentations of labourers who also take on a persona when they do their job, *Alladeen's* mediascaped stage offers a distributed network whose 'original' performance is projected and deflected. Later, we will see documentation of interviews with the operators themselves, describing the difficulty of 'getting the accent come what may' as well as their training in American popular culture. The stage shows re-enactments of more video documentation, of training sessions on the rules of baseball and the love lives of television celebrities. In restaging the performance training of the service industry, the piece thus also re-stages the unequal ground on which this circuit of mimicry occurs, one where cross-cultural training in pronunciation and popular culture occurs in one direction. This space of cosmopolitan mimicry occurs in an asymmetrical zone that compels certain performances, delocalising the Indian site of the call centre in order to address a 'global citizen' who wants to hear the language and accent tones of the highly local site of the United States. The goal of the fictional call centre represented onstage, like the nonfictional

24/7 Customer.com documented on video, is to create a system of tech support whose service is not interrupted by the jarring tones of an Other local context – nor the accompanying psychic awareness of global dependency that would come if a privileged caller decided to ask 'where are you from?'.

In many ways, *Alladeen* represented a new take on TBA's long-standing interest in the position of labour: labour as process, labour as enactment, labour as expression, labour as task, labour as supporting apparatus, labour as an 'underlying principle' that could be differently distributed through theatrical processes and mediascapes. For example, the decision to place their first production, *The Master Builder* (1993), inside the 'splitting' house of Gordon Matta-Clark was in part an attempt to explore the affect of building through a process of un-building, that is, through an 'anarchitectural' theatre. Matta-Clark's durational and anarchitectural pieces famously 'split' or 'cut' into architectural spaces in ways that opened up different perspectives on rooms, re-calibrating the perceived boundaries between and within them. In the 'splitting' of an abandoned New Jersey house at '322 Humphrey Street' (1974), Matta-Clark cut the structure in half, passing 'through all/structural surfaces' and 'beveling down/forty lineal feet/of cinder blocks/to set half the building on its foundations'.[16] The cutting released a one-inch blade of light through drywall, a window frame, a door, a floorboard and a supporting wall, showing that they were all equally vulnerable.

If postdramatic theatre consistently 'relativises' its referents, drawing radical equivalencies among its assembled signs, then *The Master Builder's* set asked its audiences to imagine a radical relativisation of material support systems, unsettling divisions between content and form, background and foreground. It was this sense of un-building that Weems hoped to cultivate in a reconstructed adaptation of Ibsen, where the steady unhinging of a home coincided with the play's expressed longings for kinship and meaningful work. John Cleater designed a set whose 'rooms' were precariously separated by walls that would be dismantled over the duration of the production. Master Carpenter Joel Cichowski built the set. And, as if to further complicate the categorical division that would have placed master carpentry in the exterior backstage, Weems decided to place this builder in front of it. Every production of *The Master Builder* began with a monologue from Joel who presented each tool on his workbench with a no-nonsense description of the creative capacities of each. Anticipating the testimonies of the call centre operators in *Alladeen*, it was the first time that the presentation of a labouring life challenged the theatrical frame and, with that gesture, the inside/outside boundaries of the theatrical space.

If both society and the theatre are dependent upon the labour of builders, then *Alladeen* offered an expanded exploration of who those builders were in the twenty-first century. The global management of labour was one of the central themes of *Alladeen,* especially at a time when a rise in 'information' and 'affective labour' drives the development of service economies. When the Builders began research in 2001 for this piece on the call centre industry, European and North American citizens were only just beginning to recognise the role of offshore labour in a global economy, including call-service industries where companies found that they could cheaply hire an educated Indian work force to field calls for technical support, international travel, catalogue shopping and other forms of telephonic personal service. The newspaper story – the 'fable' – that first triggered the idea for *Alladeen* appeared in the *New York Times* on 21 March 2001. 'Hi, I'm in Bangalore', the title read, '(but I can't say so)'.[17] The article dramatised acts of international mimicry that supported global transaction:

> Ms. Suman's fluent English and broad vowels would pass muster in the stands at Wrigley Field. In case her callers ask personal

questions, Ms. Suman has conjured up a fictional American life, with parents Bob and Ann, brother Mark, and a made-up business degree from the university of Illinois. 'We watch a lot of "Friends" and "Ally McBeal" to learn the right phrases.'[18]

As the article went on to describe the rise of the offshore customer-service industry, it quoted successful company founders who happily proclaimed: 'India is on its way to being the back office for the world.' Weems collected more articles about the offshoring of the service industries, exploring how jobs migrated from the United States to India and how a 24-hour industry depended upon a labour force in a range of time zones.

In creating a piece about the call centre industry, TBA thus sought to demystify a form of labour that at the time went largely unregistered by the consumers who depended upon it. Performance was fundamental to the mystification process within these service industries – and performance was fundamental to TBA's act of demystification as well. As TBA and *motiroti* artists learned in interviews, performance-based techniques of vocal training and rehearsal were used to train service workers to neutralise their biographical locality, creating a seamless service context whose human territorial specificity went unregistered by its clients. Builder actors thus set about researching what it 'felt' like to be trying to make others 'feel good'. They began to make lists of typical scenarios of economic and emotion management where customers try to 'get help for an inexplicably complex problem' or 'seek the wrong product' or 'try to get something for free'. They then made lists of '[w]hat the operators do (response strategies): try to help, try to make the customer happy, placate, falsely compliment, end the call, deflect, bring caller back to the business of the call, offer alternative solutions, offer bargain discounts . . . '.[19] From there, TBA actors created improvisations and scenarios of affective labour, casting themselves as individuals responsible for maintaining 'emotions of ease, hospitality, excitement, and frustration.[20] For *Alladeen* to show call centre training systems was thus to reveal the affective process by which the mystification of service occurred. It was to use the hyperbolic capacities of theatrical performance to underscore the unregistered capacities of everyday performance, exposing the new 'base' supporting global citizenship or, more precisely, the lateralised, mimetic and dynamic set of social interactions that sustain global personhood.

TBA had already begun a longer conversation about the precarious position of humans within technological systems that purported to collapse global temporalities. In part, these discussions came about in response to their own experiences as artists on an international presenting circuit. After *The Master Builder*, their second and third shows, *Imperial Motel (Faust)* (1996) and *Jump Cut (Faust)* (1997), received attention and support from artistic directors and theatre festivals outside of their native United States. Hence, the maintenance of the company and of their lives as artists depended upon a willingness to move from theatre festival to arts festival, across European, Asian and North American cities. 'We were in airports all the time', remembers Weems.[21] Company members tried to maintain their energy as performers while being in a constant state of jet lag themselves. The corporeal effect of international travel was thus something that they regularly felt in their own lives as what performer Moe Angelos humorously called 'migrant cultural workers'.[22] This theme would receive specific attention in their production of *Jet Lag* with Diller + Scofidio in 1998. Inspired by Paul Virillo's philosophising on 'speed' in contemporary culture, the company dramatised one of Virillo's signature examples where a real-life grandmother, Sarah Krasnoff travelled back and forth across the Atlantic dozens of times with her grandson, reportedly dying of jetlag. The story was paired with that of Donald Crowhurst, a man who created false documentation of himself valiantly crossing the sea in a sailboat. Joining two stories of unproductive motion and unrestful stasis, *Jet Lag* used – but also resisted – the normative time-based conventions of theatre to ask audiences what it meant to travel, at what speed and at what cost. While it used these stories as generative fables for the production, *Jet Lag* is arguably a production that de-emphasised post-Brechtian dialectical engagement regarding political themes in favour of a deep postdramatic exploration of conditions of 'perception' in a landscape where citizens occupy multiple temporalities simultaneously. It was also another project in which Weems found herself drawing upon an architectural imagination for its set design. Collaborating with renowned conceptual architects Diller + Scofidio, the theatrical process of rehearsal and the architectural process of the *charette* mutually transformed each other. Digital architecture's rendering systems were themselves projected as the story's backdrop, creating images of airplane seating and airport lobbies that simulated three-dimensions while actors moved beside and within them. Here was another chiasmic revision of the time-space conventions of visual architecture and of theatre. The theatrical bodies dynamised the flatness of architectural rendering while, conversely, the CAD-ification of the mise-en-scène seemed to render the theatre space static. In so doing, it exemplified what Hans-Thies Lehmann calls a 'postdramatic' turn away from normative 'action' and toward 'states', or the creation of an encounter that approached the condition of viewing a 'static painting' that simultaneously wanted to move.[23]

Interestingly, this kind of aesthetic reflection on movement and stasis had its parallel in the social theory on globalisation that Weems began reading in preparation for *Alladeen*. Consider, for instance, a passage she underlined in an interview with Pico Iyer, the author of *The Global Soul*:

> I begin deliberately with those dizzying surfaces and passageways –
> movement, an inundation of data, which I think reflects how the

world is today – and you have to fight your way through it to get to the stillness and the settledness and the space that begins to open up in those last two chapters. The first chapters make you almost jet-lagged, there's so much information that you can't tell right from left, east from west. In part, the book is about the passage from speed to slowness and surface to depth. To me, that's the big challenge in the global era. The need for stillness, for seceding from that world, is greater than ever.[24]

As a former dramaturg with The Wooster Group, the formal concerns around non-narrative stasis in postdramatic theatre were quite familiar to Weems. After *Jet Lag* and with *Alladeen*, Weems began to find that such formal questions could be joined to social content, especially in a globalising landscape that was confounding perceptions of speed and slowness, proximity and distance. *Alladeen* was thus an attempt to expose the mundane territory and vulnerable bodies at the centre of a world that promised friction-free connection and high-velocity travel; pushing Lehmann's postdramatic terms, it was an attempt to underscore the politics of contemporary conditions of perception.

After presenting scrims and screens that documented training programmes with their simultaneous re-enactment onstage, *Alladeen* continued by showing a call centre in action. Projected screens rose, not to reveal another digitally lush panel but instead to reveal a cast of actor-labourers, working in real time and shared space to sustain the illusion of a frictionless technological world. They navigated calls whose scripts would have sounded all-too familiar to audience members who had recently booked a flight or made a call to tech support. The actor-labourers quite literally appeared as this production's 'base', under-mounted below a screen of extended communication that showed global maps, tracked time zones, and provided updates on American news. Here, labourers struggled to 'keep the mother tongue at bay' and to engage clients with their new abridged knowledge of American popular culture. In making reservations, operators spelled out names: 'H as in Harry Potter, J as in J-Lo'. One operator with the fictive name 'Rachel' attempted to be geographically responsive when talking to a client located in San Jose – 'Oh chilly today, Sir?' – but the attempts at hyper-familiarity could also risk a misfire: 'Terrible about that elephant', she continued, reading about an animal rights case from a live West Coast newsfeed as she worked. 'What?' asked the caller. 'The elephant who was abused', she anxiously responded, 'oh . . . oh perhaps you did not read about it yet', she said, embarrassed by her overloaded knowledge of geo-trivia. As the scene proceeded, Monica received a call from someone attempting to fly to Boston and then back to 'Philly'; 'Fiji?' Monica tried to confirm. Phoebe received a disoriented call from someone trying to drive from Los Angeles to Las Vegas; she frantically tried to offer cartographical advice, 'follow this street the 15 in Los Angeles, and you take it all the way, you are going to hit this desert, now you can't miss it, because there is nothing there'. As she spoke, more screens with maps, translations and popular references appeared and moved across the stage space. The screens promised cross-global informational exchange; meanwhile, a transnational workforce rushed to keep up with the promise. The stagescape was a constantly changing composition of images, sounds and embodied actors whose actions seem to trigger each other in a percolating network of screens, speech and gesture, re-positioning referents for the real and the illusory, the client and the customer, the remote and the proximate.

So what finally to make of a cross-arts form that incorporates new media technology in the space of the theatre? As noted above, the mix of theatrical screenscapes is often celebrated and critiqued in the same terms. Such terms welcome or worry about the transformation of theatre by new technologies; similarly, they welcome and worry about the evacuation of the theatrical referent by postdramatic relativisation. Some reviews have accused TBA of reification, of producing a visually fluid spectacle that distracts from the social message. In response to

Alladeen, for instance, Jennifer Parker-Starbuck worried that 'the humour and gorgeous visual production mask an underlying critique of what it means to live as the workers or how it feels [. . .] to serve, American interests'.[25] For her, 'the gloss of the production, in effect, reperforms the central act of capitalism, the forced erasure of visible labour in the production of the commodity. While the playbill lists all of those involved in the production . . . the technological wizardry stands out not for the human production of it, but for its own slickness as commodifiable/commodied theatre'.[26] The danger here is that postdramatic – even post-Brechtian – theatre can loose its political edge in the affective engagement with the spectacle of an information society. The circulation of these labouring images within such a visual landscape risk 'erasure' of the system of human labour it is trying to expose. The possibility of this kind of reading is of course ironic, given the aspirations of the performance, but it might also be the occupational hazard of any post-Brechtian theatre that performs our enmeshment with the technologies it critiques. It also exposes debate over the political effects of postdramatic relativisation, even when post-Brechtian political dialectics are being engaged: to what degree do viewers need clarity about the 'last instance' and 'economic necessities' of a social vision in order to feel sure that the theatre is doing political work? As such a question lingers, it is still telling that, in the same review, Parker-Starbuck also voiced a recognition of her own embeddedness. 'During much of the piece, I thought back to many of the recent calls I had received – did I perceive an Indian accent? How many times did a caller try to relate to the weather in New York, or say something about the sightseeing possibilities? Later I learned that many other audience members were processing similar thoughts!' What seems interesting about this moment is that it provoked in Parker-Starbuck, and apparently in other audience members, a momentary self-consciousness of their systemic interdependency in the midst of an apparently independent interaction – receiving a phone call. It was a moment when the apparent autonomy of global technology was revealed to be fettered by a system of global dependency. As such, it seems an exemplary instance of Lehmann's political hopes for the postdramatic; it repurposed the theatre to 'make visible the broken thread between personal experience and perception'.

Some of the concerns about TBA's theatrical re-use of technology come from those of us in theatre who see the inclusion of the wireless phone, the broadband network and the digital screen as a flattening of the theatre, a way of rendering theatre a frictionless pool of visual pleasure. The critique of the mediatisation of the theatre echoes the terms in which political critiques of postdramatic theatre are lodged; postdramatic theatre's collusion with illusion robs it of materialist referents and, by extension, materialist politics. But what if we invert the gesture and decide also to see these media-based, postdramatic techniques as a means of fettering the spaces of the wireless, broadband and the digital image with the frictions of performance? *Alladeen* is not only a digital intervention in the space of theatre, but, just as interestingly, a theatrical intervention in the space of the digital. Consider, for instance, Margo Jefferson's sense of the set of *Alladeen* as 'like giant computer that supplies verbal information and visual distraction'.[27] As a giant computer with a 'set' underneath, the naturalised world of computers, digital imagesand web searches, is fitfully stalled by the social labour required to 'support' the goings-on of the screen. If McPherson is right to suggest that our contemporary experience of the web screen is that of 'volitional mobility', then the contingent lives and terrestrial specificity of a call centre show the precarity of our sense of volition and our sense of movement.[28] Staging technology here has visual, temporal and social dimensions, defamiliarising the visual, temporal and social habituations that go unregistered in the course of depending upon it. Staging technology means experiencing it at a different temporality than the temporality to which we have become habituated when the technology (usually) works. It means seeing the technology within a larger systemic dependency that is usually foreclosed and disavowed in the moment of its use.

Finally, it seems significant that TBA takes on the questions of global technology in a theatrical space, one whose genealogies are located in time-space contingencies that are not simply pre-digital but arguably pre-industrial. This is to say that they juxtapose an apparently unfettered, although occasionally pixilated world of electronic connection, with the highly fettered space of the theatre, a space where the actor onstage was obligated to show up at a certain time. It is also a space where audience members could not upload their attendance; they had to plan with foresight to buy a ticket, get the right train or to find a parking place in order to be there. To think about digital connection in postdramatic theatre is to juxtapose the apparently non-contingent world of the digital with the avowedly contingent dimensions of performance, all to expose the supporting actions that produce the experience of seamlessness. As it turns out, the digital world cannot do without the analogue any more than the immaterial economies can do without the materiality of servicing bodies. In *Alladeen* – as in other work by the Builders – there is a juxtaposition between the apparent autonomy of globalising technology and the inconvenient heteronomy of the theatre. This might be a more precise way of framing the conjunction between certain forms of performance and certain forms of technology; post-Brechtian, postdramatic new media theatre might be most interesting for its juxtaposition of the explicitly encumbered with the apparently unencumbered, a combination that is not always captured when we use the language of live/mediated or real/electronic to characterise the conjunction of performance and technology. This juxtaposition of what its artistic director Marianne Weems calls, 'New Media for Old Theatre' seems to be a particularly intriguing match between postdramatic media forms and the politics of a service economy.

Alladeen shows the bodily and sonic cultural training required to sustain a call centre in Bangalore. Its scenes juxtapose the travel plans of the most entitled global citizens with the occupational obstacles of those who are less so. It juxtaposes the screens and sounds of global connection with the bodies of workers whose headphones support digital connection. Through this particular conjunction of performance and technology, *Alladeen* asks us to ask ourselves to what degree inconvenience can be 'off shored'.

Acting, Disabled: Back to Back Theatre and the Politics of Appearance

Theron Schmidt

For some, any theatre that wants to have political relevance must find a way to overcome theatre's own limitations: it must become more real, more immediate and more authentic than the empty forms of the past. This kind of claim was exemplified by articulations in the 1980s and 1990s of the value of 'performance' over 'theatre', such as Chantal Pontbriand's assertion that 'performance presents; it does not re-present', or Josette Féral's declaration (in the same 1982 issue of *Modern Drama*) that 'performance escapes all illusion and representation' and simply '*takes place*'.[1] In *Postdramatic Theatre*, Hans-Thies Lehmann describes an affinity between his central term and features of performance art: 'postdramatic theatre can be seen as an attempt to conceptualise art in the sense that it offers not a representation but an intentionally unmediated experience of the real (time, space, body)'.[2] And yet, it is clear that the 'real' with which one has an allegedly unmediated experience in the kinds of practices that Lehmann describes is not the de-aestheticised real of the everyday, but instead the carefully constructed environment of the theatre. One possible ramification of Lehmann's influential intervention, then, might be to open up space for claiming a positive value for the theatrical, not only in distinction to the dramatic (as his title obviously intends), but also in relation to the performative.

In this way, rather than suggesting that the political potential of postdramatic theatre depends on its capacity to resist or refuse the machinery of representation, I am interested in the political relevance of artistic practices that invest in and explore theatre as an apparatus of appearances. Such practices amplify artifice rather than producing authenticity, disjoin spectatorial feelings from sympathetic identification, and proliferate sensation as not necessarily co-identical with selfhood. I will argue that a postdramatic theatre might be political because, dissevered from the drive towards dramatic illusion, it is free to be *more* theatrical, not less.

I will focus here on the recent production *Food Court* by Back to Back Theatre, which seems to typify many postdramatic tendencies as catalogued by Lehmann: 'parataxis, simultaneity, play with the density of signs, musicalization, visual dramaturgy, physicality, irruption of the real, situation/event.'[3] In addition to its formal experimentation, this work is marked, as with all of Back to Back's work over the past twenty years, by its use of intellectually disabled performers. At first glance, the apparent 'reality' of the performers' disability might seem to support the 'irruption of the real' described by Lehmann. As in Bert O. States' description of the appearance of children or animals on stage, these actors might be seen to possess a kind of 'abnormal durability' with regard to the appetite of theatre for ingesting the real and turning it into signs.[4] For a project that would seek to overcome the representational quality of the theatre, animals, children and intellectually disabled actors might all be useful because (we might think) they apparently *can't act*, and so when we encounter these beings on stage we encounter them for themselves rather than for whom they appear to be. However, this is not the claim I want to make. Rather than their potential usefulness for transforming the theatrical space, I'm interested in the implications that the appearance of these actors on stage might have for the categories of ability and disability in their extra-theatrical senses. My contention is that the distinction between abled and disabled, like the distinction between child and adult or between human and non-human, is a political distinction; and that these distinctions are matters of appearance and spectatorial relation rather than of any kind of intrinsic reality. In *Food Court*, I will argue, it is exactly the capacity to choose to appear – that is, to act – which is at stake. This is what I mean by a politics of appearance.

The connection between politics and appearance has been a recent area of exploration within political philosophy, and my argument draws substantially upon these developments. Most notably, Jacques Rancière has argued for a reconceptualising of the domain of politics that shifts attention away from the particularities of a given political discourse, and instead focuses on the pre-discursive conditions that allow for certain gestures and speech-acts to be recognised as valid while others are excluded. Rancière writes, 'Politics revolves around what is seen and what can be said about it, around who has the ability to see and the talent to speak.'[5] For Rancière and others, there is a strong connection between political distributions of visibility and aesthetic practices, such that Rancière refers to an 'aesthetic regime of politics,'[6] and Giorgio Agamben has written that 'the task of politics is to return appearance itself to appearance, *to cause appearance itself to appear*.'[7] This emphasis marks a departure from previous analyses within political theory, such as Michel Foucault's attention to the uses and distributions of power, or Louis Althusser's study of the interrelation between ideology and identity; in this more recent line of thought, the emphasis is less on the production and control of political subjects, and more on the conditions by which those subjects even come to *appear* – to be recognised and understood – as political beings in the first place.

One of the ways that this shift in political thinking is distinguished from previous analyses is evident in the distinction Rancière makes between 'politics' and 'policing'. Rancière uses the idea of the 'police' to refer to day-to-day operations of governance: the application of power as well as resistances to it. But these day-to-day operations are not politics. Instead, this activity of policing is underpinned by a distribution of roles, a distribution that is incomplete and excludes from the political order any allocated role for those whom Rancière describes as 'the part of those who have no part'.[8] Throughout his writing on politics, Rancière invokes ideas of representation, of appearance and of the symbolic value of speech and gesture to describe the operations of politics. That is to say, for Rancière, politics takes place in the realm of sensibility – the realm of the senses – and it is for this reason that Rancière asks that we consider politics as an 'aesthetic' activity.[9] The job of the police-function, then, is to maintain a particular 'distribution of the sensible': 'Policing is not so much the "disciplining" of bodies as a rule governing their appearing, a configuration of *occupations* and the properties of the spaces where these occupations are distributed.'[10] If policing is about maintaining a particular distribution of the sensible, then politics takes place through acts of 'dissensus': 'Politics consist in reconfiguring the partition of the sensible, in bringing on stage new objects and subjects, in making visible that which was not visible, audible as speaking beings they who were merely heard as noisy animals.'[11]

In this last passage, with its reference to 'bringing on stage new objects and subjects', Rancière invokes the metaphor of the theatre. To what extent is this only a metaphor, and to what extent might Rancière be suggesting that the actual theatre could be a useful place for thinking about politics? It's clear from his many writings about works of art that he identifies useful lessons for politics in artistic works, but he also explicitly rejects the idea that the political value of art might derive from 'the messages and feelings that it carries on the state of social and political issues,' nor the 'way it represents social structures, conflicts or identities'. Instead, art is political as it frames 'a specific space-time sensorium' and 'reframe[s] the way in which practices, modes of being and modes of feeling and saying are interwoven in a common sense, which means "a sense of the common", embodied in a common sensorium."[12] That is to say, theatre's relevance to politics derives – and derives *only*, according to Rancière – from the way in which it is fundamentally concerned with acts of appearance, with modes of speech and gesture, and with the production of feelings and sensations *as productions*, irrespective of the content ('political' or otherwise) of those feelings or sensations. Elsewhere Rancière declares, 'The arts only ever lend to projects of domination or emancipation what they are able to lend to them, that is to say, quite simply, what they have in common with them: bodily positions and movements, functions of speech, the parcelling out of the visible and the invisible.'[13] I take this to mean that a theatre that is politically efficacious, in Rancière's sense of the term politics, would not derive its political force from its connection to or accurate portrayal of the dynamics of a particular struggle as it takes place outside the theatre. Instead, the contribution that theatre can make must be based on its specifically theatrical properties.

If this is the case, then what is it that is specific to the theatrical, and how might this relate to the 'postdramatic'? Lehmann argues that there are political and ethical possibilities of theatre that have been 'more or less concealed by dramatic theatre'.[14] Once theatre lays aside the concerns of dramatic representation – which Lehmann characterises as being most concerned with presenting an illusion of a whole, complete and self-sufficient world[15] – then new possibilities become available. As Lehmann deliberately refuses a single definition for the postdramatic, it is perhaps most useful as a means of proposing a separation between the dramatic and the theatrical: there are an abundance of qualities and dynamics of the theatrical experience that are independent of the function of drama, although they are often put to the service of drama. Postdramatic theatre, then, opens up a space in which these operations can be foregrounded as the primary concern of the theatre. That is to say, what remains when you remove the 'drama' from theatre – when you remove the attempt to create illusions of self-contained worlds of plot and action – is not reality (nor nothingness), but the mechanism of theatre itself: the production of appearances, the staging of sensations, the interweaving of frames of sensibility. Or, to borrow Rancière's words above that could just as easily be a description of postdramatic theatre: 'bodily positions and movements, functions of speech, the parcelling out of the visible and the invisible'.

However, Lehmann seems to suggest that, having dispensed with dramatic illusion, theatre must also overcome its own machinery in order to realise its political potential. As he describes it, the ethico-political possibilities of theatre have to do with the extent to which the spectator is implicated in the situation, resulting in the cultivation of what he describes as 'response-ability': 'the mutual implication of actors and spectators in the production of images'.[16] Lehmann has also referred to this as 'the politics of perception'.[17] For Lehmann, this potential enables theatre to be a site of resistance to the growing commodification of life and human relations, as described by Guy Debord in *The Society of the Spectacle*. Lehmann echoes Debord's Situationist remedy when he proclaims:

> [T]he task of theatre must be to create *situations* rather than spectacles, experiences of real time processes, instead of merely representing time. Theatre can deconstitute to a certain degree the spectatorial habit and thereby open a space where the possibility of an intervention makes itself felt. [. . .] It realizes its modest political potential by creating ways of perception, of self-perception and implication of spectators in the theatrical process which interrupt the order of the theatre as spectacle, which is also a political order.[18]

This opposition between situations and spectacles, between real-time processes and representations, recalls some of the kinds of distinctions made between performance and theatre in the 1980s and 1990s to which I referred earlier. It also echoes a critique of spectatorship as itself insufficient for theatre to realise its political potential, such as that expressed by Tim Etchells' call for a theatre that creates 'not audience to a spectacle but witnesses to an event'.[19]

One interpretation of Back to Back's work might be to see it as embodying the kind of resistance to spectacle that Lehmann describes: the 'realness' of the performers' disability might be understood to transform the theatre-event into a situation rather than a spectacle, to which audiences feel themselves to be witnesses rather than spectators, 'to be present at it in some fundamentally ethical way', as Etchells puts it.[20] But as Caroline Wake has argued, such a distinction is based on an assumed difference between 'active' (good) and 'passive' (bad) spectatorship, a distinction that Rancière has done much to critique.[21] Rather than denigrating theatre as merely second-hand experience, of value only when it punctures its representational frame, I see in *Food Court* a sustained engagement with the dynamics of theatrical spectacle as a political realm in its own right. In my reading, the production does not aim to get at some 'real' politics behind these representational surfaces, but instead stages the idea that disability is precisely a matter of appearance as such; it is a problem of appearance (or non-appearance), and, as in the kinds of arguments by Rancière to which I referred earlier, the distribution of appearance is the domain of politics. In this way, the work is political not because it is *opposed* to spectacle but because of its construction *as* spectacle, and the theatre is used as a place to stage dynamics from the world outside the theatre, which are already theatrical problems.

Back to Back's artistic director, Bruce Gladwin, has described this engagement with theatricality as a conscious aim on the part of the company. *Food Court* followed a series of works in non-traditional performance spaces, including their widely known piece *small metal objects* (presented internationally from 2005 to 2011), which takes place in a train station with the audience listening to remotely miked performers through individual headsets. But in a post-show discussion, Gladwin tellingly described a return to proscenium theatre as 'the most challenging and thrilling thing we could do'.[22] From its opening moments, *Food Court* deliberately accentuates the mechanisms of theatrical representation, including costume, text and visibility, as intrinsically connected to the problems it raises with regard to the representation of disability. The piece begins with an entrance through a drawn curtain at the front of the stage by Mark Deans, his face immediately recognisable as having been shaped by the effects of Down's syndrome. Squirming, making a few funny faces at the audience, he squints into the lights. He looks down, picks up something from the floor that is too small for me to see, and moves it to stage-right. He stands there, looking pleased with himself, still illuminated but no longer blinded by the lights. He looks down again in order to position himself exactly, and I laugh with recognition, realising that the thing he moved was the 'spike', the small piece of electrical tape used to mark where a performer should stand or a prop should be placed. Throughout the piece, the theatricality of the event is always similarly announced. Whenever something is shown or said, we are always aware that it is being shown or said on a stage. During dialogue involving other actors, for example, Mark holds a boom mic over their heads, moving the mic from actor to actor – even though they are quite visibly equipped with individual wireless mics. And throughout the play, all the dialogue is projected as surtitles. It is a representational world within which these individual bodies appear, and they, too, are representations.

But as a spectator, where do I locate my own responsibility in relation to this world of appearances? Am I being asked to watch differently than I would watch any other theatre? In the programme notes to the Brussels production of *Food Court,* John Bailey describes a cultural tendency to regard the event itself as having a significance that is additional to its aesthetic content: 'There is a perception of theatre dealing with disability as "worthy"; that is, as having an intrinsic value that precedes the merit of the actual work done.'[23] Although Bailey describes the way this attitude can be condescending and 'poisonous', it is also immediately generative of a fissure that Back to Back draw upon in their work. In a post-show discussion, artistic director Bruce Gladwin comments,

> I think there's a tension that sits in the piece. When the actors first come through the split in the curtain, I anticipate there's a kind of reading in the audience where audience is going, 'There's a guy with Down's syndrome. I wonder if he's playing a person with Down's syndrome?' I think that's a tension that the audience is never released from. Who are these characters? What is this world that they're in? And is the intention that they are people with disabilities or that they're not? And that's something that we're interested in playing with in our work.[24]

In contrast with Etchells' analogy, here there is no easy distinction between 'audience to a spectacle' and 'witness to an event'; instead, I might conceive of my role as both audience to a crafted spectacle, *and* also as witness to an event of 'real' empowerment, self-expression, agency, etc. That is to say, I have one kind of relationship with the performers' performance, and another kind of socially mediated relationship with the performers themselves and what I assume they might be going through as they perform the actions they are performing in front of me. Indeed, my assumptions are more than likely misconceived, and to cast myself as witness is to propagate these misconceptions. Rather than seeking to resolve these complicated and problematic relationships to the event, Back to Back's theatre productions exacerbate the disjunction between these two different understandings of the nature of the event to which I am spectator: whether it is 'real' or an 'imitation', and whether I am supposed to ignore or pay attention to the performers' eccentricities of speech and movement.

After Mark, the next performer to enter is Scott Price, who calls our attention to another aspect of the theatrical apparatus by performing a mike check – but this, too, is far from straightforward, as Scott uses the mic to mimic sexual excitement. Scott is followed by a remarkable pair of entrances (Figure 9.1).

First is Nicki Holland. She stands centre stage. Staring deadpan at the audience, she is dressed in tight black sweatpants and a golden, glittering leotard, her body bulging against the tight fabric around her hips, waist and breasts. She turns to profile, her stature slightly hunched, her expression matter-of-fact. She stands there for a few beats. *This is her body. This is who she is.* She turns to the back. A few more beats, and then she moves stage-right and sits in a chair. A few moments later, performer Sonia Teuben[25] enters through the curtain, dressed in a matching costume within which all the lumpy distinctiveness of her body, too, is obvious. She repeats the sequence of poses, then joins Nicki to begin the scene. These entrances function

Figure 9.1 Nicki Holland and Rita Halabarec in *Food Court*. Halabarec's role was played by Sonia Teuben later in the tour. (Photo by Jeff Busby.)

both as presentation and representation, invoking a complex set of interrelations between appearance and reality. The reality of who they are is on display: their unusual body shapes in all their imperfections, their unique physiognomy, their blank stares. *These people are really disabled. This is what disabled people really look like.* And yet, these stage entrances emphasise that disability is a matter of appearance: it is a matter of how we see these people. Here, they are revealed, and also masked, by their sparkling golden tops, by their illumination in the stage lights, and in their moment of representing themselves.

The women begin to speak. The first dialogue of the play is a conversation between Nicki and Sonia in which they are talking about food, with Mark moving between them with the boom mic and the words appearing over their heads as they speak. It feels like verbatim text: 'Have you ever had a hamburger? No. Have you ever had hot chips? No.'[26] Nicki and Sonia's attention is drawn to Sarah Mainwaring, who enters and takes a seat stage-left, the opposite side of the stage from them. She is not wearing distinctive clothing; her hands and head are constantly moving and rotating involuntarily; she is of slim build. 'She's fat', says Sonia. The two other women tease Sarah, gradually building into bullying; Sarah never says anything, nor appears to react in any way, and the two other women comment that she 'doesn't speak'. The scene climaxes with the following tirade, noted in the script as partly improvised, with, as always, surtitles and microphones:

Fat person	Fat guts
Fat head	Fat arms
Fat face	Fat knee
Fat ears	Fat feet
Fat nose	Fat kidney
Fat brain	Fat liver
Fat daughter	Fat you

Fat skeleton	Fat diarrhea
Fat Muslim	Fat tumor
Fat Christian	Fat shit
Fat European	Fat smell
Fat history	Fat priest
Fat maggot	Fat evil
Fat beast	Fat world
Fat cancer	Fat nation
Fat monster	Fat boring
Fat freak	Fat breast
Fat witch	Fat bone

That's for you.
Look at them looking at you.

These are horrifying, powerful words, and yet as they slide around the theatre they slip in and out of their horrific signification. We see the words as text to be read. We hear them as amplified sounds. As in Lehmann's description of the postdramatic (quoted above), we are at *play with the density of signs*. We do not know if the speaker is talking to the other woman, or to a character who is represented by the woman, or repeating the things that she has been called.

The piece then moves into its second half. The transition is mediated by Mark, who speaks for the first and only time, reading lines from the surtitles as each word bounces like it is on a karaoke machine. The words indicate a shift away from the current scene. *Parataxis* (rather than narrative): 'Past the juice bar, past the Asian Hut, past the car park, past the last house, past the factories, over the creek and down the dirt road to the forest.' At the main stage of the Barbican in London, where I saw it, the curtains part to reveal the full height and depth of the stage. A translucent screen covers the proscenium opening, and the remainder of the action takes place behind this gauzy covering:

Figure 9.2 Nicki Holland, Sarah Mainwaring and Rita Halabarec.
(Photo by Jeff Busby.)

the figures are shadowy, dimly lit, casting shadows against the back of the theatre. *Visual dramaturgy*. The surtitles are visible at the front of the stage, but also pass through the screen so they are visible on the back wall, along with large video projections of shifting, indistinct branches (Figure 9.2).

Physicality. The two women accuse Sarah of having soiled herself, and force her to take off her clothes. They then order her to dance; in a dim spotlight, but obscured by the screen, we see her slowly shifting her weight from side to side, her arms moving in erratic spirals through the air. To the side of the stage, an audience of shadows slowly assembles. *Musicalisation*. The repetitive, churning music, provided by live accompaniment by 'post-rock' trio The Necks, builds to a climax.

After some time, they stop her dancing. They appear to beat her. Mark and Scott, standing some distance away, provide the sound effects using boxing gloves and the microphone. They leave her for dead: 'Wild animals will kill you. / You'll get burnt. / You're evil. / We can't rescue you. / I'm not your mother, your sister or your friend. / We're not your carers. / Guilty! / As ever!' They leave the stage, and Scott comes over to the prone body, describing his sexual inexperience and his desire to learn more. 'I need some encouragement. I'm confused of what is appropriate sexually. I'm pretty immature.' He leaves. Sarah rises, walks toward the screen separating her from the audience, and, while walking, for the first time, speaks. Her words, the last words in the show, are taken from Caliban, the speech that begins: 'Be not afeard; the isle is full of noises.' She speaks slowly, putting each word together sound by sound, and the letters of the surtitles swarm and swim across the screen until they form each word. The screen falls away, and she is alone on stage.

These representations of abuse and victimisation are hard to watch, and they're meant to be. In the Barbican post-show discussion, Gladwin describes the questions and thinking that emerged during the making of *Food Court*. He refers to *small metal objects*, the work which immediately preceded *Food Court*, as a 'feel good piece' because audiences enjoyed the voyeuristic pleasures of its site-specificity, as well as the way in which it presents characters played by disabled actors as the 'good guys' in contrast with the selfish and reprehensible characters played by non-disabled actors. For Gladwin, one of the driving interests behind *Food Court* was to push at assumed boundaries of characterisation with regard to disabled actors and/or characters by presenting disabled actors/characters who are perpetrators as well as victims of abuse. He explains, 'If you can't act evil, then you're sub-human, in a way, because we're all capable of being evil.' In an insightful commentary on theatrical work involving intellectually disabled actors, Matt Hargrave describes similar predicaments facing such actors more generally. Noting that the common definition of 'disabled' is 'incapable of performing or functioning', he asks, 'What might it mean then for a disabled person to stand in front of an audience and begin to speak?'

The fact that he is on stage speaking directly to us denotes iconically that he is disabled: he is a disabled man because he *looks like* one. But does his obvious impairment mean that he must *remain* iconic, unable to break out of the label, 'disabled man'? His disability also indexes or *points* to itself. And his appearance is symbolically loaded: disability carries connotations of 'dependency', 'affliction' or premature death. Because disability is used as a metaphor in so many stories and cultural references, the disabled actor is literally trapped in a prison house of signs. Semiotically encumbered from the start, any 'characterisation' is smothered by the 'fact' of his disability. For Hargrave, these confining assumptions about the limits of representation are exemplified by the advice reportedly given to one of the directors he interviews: 'I was told very early on in the process that these actors will only play themselves.'[27]

In Back to Back's post-show discussion about the process of making *Food Court*, it was obvious that the company directly engaged and confronted these challenges, and I was particularly struck by the extent to which the content of the work was informed by interests and challenges that were specific to the actors' own development *as actors*. Gladwin describes his job as director as being 'to put forward challenges for the actors that will help them grow and develop as performers'.[28] For example, the character ultimately played by Sarah was initially developed by Sonia, whom Gladwin describes as highly regarded among the company for her oratorical skills; the character is mute (until the end) as a result of the decision to have Sonia work with the productive constraint of not speaking during the improvisations that made up the devising process. Similarly, the opening exchange around food arose out of a desire to work with dialogue, particularly because one of the actors who originally played the scene (Rita Halabarec, who was not in the London production) tended to work primarily with monologue rather than dialogue. Mark's text – the karaoke-like moment that marks the transition between scenes – emerged because

Mark has never spoken in previous performances; Gladwin describes his strength as being with physical performance and creating strong relationships with audiences. The use of surtitles and text-captioning was a way to support him in speaking on stage. And the agonising scene in which the two women force Sarah to strip and to dance was revealed to have come almost directly out of a company improvisation. Sarah has a background in experimental performance that includes, for example, using her naked body as a tool for painting; when the actors in the improvisation ordered her to take her clothes off, they were hugely surprised to find that she nonchalantly complied.

These glimpses of the devising process, which took place over three years, reveal the extent to which the performance is the direct result of the actors engaging with challenges of theatrical appearance and representation. In addition to staging disability, the performance stages the complexity and challenges of staging itself. Rather than directly approaching broader issues of disability in culture, this piece might be understood as an account of the ways in which the actors negotiated their own experience of speaking on stage, of acting on stage, of 'being oneself' on stage. When a disabled person appears on stage and begins to speak, then, it is not the reality of his or her disability that appears, but the way that disability is already a representation – and the theatre is the place where representations are made and re-made, where they are malleable. What becomes possible here with regard to disability is the capacity to deploy it: to make it stand for something else, to falsify it, to stand to one side of it, to wear it as a costume, to use it as a dance.

Curiously, there is a kind of paradox of productivity at play, in which the peculiar kind of labour involved in the theatre might be seen to reflect and reverse some of the social problems of disability. On the one hand, if the actor is standing in for disability *in general* (in the sort of iconic function that Hargrave describes), then some kind of surplus value is extracted at the cost of the actor's individuality; it could be anyone, interchangeably representing the idea of disability. On the other hand, one form of resistance to this reductive signification would be to foreground the individuality of the actor. The actor would then be obstinately non-productive within the economy of the theatre: they are not 'really' acting, and therefore not doing the work they should be doing in the theatre, and might instead be described as doing a kind of performativity – simply 'taking place', in Féral's terms. But this is also a position of resignation, the one to which Hargrave referred in his quote from the director who was told 'these actors will only be themselves'. A third possibility, one that sits between these two positions and destabilises them, is to produce the performers precisely *as* actors, neither identifiable as themselves, nor as an abstraction, but occupying a specific and contingent representational function within a framework of appearance. In this way, what is apparent is not the actor's productivity or stubborn non-productivity, but the economy of production itself.

This is a compelling possibility because it relates to one of the arguments within disability studies that seeks to put forward a social definition of disability, rather than a medical or individualist definition. For example, in Michael Oliver's influential book *The Politics of Disablement* (1990), disability is presented as an artefact not of individual impairment but of capitalist modes of production, within which disability is constituted as a result of a system that is not capable of finding productive uses for some people. In a different system, Oliver argued, individuals would still have impairments, but disability would be differently constituted or would not be constituted at all – that is to say, disability is a function of social apparatuses rather than of individual conditions.[29] Indeed, in Back to Back's artistic statement, they do not describe themselves as making work about disability; instead, they declare that they use this ambivalent position as a perspective from which to comment on what they call 'the majority', and it is this majority that is the subject of their work: 'Family, career, sex, politics, religion, education, academia and culture are all subject to a lateral analysis from an artistic team whose defining characteristic is separation from the spectacle of their subject matter.'[30] In this way, I would argue that the relationship between the politics of disablement and the mechanisms of the theatre is not an arbitrary one, but one in which the kinds of problems that disability produces within the theatre – and also the kinds of problems that theatricality poses for ideas of disability – are interrelated.

In *The Politics of Aesthetics*, Rancière writes:

> Political statements and literary locutions [and we might add theatrical stagings] produce effects in reality. They define models of speech or action but also regimes of sensible intensity. They draft maps of the visible, trajectories between the visible and the sayable, relationships between modes of being, modes of saying, and modes of doing and making. They define variations of sensible intensities, perceptions, and the abilities of bodies.[31]

A preoccupation with the production of 'variations of sensible intensities' feels like an apt description of postdramatic theatre as typified by Back to Back. And yet one might also argue that these adjustments of perception, and the introduction of new 'sensible intensities', have always been fundamental to the work of theatre regardless of its position in relation to the 'dramatic', from forms of Greek tragedy to Shakespeare to *Food Court*. As Gladwin revealed, the company's interest in making *Food Court* was to work with this perceptual machinery of theatre: this was 'the most challenging and thrilling thing we could do'. The legacy of these modes of appearance haunts *Food Court*: its representation of brutal violence, or the lines taken from Caliban. As I have argued, this piece is not about *being* disabled but about *appearing* disabled; and Rancière's arguments help to expand upon the ways in which working on the level of appearance *is* political. That is, participation in politics is only possible if one has access to variable modes of sensibility, to multiple ways of speaking and to expanding capacities of 'acting'.

In my experience of *Food Court*, what affected me was not the sensible reality of these bodies to which I was witness, but the flickering of appearances and representations within which I was spectator: the actors' unreadable gestures and un-locatable speech-acts, the abilities of their bodies to 'mean' and their capacity to use them to make-mean. These are not instabilities introduced in order to destabilise the theatre, to challenge the law of spectacle in order to make it more 'real' or 'ethical'. But they are instabilities in appearance that are possible because of the event's nature *as* theatre. Such theatricality is not wholly dependent on the mechanism of the theatre, of course, but the theatre is a tool that helps to frame, focus and amplify these 'variations of sensible intensities'. For me, the relevance of this performance to issues of disability is not in the way that it might bring 'reality' onto stage, puncturing the theatre's representational operations, but the way in which it reveals that sense of reality to always be an apprehension, a matter of perspective, a matter of 'the way we see' disability. Theatre is both a place in which we see these appearances, and also a place that allows us to see the mechanisms of appearance. That is to say, this theatre is a place where appearance is seen; it is this that makes it political.

Parasitic Politics: Elfriede Jelinek's 'Secondary Dramas' *Abraumhalde* and *FaustIn and out*

Karen Jürs-Munby

The political can appear only indirectly in the theatre, at an oblique angle, modo obliquo.[1]

Hans-Thies Lehmann

I would increasingly like to offer secondary dramas, which then run alongside the classics barking.[2]

Elfriede Jelinek

In his essay 'How political is postdramatic theatre?' ('Wie politisch ist postdramatisches Theater?', 2002) Hans-Thies Lehmann argues that the inherent political potential of theatre as an eminently 'social' affair can only be developed if the theatre itself changes. In support, he quotes Jacques Derrida on ways of engaging with the 'genuinely political' in theatre 'by making something happen in the theatre, but not through representing or imitating something or bringing a political reality that happens elsewhere onto the stage [. . .] but by bringing politics or the political into the structure of the theatre, that is by also rupturing the present'. A repoliticisation of theatre can only be achieved if it does not accommodate itself to the order of representation but instead 'changes the form, the time and the space of the theatrical event'.[3] This changed theatre, Lehmann sums up Derrida's argument, would be a theatre that 'breaks through its aesthetic limitations by following its political responsibility to let in other voices that do not get heard and that have no representation within the political order, and in this way open the site of theatre for the political outside'.[4] The political itself, Lehmann goes on to reaffirm, must consequently be thought of 'not as a reproduction but as a disruption of the political', if the latter political was to be understood (with reference to Julia Kristeva's *Politique de la littérature*) as a 'common measure, a rule that constitutes communality, a field of rules for potential consensus'. This is so because '[o]nly the exception, the disruption of the regular shows the rule itself and confers upon it [. . .] the character of radical questionableness'.[5]

The kind of disruption Lehmann addresses is usually argued to consist in the disruption of the aesthetic by the real (in the Lacanian sense, i.e. something that escapes the symbolic order) or that of the closed fictional cosmos by performance modes that disrupt conventions and habits of perception. But does Lehmann's focus on the performance dimension imply that this is a process that can only be created through 'devised' performance, that is non-text-based collaborative creation, or can it also be initiated by authors who write texts for the theatre that challenge its conventions and its very modes of production?[6] While Lehmann in *Postdramatic Theatre* generally makes it clear that 'the discourse of *theatre* is at the centre of this book and the text therefore is considered only as one element, one layer, or as a "material" of the scenic creation, not as its master',[7] I will contend in what follows that this does not mean that the 'no longer dramatic text', as Gerda Poschmann has called it,[8] cannot play a driving role in bringing about the political as a disruption of business (politics) as usual. It is significant in this respect that Lehmann concludes his essay 'How political is postdramatic theatre?' with an extended discussion of Sarah Kane's *Blasted* as a prime example for the kind of disruption he has in mind. The sudden shift from a naturalistic scene in a Leeds hotel room to a surreal and fragmented war scene after a bomb blast midway through this play, he concludes, is 'a "rupturing of the present" in this text, which political theatre practice still has to catch up with: explosion of consciousness in a withering dramatic structure'.[9] Thus Lehmann here locates the transgression of conventional representation within the text itself, which in turn challenges theatre practice to realise a similar 'rupturing of the present' in performance.

In this chapter I would like to argue that Lehmann's conception of the political as a disruption of political consensus may also be applied to the relationship between the 'no longer dramatic' text and the dramatic tradition. Specifically I will argue that Elfriede Jelinek's new genre of the 'secondary drama' (*Sekundärdrama*) is aimed at such a disruption. This new genre – if it can be called that – is designed to be performed *together with* a classical drama and thus to come at its politics 'sideways' by disturbing it in performance. The political, I will argue, emerges here in an in-between space opened up by the disrupting secondary drama as a parasitic agent. This in-between space, as I aim to show, creates a space for questioning and dissent.

The intriguing example of Jelinek's secondary drama may also serve to reflect more widely on postdramatic theatre's ongoing relationship with drama. While the prefix 'post-' may superficially indicate a radical break with drama, a significant proportion of postdramatic theatre, from plays by Heiner Müller (e.g. *Hamletmachine*) and Sarah Kane (especially *Phaedre's Love*) to the theatre of The Wooster Group (e.g. *To You, the Birdie! (Phèdre)*) and The Builders Association (e.g. *Master Builder*), not only invokes drama in order to challenge the structures and performance conventions associated with it but uses specific works from the dramatic canon as its intertexts or material. By extension the resulting postdramatic performances often implicitly take issue with the dominant reception of their dramatic intertexts. In doing so they may also paradoxically point to postdramatic aspects, fissures and cracks already inherent in drama.[10]

Elfriede Jelinek's post-drama

The work of Elfriede Jelinek, who in 2004 was awarded the Nobel Prize for her 'musical flow of voices and counter-voices in novels and plays that with extraordinary linguistic zeal reveal the absurdity of society's clichés and their subjugating power',[11] has long been associated with the paradigm of postdramatic theatre.[12] Her theatre texts, which consist of dense montages of manipulated quotes from literature, philosophy and the media, have relinquished plot structures, psychological characters and increasingly the form of a dialogue or even designated speakers. As directors and performers grapple with the challenges posed by these resistant, 'no longer dramatic' texts, they almost inevitably result in postdramatic performances.[13] At the same time, Jelinek's work is overtly 'political', even moralistic at times. Her plays have addressed topics such as gender and class inequality, misogyny, anti-Semitism and xenophobia, right-wing populism and the repression of a national-socialist legacy in her native Austria, the war in Iraq and the global financial crisis, to name but a few. As such her texts never relinquish a level of meaning and referentiality, unlike some theatre practices among the wide variety of heterogeneous forms of postdramatic theatre.[14] Is it possible then to 'have your cake and eat it, too', to both 'thematise' contemporary political subject matter *and* allow the political 'to appear only indirectly', 'at an oblique angle', as Lehmann says? I propose that Jelinek manages to do so powerfully and that her linguistic, intertextual engagement both with mediatised 'reality' *and* with the literary and dramatic tradition through formal innovations is one of the strategies that make this possible.

In this context it is noteworthy that Jelinek's theatre texts have often been '*post*-dramatic' in a very literal sense, namely in the sense of her using and abusing classical dramas in such a way that they create a newly politicised 'afterlife' for them. We could think of her very first play, *What Happened to Nora after She Left Her Husband* (1979), in which she fused Henrik Ibsen's *A Doll's House* with his *Pillars of Society* and crossed feminist gender concerns with Marxist class concerns, having the figures constantly deliver an analytical commentary on their own character in a post-Brechtian, radically defamiliarising way. Or we could think of her more recent text, *Ulrike Maria Stuart* (2006), in which she turned to Schiller's *Maria Stuart* in order to explore the difficulty of being both a woman and having political power by 'short-circuiting' Schiller's characters of Queen Elizabeth I and Mary Queen of Scots with those of the RAF terrorists Ulrike Meinhof and Gudrun Ensslin. She explains her procedure in the essay 'Sprech-Wut' (written before *Ulrike Maria Stuart*) as follows:

> What interests me most about Schiller's dramas is this speech rage of the dramatis personae. I immediately want to add my own rage to it, it is as if they were only waiting to absorb yet more rage. Schiller's figures are charged, so to speak. [. . .] I would love to force my way into Schiller's *Mary Stuart*, not in order to blow her up into something entirely different like a poor frog that then bursts but in order to insert my own speaking into these text-bodies of the two Great Women, these female protagonists, that are full to the brim anyway.[15]

As indicated by Jelinek's imagery in this passage, the procedure here could already be described as 'parasitic'. Jelinek's citational speaking lives off the 'speech rage' of Schiller's dramatic figures and fuses it with her own rage about political issues; helping herself to 'Schiller's personnel [. . .] creates a certain surplus value. The more Schiller has done, the less I have to do.'[16]

Evelyn Annuß has used the term 'Theater des Nachlebens' ('Theatre of the Afterlife') to describe the 'distorted continuation of speaking figures that Jelinek lets appear in her texts as quotations of forms of personal representation'. According to Annuß, it is through this 'quoting speech about oneself', Jelinek's main rhetorical device, that her figures 'demonstrate the conditions of their appearance' by 'exposing their belatedness and fictionality'.[17] Importantly, this procedure goes beyond the personalisations of issues (e.g. the framing of issues in the form of protagonists and antagonists) that may obscure their political relevance: 'This constitutes the political dimension of Jelinek's work. It enables an approach to thinking about the political that refuses the reigning personalisations and opens itself up to the unpresentness [*Ungegenwärtigkeit*] of those voices that are drowned out by the current representations.'[18]

The secondary drama – a parasitic genre

It is only a small step from Jelinek's formally innovative 'post-dramas' to the new '*secondary drama*'. As a playwright Jelinek has persistently pushed for theatrical innovation in politically charged ways, not only through her own *literary* strategies but also through challenging theatre conventions and encouraging new forms of staging and acting (not least through her important theatre essays), as well as new forms of collaboration with theatre directors, composers and artists. In this spirit of theatrical innovation, Jelinek's 'secondary drama' goes further than her previous intertextual engagements with classical dramas by creating what might be called a '*parallel (inter-)textuality*' that generates relations and disturbances between the two texts through staging them *together*. In a recent commentary on this new concept, self-consciously highlighting her role as a 'supplier' of texts for the theatre industry, Jelinek wryly advertises the newly invented genre as part of her 'comprehensive range of products on offer':

> As a new business idea for the theatre industry I would increasingly like to offer secondary dramas, which then run alongside the

classics barking (or as wallpaper that is rolled up and pasted behind them). I have recently already tried this out with 'Nathan' [*Nathan der Weise*, by Gotthold Ephraim Lessing] but I now accept commissions for other dramas and will write a secondary drama for them anytime.[19]

Going beyond the creation of intertextuality through citation and references, here the sovereignty and sanctity of the original classic drama is directly invaded by the secondary drama, which disturbs and probes it in real time on stage. Nor can the secondary drama stand by itself as an independent production: Jelinek deliberately stipulates that, 'the secondary drama must never be the main play and be played alone, solo so to speak. The one conditions the other, the secondary drama emerges from of the main drama and accompanies it in diverse ways but it is always: accompaniment.'[20] (In this sense it differs from Heiner Müller's *Hamletmachine*, for example, which is mostly played 'solo', although Müller himself in 1990 famously staged it together – albeit not in parallel – with Shakespeare's *Hamlet* as *Hamlet/Machine*.)[21] In its conception, Jelinek's secondary drama is therefore not merely a literary innovation (proper to the text) but an innovation that profoundly affects theatre programming, rehearsal processes and productions, let alone the audience's experience in performance.

Needless to say that despite its name Jelinek's secondary drama is anything but a 'drama' in the Aristotelian sense but rather – like most of Jelinek's recent plays – a 'no longer dramatic' montage of texts, a *Textfläche* (text surface or plane) of polyphonic monologues, often without assigned speakers, which lends itself to postdramatic forms of staging. Interestingly the symbiotic, and as I shall propose here, *parasitic* relationship with classical drama refutes any binary ontological distinction in which the dramatic and postdramatic modes would mutually exclude each other. Rather, what I have said elsewhere of postdramatic theatre generally is especially true of the secondary drama as a new postdramatic form, namely that the prefix 'post' here is to be understood neither as an epochal category, nor simply as chronologically 'after' drama, but rather as a rupture and 'a going beyond' that nevertheless continues to entertain relationships with drama.[22]

In calling the secondary drama 'parasitic' I am taking my cue from Jelinek herself. Accused by a fellow writer of writing plays which are only 'parasitic' of current affairs and cannot be understood without their context, Jelinek has recently written an essay ironically titled 'Das Parasitärdrama' (2011). Despite the fact that she says here 'after I have already invented the secondary drama, I now invent the parasitic drama for all I care', unlike the former the latter term does not designate a new *genre* but describes *all* her plays. Here, she openly 'outs' herself as a voracious parasite feeding off mediatised contemporary reality:

> I staple myself firmly to reality as it is offered to me: amalgamated, purified, filtered through third-party opinions (and, by contrast to a proper filter, which is supposed to take these out, fortified with poisonous matters, to which I add some more, as I need something juicy for my writing [. . .]).[23]

The word 'parasite' derives from the Greek 'παράσιτος', originally meaning a person who eats at someone else's table. Three distinct meanings of the term will be relevant for my discussion: first, the social parasite who exploits the hospitality of others; secondly, the biological parasite who feeds on another organism and thereby weakens it; and thirdly, in French, and as taken up in Michel Serres' theory of *The Parasite*, a form of static or interference, that is, noise on the channel of communication.[24]

While Jelinek herself does not explicitly call her secondary drama 'parasitic', I shall propose here that it is actually 'parasitic' in analogy to the three meanings listed above: first, by 'eating at the table' of a canonical classical play and 'feeding' off the material served there; secondly, by simultaneously 'feeding' off mediated contemporary current affairs associatively related to it (as described by Jelinek in 'Das Parasitärdrama' above); and thirdly, by creating a disturbance, interference or 'noise' in performance. This third sense of course immediately resonates with Lehmann's call for a theatre aesthetic capable of disrupting the consensually agreed 'political' in a *truly* political fashion. What I would like to explore in the following is the way in which Jelinek's parasitic strategy can be described as political in this sense – on a textual level and especially at the level of the staging. What is the potential for the political effect of a 'secondary drama' in performance?

Thus far Jelinek has written two 'secondary dramas' for two great classics of the German theatre canon: *Abraumhalde* (meaning 'slag heap' or 'mining dump'), a play that was specially commissioned by the Thalia Theater, Hamburg as a text for Nicolas Stemann's 2009 production of Gotthold Ephraim Lessing's *Nathan der Weise*; and *FaustIn and out* (2011), which was written to be performed with Goethe's *Urfaust* and had its world premiere as part of the production *Faust 1-3*, directed by Czech director Dušan David Pařízek at the Schauspiel Zürich in March 2012. In the following discussion I will in each case first discuss aspects of the text of these secondary dramas, before turning to their particular staging by Stemann and Pařízek respectively.

Abraumhalde

Jelinek's 'host drama' for this project, Lessing's *Nathan der Weise* (*Nathan the Wise*), which is rightly described as '*the* Enlightenment drama par excellence'[25] and is a staple of the German canon, was written in 1779 but is set at the time of the medieval crusades. It deals with religious conflict and the appeal to mutual religious tolerance, eventually resulting in the play's conciliation of Judaism, Christianity and Islam – via the revelation that the protagonists from different religions are all members of the same family. By contrast, in her secondary drama *Abraumhalde* Jelinek persistently explores the patriarchal power structures and *in*tolerable violence of the three monotheistic religions. As director Nicolas Stemann comments: 'Everything that is silenced in *Nathan*, that has to be silenced so that Lessing's ideology of conciliation will work out, comes up in *Abraumhalde*.'[26] The text leads us, as Stemann continues, 'to the shadow side of reason, as it were. Into the psychological drive structures of religions, the claim to power of (paternal) reason, which gets rid of God in order to put itself in his place.'[27]

In doing so, the text obsessively returns to the 'Fritzl case' that was discovered in Amstetten, Austria in May 2008, as if to a trauma that can no longer be repressed. Thus, shortly after the start of the play, picking up on and twisting the opening dialogue of Lessing's *Nathan*, the text states: 'The house was burning. We will build ourselves a new one. [. . .] Where to find the land to build on? Maybe there's space in the cellar?'[28] Jelinek had responded quickly to the horrendous case, in which a father of seven had locked up one of his daughters in a cellar for twenty-four years, regularly raping her and fathering another seven children with her. The essay 'The Forsaken Place' ('Im Verlassenen') was published on Jelinek's homepage only five days after the story became known. In her theatre text she now sets the motif of the 'Grandfather-Godfather'[29] in the broader context of religion and patriarchal power. Jelinek's text, as Bärbel Lücke states, 'can be read as the deconstruction of phallocracy, as the law of the house Fritzl, the Fritzl eco-nomy'.[30] And this referent is in turn layered with the Oedipus myth, Sophocles' *Antigone* (especially the motif of the prohibited burial of her dead brother) and Lessing's *Nathan*, whose house has also been burning. The burning runs through the text as its leitmotif and linchpin, as in these very first lines:

> The house, it was burning, it was burning, can't do anything about it, it's been burning here, we will build ourselves a new one, a more comfortable one, a more comfortable one. Burnt? Burnt? Burnt? Not for ever, I hope? Resurrected from the ruins? No. Burnt burnt. My last word. (AB)

The 'here' of the house that burnt is connoted in multiple ways, a hybrid time and place[31] that could be referring to Nathan's Jerusalem during the crusades or to post-war Germany, as well as to the Palestinian territories (Jelinek's online text contains images of Gaza city being bombed by Israel) or to the Twin Towers of 9/11, yet also to Fritzl's house in Amstetten (the Fritzl's former house had burnt down; also, during Elizabeth's captivity one of her children died shortly after birth and was incinerated by Fritzl in an oven in the cellar).

In addition to the hybridity or ambiguity of place, as in many of Jelinek's texts it is also often unclear who is speaking. Throughout the text, several 'voices' are layered on top of each other or merge seamlessly one into the other. The respective speaker is an amalgamated figure (a 'Vermischungsfigur'[32]) consisting of dramatic figures, living persons known from the news, as well as a narrating or commentating meta-voice (possibly the author herself). For instance, in a passage that caricatures the erotically charged death drive of religious fundamentalists the text starts by referring to the Christian templar in Lessing's *Nathan*, then seems to move on to a 9/11 terrorist 'martyr' and his longing for the promised virgins in heaven, then morphs into being about Fritzl and his possession of the one virgin:

> It's burning, many are burning, but the self-murdered one is already with his Lord and with his virgins, with many virgins, yes, that's where he is, he who died for his faith, probably altogether

around 72 virgins (eight times nine), yes there are numerous interpretations, [. . .] I think 72 is right, who are stored there in the cellar as in paradise. Only for us. Other virgins for others, this one for me alone. (AB)

Effortlessly moving between positions, discourses and sites, the text in this way unearths overarching connections and patterns of phallocentric power that have been buried beneath the rubble, so to speak. In any performance these connections between different dramatic and extra-dramatic, contemporary discourses will potentially be heightened through the palpable interference created by the secondary drama. But how can a director possibly go about staging Jelinek's Abraumhalde *with* a performance of *Nathan der Weise*?

Stemann's postdramatic production of *Abraumhalde*

In her typically laconic (*non-*)stage directions – 'You are going to do what you want anyway', she writes – Jelinek herself suggests various ways in which *Abraumhalde* could be staged: as 'background music' or 'wallpaper', an 'endless loop', a 'litany', sometimes louder, even unbearably loud, then again inaudible. The figures 'should be enlarged, maybe through giant, *papier-mâché* heads, which they preferably wear with the face facing backwards so that they keep bumping into each other on stage, devastating the set if there is one. [. . .] There should be a multiplication and/or general enlargement of everything' (AB). The overall aesthetic she has in mind is that of American artist Paul McCarthy's grotesque actions, for example *Bunker Basement* or *Piccadilly Circus* (AB). While Stemann aesthetically adheres to some of these ideas, he does not stage Jelinek's secondary drama as parallel to *Nathan* throughout but instead as a shocking interruption half way through the play. He also makes selective use of Jelinek's text – this, too, being anticipated by her when she suggests ironically: 'You can also cut yourself off any pieces, roughly as from a long sausage' (AB).

Interestingly, Stemann stages the whole evening with postdramatic means. Lessing's *Nathan der Weise* is for a long time heard only through a giant loudspeaker suspended from the ceiling. The text we hear is spoken in a calm manner with the slight pathos of 1950s German actors, it could even be mistaken for a historical recording. We consequently perceive it with a certain historical distance, hear it as if through the mist of time. The vocal delivery may be read as indirectly commenting on the play's reception history as a so-called 'Wiedergutmachungsstück' (redemption play) in post-war Germany, after having been banned by the Nazis during the war.[33] Only about fifteen minutes into the performance do we see the actors in modern-day suits speaking Lessing's text into microphones at the back of the stage, in the manner of a live radio play. The deliberate and denaturalised way in which the actors read Lessing's text, together with the overall postdramatic dramaturgy, invites the audience to listen carefully for the messages and contradictions in Lessing's play, as much as for the seductive beauty of his poetic reasoning.

This form of 'bodiless' staging was also the result of a rehearsal process in which the director and the ensemble came to the conclusion that 'actually Lessing's ideology of reconciliation, which appeals to human beings, can only work without human beings. Any human would only disturb a play that he had designed for the purpose of being right.'[34] Stemann then sets out precisely to 'disturb' Lessing's play and to reintroduce human bodies by inviting Jelinek's *Abraumhalde* into the performance. We get a first inkling that all is not right when three figures with the large *papier-mâché* heads of the Pope, Osama bin Laden and Alan Greenspan (former head of the US central bank as the caricature of a rich Jewish banker) appear on stage and start to use gold bars as percussion instruments – while at the back of the stage the speakers of Saladin and his sister Sidha discuss how to approach Nathan for money. Money, gold and exchange are a significant motif in Jelinek's text, picking up on a motif in *Nathan* that is often underemphasised.

Jelinek's text itself enters just as the actor Sebastian Rudolph is visibly and audibly struggling with a convincing delivery of the ring parable, which contains Lessing's central message about the undecidability as to which is the true religion. At this point in the performance, an older Nathan (Christoph Bantzer) in recognisable Jewish stage costume (with yarmulke, long robes and long beard) enters and speaks up, twisting Lessing's text to confront it with the disenfranchisement and impoverishment of people in the current war-torn Middle East:

> Many years ago, there were people living in the East, people living in the East, people living in the East, who owned nothing of inestimable worth. So what? Now they still don't own it. No matter what they believe in, they don't get anything. They get nothing. They get war but they don't get it. (AB)

What is remarkable is that Stemann perversely has these 'alien' thoughts delivered by actors in traditional dramatic costume. It is as though Jelinek's speech parades as a parasitic impostor of an old-fashioned 'costume drama' performance of *Nathan* or as if Lessing's characters themselves – à la Pirandello – are starting to speak out against Lessing with the help of her text smuggled into his play.

Sebastian Rudolph at the microphone finishes the ring parable in a perfunctory manner and exits, after which all performers frantically run across the stage looking for Nathan. This ends with the line of the Christian church patriarch declaring 'No matter, the Jew shall be burnt!' which is uttered chorically by the performers – creating an atmosphere of religious fanaticism, haunted by the memory of the Holocaust. Flames are projected onto a screen and a monologue from the beginning of *Abraumhalde* is delivered by the traditionally costumed character of Recha, Nathan's adopted daughter, who is thus hauntingly associated with Elisabeth Fritzl – the line 'child and wife are our property' making the connection between them as disenfranchised beings 'belonging' to a patriarch. A giant paper role is being pulled over the entire stage by other performers – like a palimpsest being laid over the play. Then, in a grotesque sequence that has an improvised feel to it, the actors are posing to live video cameras as Islamic suicide bombers, devout Jewish women, Christian virgins, fanatically praying Muslims, Jews, Christians, and holding up the masks of Fritzl, Osama bin Laden, etc. while speaking lines from *Abraumhalde* (see Figure 10.1).

Their images being projected onto the large screen like a flood of contemporary TV images, the scenes are blasphemous and bordering

Figure 10.1 Gotthold Ephraim Lessing's *Nathan der Weise* with Elfriede Jelinek's *Abraumhalde*, directed by Nicolas Stemann, Thalia Theater Hamburg. Image shows Sebastian Rudolph, Patrycia Ziółkowska, Maja Schöne and Felix Knopp. (Photo by Armin Smailovic.)

on the tasteless. They are a '(Ver-)störung', as Ortrud Gutjahr calls it,[35] disturbing in the double sense of being both interrupting and deeply unsettling.

The evening returns to a calm reprise of Lessing's *Nathan* and its reconciliating conclusion, though not before the old Nathan has had a chance to tell the story of how he adopted Recha after his own seven sons and wife had been burnt in a Christian pogrom – the trauma at the heart of his story. In this performance the actor shouts out his 'hatred, hatred' until he collapses. Through the loudspeaker we hear the calm revelation that Recha and the Templar are really brother and sister and the Sultan their uncle. The screen goes up in front of the speakers and Lessing's final stage direction is projected onto it: 'During repeated mutual embraces the curtain comes down' – a line which we are invited to contemplate as a now highly questionable form of catharsis.

If there *was* a political message emerging from the experience of the evening it would have to do with this line from Jelinek's text spoken by one of the female performers amid the chaos: 'Didn't you say something about tolerance earlier? Personally I find tolerance absolutely inhumane' (AB). Jelinek's reference here is to Herbert Marcuse's essay 'Repressive Tolerance', where he declares: 'Tolerance is extended to policies, conditions, and modes of behavior which should not be tolerated because they are impeding, if not destroying, the chances of creating an existence without fear and misery.'[36] It is with this impetus that Jelinek confronts Lessing's message of enlightened tolerance with today's realities of religious fundamentalism and the tolerated violation of human (especially women's) rights in the name of religious freedom.

Beyond this, however, it would be impossible to 'translate' the experience of the evening into a hard and fast message. It is rather a matter of stirring up *questions* as opposed to presenting us with ready-made answers. As Jelinek generally says about her writing in relation to mediatised reality, 'The television only answers. I only ask questions.'[37] In Stemann's staging the political here is also a matter of a politicised theatrical *process,* rather than product or message. Stemann's concept, as Ortrun Gutjahr analyses, is that of a 'Werkstattinszenierung'[38] (workshop staging); and it is precisely because the actors have to come to terms with Jelinek's 'embedded alien texts' and their contemporary associations with religiously underpinned conflicts in the Middle East and elsewhere that they are able to 'speak differently' and implicitly raise questions about Lessing's *Nathan*: 'A theatrical testing space is opened up, where, rather than drawing connections between the medieval crusades and the religious disputes of the Enlightenment, the question of the heritage of the Enlightenment is encircled.'[39]

Furthermore, Jelinek's text allows Stemann to break through a certain complacency with regard to Lessing's play in a way that indirectly benefits the classical drama. Michel Serres, who often emphasises the creative and productive aspects of the parasite, at one point says that 'the parasite is a thermal exciter'.[40] I would argue that the secondary drama in this sense also allows Stemann to 'raise the temperature' of the performance and heat up the issues it deals with. Stemann himself has concluded that this allowed him to 'return the hatred to [Lessing's] play – but also the life'.[41] In this sense, the secondary drama does not simply weaken or kill the 'host drama' but also lends its questions renewed political relevance and vitality through its postdramatic disruption.

FaustIn and out

Like *Abraumhalde*, Jelinek's considerably longer text, *FaustIn and out*, concentrates on historical and contemporary issues that have suffered from cultural repression, this time even more radically from a female/feminist perspective. It does so by returning to the figure of

Margarethe in Goethe's *Faust*, the innocent young woman who with Mephisto's help was seduced by the young Faust and who ends up being incarcerated as a child murderess. While in Goethe's *Urfaust* this so-called Gretchen tragedy had still occupied a central place, during his lifelong work on the Faust material it was increasingly relegated to a mere 'leg on Faust's educational journey', as the director Einar Schleef remarked.[42] Jelinek associates this Gretchen material not only again with the tragedy of Elisabeth Fritzl, who was incarcerated by her own father, but crucially also with the precarious economic situation of women in our contemporary post-credit–crunch capitalism. 'Jelinek's undead Gretchen [figures] are women who have been deprived of their human dignity and human rights [. . .] But they are also the abused and powerless of our neo-liberal stockmarket-fuck-and-fun society',[43] as Bärbel Lücke comments. The secondary drama thus also implies a renewed focus on the tragedy of women as the still 'second sex' (de Beauvoir).

The text consists of large chunks of monologues – a dialogue develops only much later – which are attributed to the figures 'GeistIn' and 'FaustIn', with Jelinek specifying that 'at least FaustIn must be a woman'.[44] Both figures, who in their speaking incorporate male as well as female voices, are later temporarily replaced by competing doubles (GeistIn 2 and FaustIn 2). While Jelinek abdicates any authority over the staging – she first declared in *Sports Play* (*Ein Sportstück*): 'The author doesn't give many stage directions, she has learnt her lesson by now'[45] – her 'suggestion' for the staging includes 'two television sets on which scenes from *Urfaust* are running, which could also partially be played on stage, be filmed and projected' (FAU). In front of these television sets, sitting in two armchairs, are GeistIn and FaustIn, each as a 'one person chorus' (*Einpersonenchor*, FAU). This sketch of a possible staging perhaps implies that this secondary drama as a live commentary is supposed to 'upstage' the screened primary drama ('perhaps the original Faust only as a film', FAU). At the same time, it could be read in such a way that the figures, as mere television spectators in their private 'dungeon', have been banned from the public – although by putting them on stage, Jelinek arguably reintroduces them into a public space. The 'one person chorus' paradoxically identifies the figures as isolated *but* collective figures. Lücke suggests that we can apply Schleef's thesis of the expulsion of woman and the chorus from classical German drama to this play: 'By giving the conquered woman in patriarchy [. . .] a voice in the polyvocal one-person chorus, and by making us aware of her displacement from society, [Jelinek] connects up with ancient theatre and restores the lost tragic consciousness – even if only ironically.'[46] The spelling of 'FaustIn' and 'GeistIn' with a capitalised 'I' for the feminine ending – a progressive spelling originally adopted by feminists to indicate the male bias in the German language – already alludes to the Women's Movement's demand for equality, implicitly posing the question of what women's equality really amounts to nowadays. Twisting Mephisto's advice to the young student that he just needs to learn to lead women ('Die Weiber lerne führen nur'), GeistIn as a modern day Mephisto figure asks: 'Teach women to lead? We would rather have reason to disarm them. For they are already leading' (FAU). However, Jelinek's text goes on to allude to a widespread contempt for women that is symptomatic of a backlash against their efforts for emancipation, as well as alluding to women's 'media driven self-oppression',[47] real gender discrimination in training and education, higher unemployment for women ('Ladies first', as the text sarcastically states, FAU), and economic as well as sexual exploitation. While Jelinek in the beginning still seems to caricature women's need to always run to the doctor, the voices gradually lead us deeper into the day-to-day hell of the contemporary 'undead Gretchen figures', the Elisabeth Fritzl and Natascha Kampusch Gretchens in the cellar, on the one hand, and the 'female workers of the neo-German precariat',[48] on the other hand. With reference to Joseph Vogl's analysis of the financial crisis, Jelinek articulates how the 'future is already mortgaged for other futures' (FAU), leaving these women *without* a future. In the play's finale all voices are increasingly coming together, now forming more of a dialogue (potentially a kind of consciousness-raising group). However, in the end, GeistIn's final insistent words 'Rette? Rette dich!' (Save? Save yourself!) and FaustIn's lapidary response, 'What?' (in English in the original) leave it open, whether there is a 'way out' for the Gretchen revenants or whether they are simply 'out'.

Pařízek's postdramatic staging of *FaustIn and out*

For the premiere of *FaustIn and out* as part of his postdramatic *Faust 1–3*, suitably timed to coincide with International Women's Day, Dušan David Pařízek comes up with a clever 'site-specific' staging within the Schauspielhaus Zürich: while Goethe's *Faust* is being shown in the theatre's main house, Jelinek's secondary drama starts at the same time in the small rehearsal studio, the 'Musikzimmer', in the basement of the theatre. As the theatre announces on its website, a small audience of around thirty spectators will be able to attend Jelinek's secondary drama – women will be given preference for ticket allocation. The actresses and 'spectatoresses' will thus be 'incarcerated' together. According to the website (availing itself of Jelinek's ironic text), they 'form a circle, according to the motto: we participate in women's form in the women's forum. We always participate when it's about Woman. We are in best form, albeit in female form.'[49] While this 'site-specific' arrangement is bound to segregate the audience not so much in terms of gender (there actually were some men among the cellar audience on the evening I attended) but more likely into Jelinek and Goethe fans, this spatial segregation from the start also serves to highlight theatre's conventional production hierarchies: the classics in the main house, experimental theatre in the smaller, cheaper studio space – which very often happens to be situated in the basement of large theatres or arts centres.

Having chosen to attend the performance in the cellar, we are led to a soundproof room below the main stage where chairs line the walls. The three actresses (Pařízek has added a 'GretIn' to Jelinek's FaustIn and GeistIn), dressed in white lace dresses underneath trench coats, act their way through a dramaturgical structure chalked on the back of the door (with headings such as 'Disarming women!', 'Off to the cellar' and 'Above me only my father'), sharing the text and addressing it directly to the surrounding audience members (see Figure 10.2).

There are moments when the performers invite the solidarity of female audience members, addressing them directly as if in a doctor's waiting room, and other moments when they provoke male audience members, as for example when the line 'Women exist to get fucked' gets repeated to male audience members with an invitation to complete the line: 'Women exist to . . .? Women exist to . . .? Eh, eh?' As they talk, dialectically moving between the positions of perpetrator and

Figure 10.2 *Faust 1–3* with Elfriede Jelinek's *FaustIn and out*, directed by Dušan David Pařízek Schauspielhaus Zürich. Image shows Franziska Walser, Sarah Hostettler and Miriam Maertens. (Photo by Toni Suter / T+T Fotografie.)

victim, images of women in captivity can become painfully vivid in our minds – at least this was the case in my personal experience of the performance – but it is not as though we really feel like one of them by being put in this situation in the cellar. Rather the performance invites us to reflect on the sociopolitical conditions that make such oppression possible.

There are TV screens in the cellar on which we catch glimpses of the performance upstairs where two actors play with the material from *Faust I* and *II*. At the same time Jelinek's secondary play is sporadically transmitted onto a screen as part of the latter production in the main house, thus interrupting its focus on the main protagonist and acting as a constant reminder of the 'undead' Gretchen. The two performances thus mutually disturb each other via live video link, with the effect that both audience groups have the feeling they are missing something – the downstairs audience feeling excluded from 'high culture', the upstairs audience sensing there's something going on underground which is being repressed in Goethe's lofty verses. About seventy-five minutes into the performance we hear loud bangs and see the Faust actors from above hacking their way through the stage floor with an axe. They knock on the door and 'liberate' us. We are asked to don the trench coats stashed beneath our seats and make our way to the main stage where we stand awkwardly for a few minutes facing the other audience as a collective of intruding 'GretInnen'. For the rest of the performance, Goethe's and Jelinek's texts are interlaced and mutually disturb each other.

Hearing voices in the in-between

In *Faust 1–3*, too, Jelinek's parasitic secondary drama has the potential to act as a 'thermal exciter' in the idealist-humanist debates on human progress in modernity that inevitably surround Faust productions, as well as putting the question of women's progress (or lack thereof) back on the agenda. The locus of the political in both performances, I argue, appears in the *interstices* between the classic 'host' play and contemporary reality, a liminal space opened up by Jelinek's parasitic 'secondary drama'. According to Michel Serres, '[t]he position of the parasite is to be between',[50] the parasitic is the relational *par excellence*. Both *Abraumhalde* and *FaustIn and out* open up an in-between space where the actors can play with both texts as material.

Paradoxically, too, in both of the discussed productions, the parasitic intrusion of Jelinek's text also serves to bring out the postdramatic aspects *within* the classic texts. For neither are 'pure dramas', as it turns out: Lessing called his play a 'dramatic poem' and considered it unstageable, while Goethe's *Faust*, in its sprawling, stylistically heterogeneous 'self-reflexive playfulness', has been called 'proto-postmodern'.[51] The disruption of a conventional reception of these texts by the parasitic intruder here also indirectly, *modo obliquo* releases the political dynamite contained within the original. Despite the fact that Jelinek's secondary dramas do not give up on 'thematising' political issues, the postdramatic stagings discussed here allow for an experience of the political as a disruption, a 'rupturing of the present'. By changing the form, the time and the space of the theatrical event, they allow us to perceive voices that often do not get represented, either in classical drama or in our contemporary political discourses. The uncanny and urgent 'unpresentness' of these voices is brought home by FaustIn's penultimate lines:

> I scream loudly, so that all awaken. But who should hear me? The oven? The worm? The dog that I don't have? The children? The day that dreads the dawn before it even sees us. But down here it won't see us anyway. The day.

Phenomenology and the Postdramatic: A Case Study of Three Plays by Ewald Palmetshofer

Jerome Carroll

Hans-Thies Lehmann begins the essay 'How political is Postdramatic Theatre?' with the striking assertion that there is a qualitative distinction between theatre (and art in general) and politics: 'I start with the simple premise that theatre and art are initially not politics, but rather something else. Precisely because of this the question arises at all about a possible connection between the political and its manifestation in art.'[1] This statement expresses Lehmann's view that theatre's political force depends on its substantial separation from political norms, which among other things includes its eschewing of the presentation or critique of such norms by discursive, thematic means. One can allow for some tendentious overstatement: we shall see in what follows that Lehmann is concerned to conceptualise theatre as a space for the production of meaning that is as free as possible from meanings imposed on it from outside that space. However, my view is that this position unnecessarily restricts what can be counted as contributing to art's political force, as well as setting up a questionable separation between, on the one hand, politics and the norms by which it is made manifest and, on the other theatre, and the dismantling of those norms. My concern in this chapter is, conversely, to explore the potential for phenomenology as an approach to analysing theatre that might counterbalance this somewhat polarised and dichotomous conceptualisation of the political or socially critical force of postdramatic theatre. First, I will sketch out two conceptions of phenomenology – one of which I will prefer to the other. Secondly, I will draw out the implications of this notion of phenomenology for theatre and the presentation of 'political' material. In the third section I will analyse the work of the Austrian playwright, Ewald Palmetshofer, in the light of these ideas, and draw conclusions about the specifically phenomenological presentation of politics in his plays. Finally, I will return to Lehmann's conceptualisation of the political force of theatre that is labelled 'postdramatic', comparing it to the phenomenological approach.

Phenomenology: Corporeality or 'discipline of the imagination'?

The theoretical background for this chapter is the body or school of thought called phenomenology. In my view one can distinguish between two dominant conceptions of phenomenology, and consequently between two views of its relevance for theatre and for the political significance of theatre. The first view reads phenomenology as an attitude that reasserts the separable components of experience. As Robert Sokolowski puts it:

> In the natural attitude we head directly towards the object; we go right through the object's appearances to the object itself. From the philosophically reflective stance, we [. . .] look *at* what we normally look *through*. We focus, for example, on the sides, aspects, and profiles through which the cube presents itself as an identity. We focus on the manifold of appearances through which the object is given to us.[2]

The corollary of this approach is the emphasis of the *components* of theatre, in particular its corporeal aspect, highlighted in several of the attempts to integrate phenomenology into the analysis of theatre in the past thirty years, such as Bert States's *Great Reckonings in Little Rooms*. States begins his discussion emphasising theatre's component parts, 'in the sense that it focuses on the activity of theater *making itself* out of its essential materials: speech, sound, movement, scenery, text, etc'.[3] More recently Andy Lavender refers in similar terms to how productions of *Hamlet* by Peter Brook, Robert Lepage and Robert Wilson 'trade in a phenomenological theatre, exploiting qualities of space, sound, movement, rhythm, visual image and the body of the performer'.[4] In these terms theatre is no longer merely the site for the dramatic presentation of a story, rather recent work in performance is seen as freeing theatre from drama's traditional obedience to the representative duty of creating a 'fictive cosmos'.[5] As such, for States and others these components are not just the materials of theatre, but something of which a residue remains after all semantic explanation or analysis. 'Political' value is found in the stage's unique features, for instance that, unlike many other cultural forms, the stage and its actors are really *there* in front of us, at the same time both 'make-believe and radically actual'.[6] Since Artaud, this liberation has also been couched in the more philosophical terms of the 'representational' status of the stage: the focus on performance highlights the stage's exceeding of 'mere' representation of what is already given. This shift also gets expressed as a turn against conceptual meaning, in favour of corporeal experience, inasmuch as it goes some way to overturning or at least resisting the tendency for meaning to conceal or swallow up physical perception, the way bodies on stage disappear into the meaning of the piece. Nuki Shigeto refers to States in this regard:

> A theater piece is not completed with its textual meaning, but with its performance on stage realised through the voices and bodies of

living actors. As Bert O. States (1985) says, those who are interested only in the meaning of the story of Macbeth can stay home and read the text.[7]

The second conception of phenomenology is as a study of the structures of meaning that organise experience or consciousness – what Bruce Wilshire calls the 'discipline of the imagination.'[8] The point that this variant of phenomenology seeks to make is that any assessment of what counts as reality has to take account of the fact that any and all experience is pre-disposed by a range of assumptions, attitudes and values. What is striking here is that these two conceptions of phenomenology seem to be at odds: the first emphasises the largely sensory or corporeal components of perception, to some extent divorced from meaning; the second emphasises the ideal realm of consciousness and imagination. One is unquestionably present and in some sense *immediate*; the other is intangible, and seeks to draw attention to the very process of mediation. Moreover, Wilshire's 'discipline of the imagination' may be seen as working in the opposite direction to the kind of separating out of sensory elements like the 'space, sound, movement, rhythm, visual image and the body' of theatre, insofar as one of the primary concerns of this second variant of phenomenology is to account for subjectivity and experience without dissecting it.[9] Maurice Merleau-Ponty expresses most clearly phenomenology's concern to do justice to the *holism* of experience: 'It is impossible to decompose a perception, to make it into a collection of sensations, because in it the whole is prior to the parts.'[10]

This holism is not only a comment on how our experience is in part determined by a complex web of assumptions, attitudes and values, but it also sets out a significantly new idea of the connection between the self and the world. The point is that the way consciousness works, the way it is both informed by *and* shapes our experience and understanding of the external world, does not admit of a clear-cut separation of 'internal' mind and 'external' matter or world. By the same token, phenomenology puts to one side the aspiration to objective knowledge of the natural sciences. As Stanton Garner puts it in *Bodied Spaces*, the concern is 'to redirect attention from the world as it is conceived by the abstracting, "scientific" gaze (the objective world) to the world as it appears or discloses itself to the perceiving subject (the phenomenal world)'.[11] The distance between phenomenological and objectivist epistemologies is made clearest by the claim, voiced by David Stewart and Algis Mickunas, that phenomenologists 'make no assumptions about what is or is not real; they rather begin with the content of consciousness – whatever that content may be – as valid data for investigation'.[12] In their concern to refute the positivism of the objective view, Stewart and Mickunas ostensibly contravene the central phenomenological principle that any grasp of what is real *necessarily* involves a range of assumptions and attitudes. However the point here is that the phenomenological approach wants to make no 'hard and fast' rules in advance, a priori, about what can contribute to any grasp of reality.

Phenomenology and theatre

So how does this conception of phenomenology's holistic, non-objectivist epistemology relate to theatre? In Garner's view, very closely indeed: he describes the theatrical stage as a 'non-Cartesian field of habitation which undermines the stance of objectivity and in which the categories of subject and object give way to a relationship of mutual implication'.[13] Alice Rayner is even more pointed in aligning theatre with non-objective phenomenology, describing the stage's capacity to resist the dualism that posits discrete subject and object as the defining quality of 'theatre': 'Any point at which dualistic, oppositional thought is invoked but then breaks down might be said to be theatrical.' Theatre, according to Rayner, aims or at least should aim to work against any epistemological or ontological premise that 'divides the world into oppositions of true and false, real and unreal, visible and invisible'. Rayner's recent analysis of theatre practice focuses on the role and status of ghosts on the stage, which are seen to present 'images that confound the real and representation, about the return of the past to the present, materiality and memory, about self-deception and action'.[14] This approach clearly tallies with the above characterisation of the phenomenological attitude as one that resists making hard and fast assumptions about what is real and unreal.

There are several implications that follow from this attitude that one might pick up on, not least the issue of relativism. Does having no hard and fast premises or assumptions about what is real or true also preclude drawing conclusions about what is real/unreal or true/false? Is phenomenology – and with it theatre that might be classified as 'phenomenological' – uninterested in substantiating or verifying truth claims concerning the reality it presents? In that case what becomes of theatre's critical function or its capacity to offer generalisable or even transferable insights about the world? What would this mean for the politics of theatre? How is a critical perspective possible in theatre that seeks to interweave the real and imagined and leave their ultimate status indeterminate? Conversely, what might be gained from a 'phenomenological' approach to theatre that is more circumspect about dividing things into real/imagined, or internal/external, or at least that is more flexible about such categories? And what implications would such analysis have for questions of political consciousness and political critique, particularly as regards theatre that is characterised as 'postdramatic'?

Palmetshofer

In what follows I will suggest that this refusal to separate the real and imagined, the 'external' and 'internal', is crucial to the political force of some theatre. In particular I will sketch out what a phenomenological approach to postdramatic theatre might look like with reference to three plays by the contemporary Austrian playwright Ewald Palmetshofer: *wohnen. unter glas* (written 2006, premiered 2008), *hamlet ist tot. keine schwerkraft* (written 2007, premiered 2008), and *faust hat hunger etc.* (written 2009, premiered 2009). His work postdates Lehmann's list of practitioners of postdramatic theatre,[15] and the retention of character, fictive cosmos and the still conventionally authoritative play text suggests that, if anything, Palmetshofer's work should be categorised in terms of Gerda Poschmann's 'no-longer-dramatic text'.[16] However, several aspects of these plays might reasonably be classified as postdramatic: in terms of plot and thematics they eschew plot or 'generative action'[17] and they abstain from coherent thematisation of political issues; in terms of language and characterisation, they have a specific focus on language whose referential quality is impaired, at the same time as constantly putting characters' identity under question, with specific utterances shared among those characters. This might suggest Palmetshofer's plays lend themselves to performative practice and to phenomenological analysis, which – according to the first understanding of phenomenology above – would attend to the components of performance that we have associated with the first definition of phenomenology: voice, text and audience, if not body and stage. Certainly it is notable that most productions of Palmetshofer's plays thus far have used only minimal realistic scenery and props, and have largely eschewed naturalistic dialogue and treatment of character, treating the pieces more or less as *Sprechstücke*, albeit with some minimal onstage activity. My focus is slightly different, however, and more in line with the second conception of phenomenology: I want to argue that the conception of self and society presented in his plays is phenomenological. I will argue that Palmetshofer's plays do more than most to explicitly thematise issues of the interiority of the individual and his or her connection with the 'external' world, as well as engaging with the difficulties that this poses for direct and determinate answers to questions of political consciousness and critique. As such I think that a 'phenomenological' analysis of his plays is indispensable to bringing out their social and political significance.

From the outset, the interweaving of self and world in Palmetshofer's plays is presented as a problem, primarily in the ostensible absence in his plays of what one might call 'subjective interiority'. This implosion of subjective interiority or agency is manifested in the first instance linguistically, in the artificial, repetitive and fragmentary language of the protagonists in all three plays, and in the shared delivery of sentences and meaning. (In this respect Palmetshofer's plays might be seen as coming in the wake of those of René Pollesch.) So, for instance, the dialogue in *wohnen* is littered with non-standard syntax, such as verbs missing from ends of sentences, unclear referents, missing information, uncompleted ideas, unanswered questions, contradiction, repetition and general ambiguity, particularly with regard to seemingly pregnant, meaningful words. In *wohnen*, Babsi, one of the characters – all university friends meeting up after years apart – is talking obliquely about her old friend Max's inability to have an orgasm, expressed in the metaphor of climax, or 'Höhepunkt'.[18] Max takes up this word minutes later, but this time the concept applies to the sense that modern life is bereft of any kind of special achievement or experience, the kind of idea – whether illusory or not – that we need to sustain our interest in existence (W 293). There is no attempt to spell out the specific meanings or indeed links between these two uses of the same term, and it is not too much to say that this slackness of communication and elision between ideas, combined with the impaired referential quality of the text as a whole, seems to reflect a general disintegration of the autonomous subject. The lack of specificity and the lack of specialness – *Höhepunkte* – in the lives of the protagonists combine to give the sense that there is nothing to 'externalise', no inner life worth expressing.

This repetitive, ambiguous and seemingly pregnant language sounds like Pollesch's discourse theatre, but this is not to say that Palmetshofer's plays are peopled by Pollesch's post-human avatars; I say this is in spite of their diminutive names: Jeani, Babsi, Caro, Dani, Mani, etc. Rather his figures are always firmly embedded in familiar communities, and here the adage is bitingly accurate: familiarity breeds contempt. In *wohnen* it is the university friends reunited whose repeated expressions of pleasure at seeing one another again ring hollow, and who now share only the creeping sense that they are no longer where the action is – their social exclusion expressed in the subtitle 'unter glas': the glass ceiling that constrains upward mobility; in *hamlet*, the (figuratively) incestuous and self-obsessed family, disoriented and rendered impotent by a globalisation that passes them by; in *faust*, the self-satisfied but ultimately empty petit-bourgeois social merry-go-round of the thirty-something neighbours, in which the quest for more meaningful experience can only be pursued at someone else's cost. In all cases, the shared and broken sentences do not simply indicate automata, but also that the characters are products of their milieu – and as products they are all what in the retail world might be called 'slight seconds'.

The point is that community, like language, is presented as a double-edged sword in Palmetshofer's plays, especially in *faust*. On the one hand it precipitates feelings of belonging and integration, explicitly thematised in the integration of outsiders into the neighbourhood.[19] But it is also highly suffocating. One of the neighbours, Robert, refers to the welcoming community in grotesque – and sexual – terms such as a 'Gemeinschaftskörper' (collective body) which makes 'Gemeinschaftskörperöffnungen' (openings in the collective body) to allow others in and a 'Gemeinschaftsmaul' (collective mouth) that utters the invitation (F 519). Community is presented only as exterior veneer, its skin-deep nature reflected in the highly banal and self-reflexive conversations about recent shared times, about who they invited, what they did, and how welcoming they are (F 515–19). But engagement in the community is also self-serving: *faust* presents a social world in which neighbourliness is little more than an intensely narcissistic keeping up with the Joneses, evidenced for instance in the thinly veiled rivalry that motivates the competitive hosting of dinner parties (F 520). This rivalry is crystallised in the speeches made by the men hosting dinner parties, such as Fritz's discourse on truth and happiness.

The main idea in Fritz's speech is that the old models of universal truth and autonomous individuality are outdated in an era of dwindling resources and mass society (see F 513–14). Here the effacing of individual identity is presented as a consequence not just of social conformity, but also of the all-pervading consumerism of late capitalism, suggesting a vestige of focused 'political' critique: 'As long as the stream of commodities, which is of course external, obviously it is external, the world, as long as it goes through you, you have an inside, my friend, it doesn't come from anywhere else, the inside, but from the outside' (F 513). Identity-forming aspects of experience like love, dreams, aspirations and self-image are seen to come only from external sources, not least cinema: 'bloody Hollywood-contaminated trash-dream' (F 527). This infiltration of our thoughts and attitudes seems to leave little room for an autonomous self, and Fritz suggests that we simply have to hold ourselves open to this stream. Here there is no residue, no remnant that can be charged with emancipatory force. Any self-consciousness is described as nothing more than a by-product of neurological activity (F 526), and Paul asks what remains if everything and everyone is nothing more than 'Äußerlichkeit', exteriority (F 526). In *hamlet* Dani castigates her feelings as 'trash in my brain'.[20] In *wohnen*, any fulfilment that our inner life offers is seen to only work briefly and in any case is said to amount to little more than self-deception, an indication that we have succumbed to the consumerist 'Glücks-Lüge', or 'deceit about happiness' (W 305). So far so dismal.

The explicit reference here to the topos of inner and outer that I have discussed above is notable, and seems to have a number of implications. First, it seems to be informed by the phenomenological insight, discussed above, which states that the range of what must be taken to count as real is to be expanded. This in turn marks an insistence that experience and identity, while 'highly personalised', are also socially constructed, 'already established code of interpretation'.[21] Here I am citing the writings of Alfred Schutz, a figure primarily associated with sociological phenomenology. This social construction might be taken to suggest that no objective perspective on the society we inhabit is available to us, but it also carries much critical force in Palmetshofer's work, suggesting that our 'external' aspect is essentially a process of imprinting of received values and attitudes onto a clone-like subject. That said, occasionally in Palmetshofer's work the interwoven nature of inner and outer is expressed more benignly. This is the case in the character of Anne, the Gretchen-figure and most positively portrayed character in *faust*, whose identity is forged through a song, 'my song' (F 526), although even here Anne herself castigates the 'pathetic' nature of self-identity.

Elsewhere the play adheres to a more conventional – bourgeois – conception of subjecthood, for instance inasmuch as the individual's inner space is characterised as a source of strength and resistance (F 511), a point of refuge from the aforementioned 'stream of consumables' (*Warenstrom*, F 513). It is worth noting that this capacity for holding oneself apart is gendered, a male quality: Tanja and Ines, in a typical sharing of dialogue and confusion of roles, report their partner's verdict that one needs to keep one's outer self quite different to one's inner self: 'Then from that grows another, an inside one, that is completely different to this external one' (F 534). Likewise in *wohnen* it is Max who is said to have the capacity for this interiority, which is referred to as a locus of freedom: 'Max is totally internal. He is. Internal. Completely on his own. He doesn't need anything. [. . .] He is free. [. . .] Max doesn't need external things' (W 308). This interiority is seen as authentic, largely on the basis of the refusal to play the game of keeping up the appearance of being happy and fulfilled, of subscribing to the aforementioned 'public deceit about happiness' (*öffentliche Glückslüge*, W 305). But it is notable that this freedom is not discussed in terms of 'positive' behaviour or the freedom to opt for values that might be shared, but is largely 'cerebral', a kind of stoic turn inwards, whereby one is able to insulate oneself, for instance from the pernicious effects of economic disadvantage or social exclusion. But in the course of the discussion among the old university friends in *wohnen* it becomes clear that the price of such self-determination is that it is largely private: 'For you. Afterwards, completely privately and secretly you make something great from these dead things' (W 295). To others, this inward turn looks like selfishness, as Jeani passes verdict on the recalcitrant Max: 'He is internal and free and doesn't give a shit' (W 308). Here and elsewhere Palmetshofer's dialogue often hints at a solipsistic world view in which individual characters are separated from the inner lives of others, never able to know what is going on underneath the surface. In *faust* Fritz claims that one invests in people's inner being 'auf Pump' – on the 'never never' (F 538). He asserts that one cannot invest in a 'soul' in an economic way, as it comes 'out of nothing, or perhaps just not at all' (F 538). One of the more poignant verdicts in the play, this is a highly ambivalent statement, suggesting that it is hard to tell whether the soul manifests itself intangibly, mysteriously or whether in fact it is simply not manifest at all. The bleaker of the two alternatives seems to be confirmed, as Anne – the Gretchen figure in *faust* – when she goes into the woods to bear and kill and bury her baby, states in her monologue 'that there is no person inside the person, not in me, not any more' (F 553). The double meaning seems to convey the strongest moral message of the play: that there is no baby inside her, but no humanity (as characterised by compassion and altruism, among other things) either. One suspects the two are interconnected: our inability to contain others within us is an indictment of our humanity. Here once again, things are couched in terms of the topos of internal/external – this time with a strong moral inflection.

This presentation of characters as automatons or sociopaths – either lacking in an inner core of agency or as incorrigibly selfish – raises the question whether a view of man's internal/external nature arises in these plays that is more in line with the phenomenological insights I started with. Certainly, it is hard to speak of any 'holist' treatment of character, as might be sketched for instance with reference to an imaginative lifeworld, in cases where the characters' lack of personal fulfilment precipitates an unbalanced self-orientation. This selfishness is evident in the references to conventional, 'external' political issues in the plays, which tend to be crassly simplistic or simply self-serving, inseparable from personal preoccupations. This is most clearly thematised in *hamlet*. Caro, the mother, remarks that thousands of people are dying in other countries, 'in Africa, for example' (H 431). This is expressed with some jealousy, as she is wishing death on her own aged mother. Her son, Mani, asserts that those in Asia are better off because they eat rice, have less cancer, and live 'completely in the moment, totally in the here and now and totally happy' (H 425). These far-away locations emphasise the ignorance and prejudice that attends the discussion of this global perspective. Mani's only response to the sense that the world is 'in decline' is to masturbate, 'on the floods and the bombs, about the Pope and drought and about the East, you wank hard about the Middle East' (H 413). The self-orientation and fruitlessness of this act contrast notably with Anne's pregnancy, and Mani's crass claim that masturbation is the 'religious act *par excellence*' seems to reiterate the solipsistic attitude registered above: 'alone at home with you and the world' (H 413). This 'and the world' hubristically suggests that the challenges posed by the world can be captured in, reduced to, this act. The sister, Dani, is more despairing and disparaging that her own 'emotional crap' (*Befindlichkeitsscheiße*) is the 'only politics' available to her (H 444), but her comparison of the euphoric moment of meeting Mr Right with catastrophic world events is still jarring: 'that is your event, you think to yourself, that is your revolution, your Hiroshima, your 9/11, your rebirth' (H 405).

But this complaint of Dani's is itself one of a number more or less coherent articulations which take the form of Palmetshofer's recurrent use of monologue, during which protagonists express their thoughts and fears, in ways that – centrally for my argument – interweave the personal and the political. This monologue introduces a self-reflexive element akin to that of an intra-diegetic narrator in a novel. And while it is potentially drama's most solipsistic mode, in Palmetshofer's work the monologue invariably thematises the relationship between inner and outer self and world in a more sustained and insightful way than the exchanges in that world. Like her daughter, Caro in *hamlet* laments the tunnel vision of the housewife's limited horizon. (H 418–19) In *faust*, Fritz holds forth on our capacity for happiness being impaired because we resist impulses from outside, and that old models of individual fulfilment or universal truth are outdated (F 511–14), Anne discusses the pathetic nature of self-identity (and the failure of women's movement) (F 522), and Tanja self-identity and the mass media (F 526–7). In *wohnen* Max also addresses the self/world interface, describing how the desire for consumption has become sexualised, characterising consumption as the attempt to fill an existential hole which products do not fit (W 303–4).

In my view, these frustrated monologues are one of the clearest 'vital signs' on the part of Palmetshofer's characters of a more sustained capacity for understanding and for articulating the difficulties that the contemporary situation throws up, even where an alternative mode of being is not obviously on the table. Of course, this understanding and articulation of their situation is of little comfort to the protagonists who are delivering these monologues. The discourses are largely an expression of their exclusion: decisive action is not available to the protagonists. Notably, the sense that decisive action is once again elsewhere is expressed in the topos of inner and outer: 'Outside./Not we./Outside./External' (W 326). And of course my point is that even the protagonists are not simply 'internal': the play makes clear that the internal and external can barely be separated. The emotional and the economic are interwoven. Happiness is described in *hamlet* as a 'economic function' (H 424), and the thoroughgoing economisation of reality in late capitalism manifests itself in a situation in which a lack of (mental) perspective is intertwined with a lack of (economic) prospects (both words are denoted by the term *Perspektive* in German), where depression and self-doubt is shown as inseparable from social and economic exclusion. Mani describes himself and Dani as 'two planets that no one inhabits' (H 446), a feeling that one is unattractive that is the correlate of the weightlessness of the subtitle: 'without gravity' (H 446). This feeling of weightlessness is an emotional, internal feeling of meaninglessness in those who have no 'external' economic role (H 435). In my view this interweaving of the emotional and the economic, the internal and the external, is the most convincing articulation of political issues that Palmetshofer's plays offer.

The phenomenological sense that there is no clear-cut separation of 'internal' mind and 'external' world also sets clear limits in the characters' capacity for self-understanding and critique, which lacks a vantage point for objective analysis, or even insights about decisive forces that govern their experience. This gives the characters' articulations of their situation a claustrophobic quality, as if they are banging on the inside of a cardboard box from which they cannot escape. Mani articulates the half-baked nature of his and their capacity for analysis, lamenting the sense that any kind of insight he has is momentary and not cumulative, lacking continuity: 'no, your moments don't make a line [. . .], a now and a now and a now and between them no line' (H 424). He contrasts 'moment' with 'a story and narrative' (H 446), and here the common ground is also apparent between this pairing and the terms of my discussion of phenomenological approaches to theatre above, namely the contrast between immediacy and that which is mediated. But it is also in these monologues that Palmetshofer's plays come closest to a coherent 'story'. According to this reading, the depiction of a lifeworld in which meaning is fragmentary or shared, and in which interiority is limited to internal battles with consumerism, impotent solipsism, hubristic onanism, or to lamentations about the pathos of self-identity, might be just as valid or insightful as offering of an objective, critical vantage point for analysis.

Postdramatic theatre

So what does this interweaving of internal and external that I am aligning with phenomenology have to do with postdramatic theatre? The shape of the overlap between a phenomenological approach and postdramatic theatre depends, of course, on one's definition of each term, and the kind of postdramatic theatre one is talking about. For some theorists, such as Nuki Shigeto, phenomenological analysis is particularly appropriate for theatre that has dispensed with the presentation of specifically 'dramatic' action, what she calls 'a theatre that got rid of narratives', because it is suited to analysing 'stage performance per se'.[22] I registered above the ways in which the focus on performance in recent theatre is seen by theorists to have liberated the stage from certain epistemological frameworks, and this issue of the ontological or epistemological status of performance and its relationship to 'external' referents is also central to the claims made on behalf of postdramatic theatre in Hans-Thies Lehmann's theoretical writings. In the Epilogue to his seminal *Postdramatic Theatre*, in which he addresses the question of the political force of theatre that has eschewed conventional dramatic elements, he characterises postdramatic theatre as casting off theatre's traditional function of re-presenting the world outside the theatre. Dramatic theatre has traditionally derived its critical, political force from its capacity for insightful portrayal of and discursive commentary on 'external' social and political realities, and has done so through the medium of action, thematic dialogue, character, and by virtue of all these through the generation of a fictive cosmos. Lehmann refers to this as the 'reproduction of the political as it appears in everyday theoretical, political discourse'.[23] By contrast, recent experimental performance practice has been labelled 'postdramatic' by virtue of the extent to which it eschews some or most of these categories, and with them the claim to mimetically represent reality. Rather, it is claimed itself to *be* a kind of reality, which Lehmann refers to both in the Lacanian terms of an 'irruption of the real'[24] and in terms of the reality of the *performance*, as 'more presence than representation, more shared than communicated experience, more process than product, more manifestation than signification, more energetic impulse than information'.[25] He is ambivalent about this: at points in the discussion he claims not to be interested in conception of performance as 'reality' in itself: in the Epilogue he precisely disputes the conceptualisation of theatre as a direct political 'act'.[26] But in the German version Lehmann does refer to theatre's 'event-character',[27] emblematic of which is the new status of the performer and the audience in postdramatic theatre, as opposed to dramatic theatre's emphasis on the fable or the concerns of writer or director.[28] Further evidence for the particular 'reality-status' of performance is apparent in Lehmann's recurrent emphasis on the 'concrete' or sensory (i.e. corporeal, visual, auditory, etc.) aspects of theatre, insofar as these resist the traditional subservience to the (conceptual, discursive) 'meaning' of a piece.[29] Here the overlap is apparent with the first conception of phenomenological theatre discussed above.

This rejection of a conceptual, discursive approach to stage meaning touches on a couple of key aspects of Lehmann's politics of theatre. First, he takes the view that coherent discourse does not reflect our experience of an increasingly complex and opaque globalised and mediated reality. Secondly, he is concerned that the model of meaning that sees the stage as merely reproducing pre-existing reality or discursive norms closes down avenues for the determination of that meaning by actors or audience, who are reduced to mere conduits or passive recipients of pre-established meaning. The exclusion of the audience is particularly pernicious for Lehmann because it replicates within the theatre a relationship to reality that he characterises, following Althusser, as being separated into two temporal frames which never match up: 'Thus, the experience of a split between two times – the time of the subject and the time of the historical process – is the core of political theatre, as Althusser points out, and this in fact hits the nerve of the problem of politics as a subject for theatre.'[30] Lehmann however does not want this schism to be unified at the level of action, character or thematics. Indeed he sees conventional political theatre, and in particular that of Brecht, as an illusory attempt to unify these two time frames.[31] Concerned not to falsely reconcile this schism between the personal and historical, Lehmann rejects conventionally dramatic approaches to character and action because he views the faith they indicate in comprehensible causal connections and individual agency as an *erroneous* representation of the individual's experience of political and economic reality in advanced capitalism. In notably Brechtian terms, he argues that the individual's lack of oversight over and control of complex economic processes means that presenting individual 'occurrences' as causal 'action' is illusory: 'In present society, almost any form has come to seem more suitable for articulating reality than the action of a causal logic with its inherent attribution of events to the decisions of individuals.'[32]

Lehmann sees this schism between personal and historical world views as being exacerbated by the role of the media, in what he characterises, with Guy Debord, as a society of the spectacle. In this connection Lehmann cites Samuel Weber, using terms that share the twin topos of inside/outside and subject/object that I have deployed above: 'If we remain spectators/viewers, if we stay where we are – in front of the television – the catastrophe will always stay outside, will always be objects for a subject – this is the implicit promise of the medium.'[33] Here his concern shifts slightly – but crucially – from the subject's status as a political and economic agent, to that of an agent of meaning, and it is on this terrain of meaning that Lehmann joins the battle with the forces of capital and mass media. That is to say, he is primarily concerned about the separation of production and reception of theatrical meaning, which he sees as fundamental to the model of the spectacle. In this he may be aligned with Rancière, who himself cites Debord, 'What in fact is the essence of the spectacle for Guy Debord? It is exteriority. [. . .] "Separation is the alpha and omega of the spectacle."'[34] Both Lehmann and Rancière think theatre responds inadequately to the dilemma of the spectacle if, by virtue of its strategies of representation (e.g. treating the stage as thematic mouthpiece of the author or as a faithful mirror of external reality), it perpetuates this separation, ultimately promoting indifference in the recipient. '"Good" theatre is one that uses its separated reality in order to abolish it.'[35] For Lehmann this 'good' theatre is postdramatic theatre, which generates a situation in which the production of meaning is *shared* (thereby reigniting a collectivism that he also sees as having been sacrificed at the altar of bourgeois individualism).[36]

As such, Lehmann conceives of postdramatic performance as resolving the crisis of the schism that separates individuals from the historical processes by generating a collective space in art. But arguably the way he describes this political value of performance reconnects the agent with processes of production *only* at the expense of separating theatre from 'external' reality. Indeed, this separation is precisely the means by which Lehmann reckons the indeterminacy of the performance situation is secured, on which its collectivism and creativity depend: namely, by releasing it from the obligation to faithfully represent external reality or to impart clear, thematic, politically 'engaged' instruction. This is why Lehmann makes a virtue of this separation of theatre from extra-theatrical reality in *Postdramatic Theatre*, where he not only rejects theatre that attempts to portray – naïvely intact – causal relations and agency, but absolves theatre *in toto* of the requirement to treat political or social issues thematically or discursively as well. This is also the point of his categorical distinction between art and politics that I started this chapter with. The position Lehmann takes here – or at any rate his theoretical articulation of it – strikes me as an unnecessarily restrictive one, which seems to overlook, or at least understate, the vital connection between theatre – even postdramatic theatre – and the wider norms and attitudes that are its lifeblood. What occurs on the stage, and even how it is presented, is hard to separate from a web of attitudes and assumptions, some of which are to do with the institution of theatre, some of which are to do with the attitudes that extend beyond the confines of theatre, for instance conceptions of subjectivity and agency. Palmetshofer's examples of failed agency and partial interiority are a case in point.

That said, more recently Lehmann has referred to 'the impulse to re-open the dialogue between theatre and society by taking up more directly political and social issues, [. . .] even if there are no solutions [. . .] to offer', or indeed 'a specific ideological viewpoint'. This, he concludes, involves 'not so much a return to socially engaged drama' but 'a remarkably steady focus [. . .] on the exploration of everyday life [. . .] which we only think we know well'.[37] This combination of a focus on everyday life and an engagement with political and social issues that is not reducible to clear solutions that are underpinned by stable ideology is precisely what we have found in Palmetshofer's work. Both aspects are essential to the interwoven nature of 'internal' and 'external' in his plays. In my view Lehmann is more convincing when he is more tentative about the issue of 'externality'. In *Postdramatic Theatre* he discusses those points where onstage action does partake of referentiality, which in the postdramatic mode is characterised by connotations that do not translate into clear, discursive meaning. This indeterminacy leaves an external reference that is only vestigial, which Lehmann refers to as the 'partial perspectives and stuttering answers that remain "works in progress"'.[38] Palmetshofer's plays can very well be interpreted as a 'stuttering answer'. His bleak assessments of the lack of subjective interiority, in discursive, thematic statement as well as in the dialogue and characterisation in his pieces, indicate the repressive, problematic side of norms. The treatment of community and collectivity also tends towards the suffocating, but not without a sense that this is also inevitably where much identity and belonging comes from.

And to return to another of Lehmann's antinomies, Palmetshofer's treatments of agency also suggest that the historical and subjective may be said to 'match up', in the sense that we do experience the failure of agency at some level. The faltering critique and partial self-diagnosis confirms Althusser's sense of a schism between personal and historical realms, but his pieces also show that in certain respects the personal and the historical dimensions cannot be anything but interwoven. That this connection between the personal and historical is not presented as a solution to the problem of agency and critique suggests that these problems cannot be solved in the theatre, but only economically and politically. And in this respect I think it is notable that Palmetshofer does not seek a point of reconciliation outside of these environing norms and mechanisms of identity. That the characters' fragmentary diagnosis stops short of insights about the decisive forces that lie behind their experience arguably adds to rather than detracting from the plays' political force. This fragmentary treatment of themes such as subjective interiority and political agency might be seen as offering us an example of articulating or at least expressing resistance from *within* these norms, *without* resorting to a resolution of the crisis of agency in some sphere beyond the one in which that crisis has come to a head. Put another way, I want to suggest that a phenomenological understanding of theatre offers a mode of critique that does not rely on the objectivity of its representation or the strength of its critical discourse, but at the same time does not dispense with this external relation.

Performing the Collective. Heiner Müller's 'Alone with These Bodies' ('Allein mit diesen Leibern')[1] as a Piece for Postdramatic Theatre

Michael Wood

As Hans-Thies Lehmann writes in 1987, 'the politics of a text is not determined by the theses it contains, rather by the manner in which it organises these [theses] and itself. Not the politics *in* the text, rather the politics *of* the text.'[2] To paraphrase Lehmann's statement: the political is formal. It can perhaps be taken for granted that the postdramatic theatre text is a text which experiments with form, but it would be well worth taking a closer look at the role formal experimentation plays with regard to the politics of theatre. Lehmann's assertion was made well before the vocabulary of the postdramatic or the 'no-longer-dramatic', to use Gerda Poschmann's somewhat more clunky terminology,[3] was coined. Here, Lehmann is explicitly referring to the works of Heiner Müller. Born in Saxony in 1929 and composing most of his oeuvre in the German Democratic Republic (GDR), Müller's work both engages with and transcends his own socio-historical context. Müller is regarded by many as both a pioneer and central practitioner of postdramatic theatre in terms of his work as writer and director: thus we find constant references to him in Lehmann's monumental study, *Postdramatic Theatre*.[4] Likewise David Barnett's *Literature versus Theatre* discusses many features of Müller's work which would allow us to designate it as postdramatic, in the sense of challenging the categories of classical drama, through often being bereft of plot and/or dramatis personae, and tending to disrupt traditional notions of temporality on stage.[5] Müller's work is not exemplary of postdramatic theatre, but provides us with a historically influential model for the politics of postdramatic theatre: that is to say, for what it can do, and how it can go about doing this.

In the following, I shall examine the textual politics of Müller's work, through the lens of a short, so-called lyric text, 'Allein mit diesen Leibern' ('Alone with These Bodies'). As we shall see, Müller's theatre is not one of consensus, that is, the formation of fixed, stable opinions to which everyone in a collective of subjects subscribes, but rather, one of 'dissensus'. It is this that qualifies Müller's theatre as one of 'politics', to borrow the terminology of contemporary French philosopher Jacques Rancière.[6] Rancière, too, sees politics as a formal category, whereby politics shares with aesthetics its foundation on the *organisation* of the material within it, and adopting the framework of his theories of politics and democracy allows us to conceive of politics as something integral to the postdramatic aesthetic. Müller's form of political theatre is one which relies on theatre as a means, through performance, of eliciting a response from its audience, and this serves as a central archetype for the political potential of postdramatic theatrical forms: presented with the social medium of the theatre, the role of the recipient is to actively harness the potential encoded within the performance and convert it into a form of movement, in which various spectators may construct their own readings of the material presented to them. The audience's movement is not guided by a consensus of interpretation among the collective recipients, but is coloured by the possibility for and emergence of a collective punctuated by difference and individuality. Indeed, as we shall see, the very possibility for individual experience is predicated by the individual spectator's belonging to a collective which partakes in a shared discursive space, be it within or outside of the theatre. The potential efficacy of Müller's theatre is described by Georg Wieghaus, who writes that Müller's intention is the 'disruption of a superficial, social consensus'.[7] In so doing, the role of Müller's theatre, and indeed postdramatic performance, is to bring a democratic collective into existence in the auditorium.

Why a 'poem'?

It may be asked: why a poem? The choice of a poem could seem to be at odds with the intention of exploring and developing a thesis on the politics of theatre: it might appear to be taking one genre with its own form, and attempting to impose it on another completely different genre. Yet, in the case of Müller, the notion of genre is problematic to say the least. It would be fair to say that Müller 'doesn't do genre': throughout his career, genre distinctions are not watertight, and are continuously transgressed. His 1985 text, *Bildbeschreibung* (*Description of a Picture*), for example, is contained in the 'prose' volume of Suhrkamp's complete works edition, yet is handled by almost all critics as a theatrical work.[8] It is seemingly printed as a block of prose, but several things about the text suggest that it is a work for the stage: Müller's comment at the end that it is written 'in an extinct, dramatic structure';[9] the fact that it was written for the stage;[10] its repeated performance.[11] Conversely, his 1968 'play' *Der Horatier* (*The Horatian*) is ostensibly formally a piece of epic poetry; yet it is published as a play and performed on stage, including in a production at the Deutsches Theater 1988–91, directed by Müller himself. We can find numerous other instances in Müller's output in which conventional genre rules are confused and genre distinctions disappear altogether.[12]

The traditional genre markers are, however, readily assigned to Müller's literary production in its reception. The recent Suhrkamp *Werkausgabe*, for example, divides Müller's work along the lines of both genre and chronology, dividing his texts into poetry, prose, plays, writings and interviews. While this chronological organisation does not pay heed to the often painstakingly long gestation period of many of Müller's texts, and, in his view, amounts to the 'colonialist politics' of periodisation,[13] what follows from this genre categorisation is that Müller's works are received in different ways: both Marcus Kreikebaum and Katharina Ebrecht concentrate their studies solely on 'poems', and Uwe Schütte's recent book focuses purely on 'prose'.[14] Furthermore, this distinction between genres in Müller's work leads to some rather alarming conclusions, such as Jonathan Kalb's assertion that Müller was 'not a strong lyric poet'.[15]

Treatment of Müller's texts within the framework of their ontologisation along the lines of genre therefore leads to some difficulties when considering his apparently 'poetic' and 'prose' works. Genia Schulz, for example, in her 1980 study of Müller, sees such pieces merely as aids to the interpretation of the theatrical works, and therefore not to be treated as self-sufficient texts in their own right.[16] That such works were initially printed alongside larger, apparently more significant theatrical works in the original Rotbuch editions would appear to support this thesis. Thus, poems from the years in which Müller was more active as a playwright than a poet (i.e. between about 1956 and 1989) tend only to be read as ciphers, aiding us in our comprehension of the plays, and the man behind their composition. Yet the basis for this ontological status of Müller's poetry is a set of somewhat arbitrary distinctions between what counts as 'prose', 'poetry', and 'plays'. Schütte, for example, decides to consider anything printed in block text as 'prose',[17] a decision which, as we have seen from the example of *Description of a Picture* above, is immensely difficult to substantiate. Thus, I would like to examine whether we could consider the so-called lyric text, 'Alone with These Bodies', as a piece of postdramatic theatre. Following this, I shall examine what can be gained from reading it as a play. As we shall see, this can offer us a model for the political efficacy of postdramatic theatre, as well as provide us with rich insights into textual production within the so-called postdramatic mould.

Reading 'Alone with These Bodies'

'Alone with these Bodies' was composed around 1975–6 and first published in the 1977 Rotbuch edition of *Germania Tod in Berlin* (*Germania Death in Berlin*).[18] For reasons which will become clear below, I have taken the liberty of translating it myself:

ALONE WITH THESE BODIES
States Utopias
Grass grows
On the tracks
The words decay
On the paper
The eyes of women
Grow colder
Farewell to tomorrow
STATUS QUO[19]

Taken as a piece of commentary, it would perhaps be correct to presume that the text self-consciously comments on questions relating to Müller's plays, the political position of the playwright in the mid-1970s, and to theatre itself: we may see, for example, an image of dialectics at a standstill, and a sense of historical pessimism, which could well aid us in a reading of *Germania Death in Berlin*; and we shall meet readings below which could help to elucidate all three of these matters. Yet, to read the text purely as commentary surely limits the signifying capabilities within it. The language is packed with dense, polysemic signs: rather than finding a single possible meaning, that is, a definitive comment on a state of affairs in the world, we are confronted with multiple meanings, as my reading of the text will show. Structurally, the text for the most part appears to be organised into couplets: while the 'title' and lines one, eight, and nine seemingly stand alone, the other lines elide into pairs of grammatical, short sentences. Nonetheless, there is no punctuation in the poem. Therefore, despite adhering to the rules of capitalisation of the first letter of new sentences, and (in the German at least) the capitalisation of the first letter of the first word of a line and of a noun, there is nothing else to indicate that the lines cannot freely flow into each other, creating new connections.

The title, 'Alone with These Bodies', is generally regarded as an initial statement of pessimism. For Janine Ludwig, the bodies, or, to use the original German term 'Leiber', can be one of two things: either they are the mere bodies, that is, the corporeal husks of the lyrical subject's 'zombie-like fellow people' who roam the world unthinkingly;[20] or, in Ludwig's words, 'what is more likely, [. . .] the dead of history'.[21] Ludwig reinforces this idea by positing the presence in the poem of a lyrical subject, who expresses a sense of solitude as one who has fought for the states and utopias of the first line. Furthermore, according to Ludwig's reading, the states and utopias mentioned in the first line count among the deceased fallout of history.[22] A reading in which zombies and death figure is offered somewhat simplistically by Marc von Henning's English version of this text, which translates the German term 'Leiber' with 'corpses'.[23] Starting the text with a vision of death already arguably predisposes us to a certain response to it. We shall return to the reconsideration of the title further below.

When reading the text, we see that in line one what we may take to be a lyrical subject apparently contemplates states and utopias.

Initially, we might like to read these as a form of diametrical opposition: a state as an instantiation of a political system with all of its imperfections, versus the utopia, an idealised state which has not necessarily taken material form. What this would suggest is that the two differ in regard to their materiality and to their perfection. In terms of Müller's thought, the state in which he lived (the GDR) was not a perfect state, but rather an imperfect form of socialism. Then again, inhabiting a self-proclaimed *Übergangsgesellschaft* (transitional society), Müller was more than aware that the state and the utopia cannot be considered in terms of opposition, but, to use a term from Jacques Derrida's vocabulary, are more united in *différance*: the state strives towards becoming the utopia, only then to become a state, which precludes the very existence of the utopia in the first place.[24] Furthermore, we may ask: are these states and utopias the corpses of history, or living bodies of the present? They can, indeed, be in the present, albeit with differing material status: the state functions, albeit imperfectly, and at the same time there thrives a desire for a change to the established order and for a utopia which may one day exist.

The second image, in lines two to three, is ambiguous to say the least. Ludwig reads it as one of stagnation: grass grows on the tracks, hindering the movement of the train of revolution in its path towards the future.[25] Initially, however, the idea of grass growing sounds optimistic. In Müller's earlier play, *Mauser* (1970), the motif of grass represents the flourishing of individuals. Yet, the authoritarian chorus presents a paradoxical situation: 'Still we must | Tear out the grass, so that it stays green.'[26] That is, for order to be maintained, the individual who presents a challenge to that order must be neutralised. This reading is supported by a passage of Müller's 1992 autobiography, *Krieg ohne Schlacht*, in which he states, that '[h]umanity gives itself a purpose; the path to its goal demands control, organisation, discipline, selection. When it's about the emancipation of humanity, the enemy is an enemy of humanity, that is, not human.'[27] That is, utopias with a clear vision of the future work towards the neutralistaion of individual dissenters, finding legitimisation for this destruction through a clear Schmittian friend/foe binary. According to the above reading, therefore, the tracks upon which the grass grows might represent the Marxist teleological view of history of which Müller is heavily critical.[28] In this sense, they offer an association with the train tracks leading to the extermination camp of Auschwitz, an all-too-chilling embodiment of the technologised rational progression of history towards humanity's own self-destruction.[29] Thus, the grass growing and flourishing offers a possible future in which the destructive force of history is covered over. Nevertheless, the German phrase, 'Gras über etwas wachsen lassen', that is, 'to let the grass grow over something' resembles the English idiom of sweeping something under the carpet: we sweep something under the carpet in order to forget about it, but it is still there, right under our noses. Thus, while the destructive force of history is covered over, in our forgetting it, it haunts us still, like a spectre.

Following this in lines four to five is the image: 'The words decay | On the Paper'. This may refer to a lack of ability on the part of language and the old words to play any part in the time and the world inhabited by the author or the recipient: once written down, they merely decay, becoming impotent. This again suggests the motif of stagnation: not least, on an autobiographical level, it perhaps signifies Müller's concerns with his ineffectuality as a writer in bringing about any change in the world.[30] Nevertheless, we may read this differently: as soon as the word touches the paper, it ceases to be a truth, but rather becomes a moment of openness to interpretation, a polysemic sign.[31]

The image in lines six to seven is perhaps the most perplexing of all. Is it a personal reference to Müller's love life? Or is he pondering the demise or hindering of social interaction in general? A key to interpreting this image may be that, in Müller's works in this period, female figures are usually the possessors of a utopian revolutionary power.[32] The fact that their eyes become colder may be read in terms of the freezing of revolutionary hope: history becomes stagnant as the winds of change petrify into the 'frozen storm' which we find at the end of *Description of a Picture*.[33]

The final two lines emphasise a clear image of stagnation. As the 'lyrical subject' waves farewell to tomorrow, all that is left is the eternal return of the same, the 'STATUS QUO' of the last line. But, we may ask, will we read this 'tomorrow' as denoting the next day according to a teleological version of history? That is, the next rational step in the progression towards a predetermined utopian future? Or are we to read this as a recognition of the impossibility of any future? Furthermore, there are two senses of 'farewell' here: in the original German, 'Abschied von' may mean either that it is tomorrow which bids its farewell, or that someone or something bids farewell to it.[34]

Thus the text, as analysed above, is full of numerous possibilities: each line or pair of lines can be read in a variety of ways, and the preceding analysis by no means exhausts the possible interpretations of it. This further implies that no definitive and final meaning of the text can be ascertained. If we read the text as a commentary, we attempt to get something out of it, that is, a message, but that is to force a reading upon it. In assessing it aesthetically, as a text in its own right, the text has a chance to speak and offer an immense potential for different interpretations. Furthermore, taken as a whole, and combining the lines in different ways to create new images, the visions presented in 'Alone with these Bodies' may indeed call each other into question: while some of the images within it indicate becoming and, at that, a change of state in the things described, do we really arrive at a status quo, or is the poem in fact caught in an eternal recurrence of the same? Nonetheless, it is clear that the poem ends in stagnation of some sort, rendering, in Schulz's words 'a moment of death and standstill, which is experienced by the individual consciousness as well as by stagnating history'.[35] The individual, solitary reader of a poem can react to this stagnation and the images within the poem in his/her own way and, in interpreting the poem as s/he sees fit, consider ways of generating his/her own movement out of the status quo, which may feed into his/her own individual behaviour or modes of production.[36] It is, however, in the collective of a theatre audience that a larger, perhaps political, motion out of this stagnation can be generated. So, we might ask: what might be gained from reading this text as a piece of theatre?

The 'politics' of theatre

Before I illustrate what reading 'Alone with These Bodies' as a piece of theatre can show us, it would be useful to briefly outline the social function that Müller ascribes to theatre. The political programme of Müller's theatre can perhaps be summed up with reference to three important quotations. In an interview from 1985, he lauds the directorial practices of American director Robert Wilson, saying:

> Wilson never interprets [. . .]. There is a text, and it is delivered, but not evaluated and not coloured and not interpreted. [. . .] I think that's important. It is a democratic conception of theatre. Interpretation is the work of the spectator: it must not take place on the stage. This work must not be taken away from the spectator. It is consumerism, to take this work away from the spectator, spoon-feeding. That is capitalist theatre.[37]

Müller returns to this idea of a 'democratic' form of theatre in an interview in which he discusses his work directing his 1956 play *Der Lohndrücker* (*The Scab/The Wagepresser*) at the Deutsches Theater in 1988. In this case, he speaks of the use of broad brushstrokes in painting as analogous to his method of directing:

We tried something similar with the dialogue, which was just spoken in a way, whereby it could not be evaluated. You cannot say who is right or who is wrong. It is more a case of leaving out nuance and emphasis, which lets a sentence be interpreted by each spectator, according to his own experience.[38]

In the two citations above, we can see that Müller is concerned with the ability of theatre to allow spectators to undertake their own interpretative work, and not to provide meaning for them: the generation of meaning is the work of the spectator on an individual basis. This is fundamental to the creation of a democratic theatre. The engagement of the spectator is also to be achieved through presenting dense, metaphorical language, which allows spectators to respond to a performance in a multitude of ways. Despite Müller's reference above to the spectator in the singular, he understands the individual to be partaking in the activity of meaning-generation collectively. In an interview in 1986, he states that collective experience is fundamental to the experience of the individual:

I believe people can only have experiences collectively. The individual doesn't have experiences. Collectives have experiences. But, because collectives are usually organised in such a way that the experiences are suppressed again straight away, it's about preventing this suppression process or disrupting it.[39]

In this passage, Müller emphasises that there are social conditions underlying all experience both within and outside of the theatre, but that the formal constitution of particular forms of collective forbid the emergence of particular experiences which do not conform to the general consensus of the rest of the collective. In the context of the theatre, what Müller calls for amounts to a collective of audience members, who share the same socio-historical context and are seated together in an auditorium, but in which consensus is forsaken, as the spectators may produce divergent readings of their collective experience. Müller clearly sees the role of theatre as one of allowing for a democratic collective to emerge through the experiencing of what takes place on stage. Away from centralised meaning and any sense of a pre-packaged ideology, the individuals in the collective space of the auditorium are encouraged to generate their own meanings of a performance. They may not achieve a synthesis of meaning, arriving at a definitive and fully formed interpretation of a performance, but are nonetheless responding to the material in a productive way, and as individuals within a collective.

Müller states that the function of art is 'to build islands [. . .], where fantasy can still reproduce itself'.[40] Thus, for Müller, theatre serves 'as a laboratory, in which situations or even social, collective fantasy can be made productive or even can first be created'.[41] That is, an experience which, in its interaction with the spectators, opens up a world of imagination and generates possibility for them. The activity of the audience is, according to Lehmann, integral to postdramatic theatre practice,[42] which engages spectators in 'the mobilisation of their own ability to react and experience in order to realise their participation in the process that is offered to them'.[43] The result of encouraging active participation on the part of individual spectators is that a collective is formed that is not bound by consensus, but rather by internal difference. This is described by Lehmann thus:

> The 'community' that arises is not one of similar people, i.e. a community of spectators who have been made similar through commonly shared motifs [. . .], but instead a common contact of different singularities who do not melt their respective perspectives into a whole but at most share or communicate affinities in small groups.[44]

The result is, in Lehmann's words, 'a community of heterogeneous and particular imaginations'.[45] Despite Lehmann's usage of the term 'community' (*Gemeinschaft*) over 'collective' (*Kollektiv*) or 'society' (*Gesellschaft*), which brings with it a different ideological weighting to that found in Müller's writings,[46] it is here that we cannot help but see a similarity with Müller's conception of the creation of 'islands [. . .] of disorder' in the audience.[47] That is, at the heart of both Müller's practise as director and playwright and Lehmann's interpretation of the postdramatic lies a clear similarity in the potential political role of theatre and how it can be effected. Postdramatic theatre practise, that is, focuses on the role of the spectator as that of becoming part of a collective, which is of equal importance for Müller.

We can see convergences here too with Rancière, and begin to indicate the suitability of his critical vocabulary for talking about postdramatic theatre: using Rancière's terms, the collective enacted through the postdramatic is characterised by dissensus, and in this sense, is a space of 'politics': the established modes of being, embodied in ways of acting, saying, and thinking (what Rancière calls the 'distribution of the sensible'[48]) are disrupted, giving space for the presence of alterity, and a reconfiguration of the sensible.[49] This generates an entirely new world of possibility,[50] with no centralised locus of meaning, and thus entertains the potential for new ways of experiencing and consequently inhabiting the shared discursive space of the world, challenging the stability and hegemony of consensus.[51] This figures, too, as Rancière's definition of democracy: 'Democracy is more than a social state. It is a specific partition [distribution] of the sensible, a specific regime of speaking whose effect is to upset any steady relationship between manners of speaking, manners of doing and manners of acting.'[52] Rancière conceives of such a collective being rendered in a way not dissimilar to that described by Müller: 'If there exists a connection between art and politics, it should be cast in terms of dissensus, the very kernel of the aesthetic regime: artworks can produce effects of dissensus precisely because they neither give lessons nor have any destination.'[53]

'Alone with These Bodies' as political theatre

It is this politics which emerges from 'Alone with These Bodies'. If we consider 'Alone with These Bodies' as a text which might be performed on stage for an audience, we can see its politics, and begin to imagine how this politics is enacted by it. The 'poem' (again, using scare quotes) bears the hallmarks of many other works of this period of Müller's literary production: an apparent dialectical movement, or the calling of it into question; rich, densely polysemic images; condensation; brevity; and stagnation; and formally, there are no dramatis personae, there is no character attribution, and no lyrical subject, i.e. addresser. Inasmuch as it bears these traits, it has much in common with a theatrical work such as *Die Hamletmaschine* (*The Hamlet Machine*) (1976–7) or much of *Der Auftrag* (*The Task/The Mission*) (1979). It would seem, therefore, that it is just as performable as the aforementioned texts: it will present similar issues regarding staging and the handling of the text (not least because of its brevity). Furthermore, the dense, highly metaphorical language of this poem is characteristic of countless other 'plays' by Müller, despite being considered a facet of 'lyric poetry'. But for Müller, it is precisely this metaphorical language which can allow theatre to fulfil its political function: rather than communicating fixed authorial meaning through allegory, Müller's texts engage their recipients in a creative process through metaphor. In Müller's, albeit characteristically borrowed, words, 'the author is smarter than allegory, metaphor smarter than the author'.[54]

The text ends with the motif of stagnation: the movement within it is a seemingly temporal one, as grass grows, and eyes become colder; yet, despite the temporal progression implied in these lines, at the end we are met with the ultimate denial of movement. There is no more tomorrow, but a large, looming 'STATUS QUO', printed in block capitals so as to take on the form of an immovable giant. The images in the text therefore aggregate to create a web of signs which resist movement, as the text is caught in a constant circle, endlessly returning to the status quo. In this sense, the text could indeed be considered pessimistic: there is no escape from the circular process of history, and there is the implication that we too will become nothing but the bodies of history one day. But the possibility for movement lies outside of the text: the text is not a finished work, but requires the creative input of the recipient.

Yet, we may ask: how might a director want to stage 'Alone with These Bodies'? Postdramatic theatre practitioners would appear well suited to a text such as 'Alone with These Bodies'. Not least, according to Lehmann's interpretation of postdramatic theatre, the theatrical text figures as yet another equal element of performance along with the bodies on stage and the space of the auditorium itself, and is not necessarily presented for its meaning, but may be deployed rather as acoustic material.[55] For Lehmann, this treatment of text and voice leads to the formation of a '*soundscape*' which 'creates a space of association in the mind of the spectator.'[56] The text could therefore be easily de-semanticised, and spoken in various ways, enhancing its polysemic qualities. If we look to the possibilities for performance of other texts by Müller which lack traditional dramatic characteristics, such as *The Hamlet Machine*, we can further imagine the numerous ways in which 'Alone with These Bodies' could be staged in the postdramatic mould.[57] Indeed, the very brevity of the text, and the temporal questions raised by it (i.e. the almost paradoxical growth towards stasis, and the eternal recurrence it seems to suggest) already recommend themselves to the aesthetic of the postdramatic: Lehmann notes the preponderance of 'an *aesthetic of repetition*' in postdramatic theatre, which further serves to de-semanticise the text and call for its constant re-evaluation through the repetition of elements of performance.[58] As much as Müller's text seems in one sense to be caught in a repetitive loop with neither beginning nor end, if staged in certain ways, it may, again in Lehmann's terms, 'gain the dimension of the *time "shared"* by the performers and the audience as a processuality that is on principle open and has structurally neither beginning, nor middle, nor end'.[59] To this extent, it would seem that 'Alone with These Bodies' not only could be performed as a piece of postdramatic theatre, but much within it addresses the development of a theatrical aesthetic which we now label 'postdramatic'.

In the setting of a collective experience, that of being in the auditorium, the recipients of 'Alone with These Bodies' can indeed be rendered democratic in the way suggested by both Müller and Lehmann. As already stated, the piece is rich in the possibility for numerous readings. Furthermore, the breakdown of movement in the text serves as a form of question mark in the Foucauldian sense: for Michel Foucault, questions marks 'must be left in suspense, where they pose themselves, only with the knowledge that the possibility of posing them may well open the way to a future thought'.[60] Thus, through stagnation, Müller's text encourages movement out of the circular motion of history. These ideas are suggested in the text of 'Alone with These Bodies' itself. The bodies of the title are ambiguous, but it is notable that Müller uses the German word 'Leib' as opposed to 'Körper' (a more material way of understanding the body), or 'Leiche' (corpse).[61] He is pointing to a more phenomenal understanding of the body which we find in postdramatic theatre: in the space of the theatre, the audience and performers are linked by their possession of phenomenal bodies ('Leib-Sein') into a form of collectivity; undoing the aesthetic distance rendered by the purely semiotic, representational body ('Körper-Haben') of the actor in classical drama.[62] If seen in this way, then we can shed new light on the title of 'Alone with These Bodies': it is only ('allein') *with* ('mit') these bodies ('diesen Leibern'), that is, in 'the collective of audience–actors',[63] that there is any possibility of an escape from the status quo. Words rot on the page, precisely because it is only in the social realm of the theatre where they can take effect on a collective. And in being heard and experienced in all their polysemy, they can enact the democratic collective Müller seeks to create. For Müller, this collectivity is one in a state of constant movement, with ever-evolving possibilities for difference and newness. In the words of the critic Fabian Lettow, Müller's audience is a collective characterised by 'non-completion'.[64]

A challenge

The very possibility of enacting the democratic collective to which Müller aspires is contained within the form of the text. He himself is conscious of this: citing the French film-maker, Jean-Luc Godard, he states that 'the task is not one of making political films, but of making films politically. So, it is about the treatment of material, the form, not the content'.[65] That is to say, for Müller, as with Godard in the case of film, the politics of theatre is a formal matter. The play of signifiers and the circular motion in 'Alone with These Bodies' demonstrate a model for the textual politics of a postdramatic theatre: that is, a theatre which actively encourages the creative production of its audience, without attempting to achieve a consensual community. Yet, Müller's – and arguably postdramatic theatre's – politics does not end there. Through experimentation with form, postdramatic theatre pushes notions of genre to their limits, and calls them into question. The borders between 'prose', 'poetry', and 'play' are blurred, as the traditional notions regarding what constitutes a theatrical text are left behind. The hierarchy of genre is mimetic in Rancière's sense, in that it reproduces the hierarchies of the political realm.[66] The postdramatic, conversely, is not: by refusing to ascribe to traditional genre markers, it disturbs our expectations of how to treat a text, disrupting the hierarchical order. As Poschmann astutely notes, even within the postdramatic theatre text, the hierarchy of 'main text' (such as dialogue) and 'secondary text' (such as scene titles and stage directions) dissolves.[67] As this glance at Müller illustrates, writers of postdramatic theatre write texts which defy and transgress the boundaries of form. In doing so, they demonstrate the very real revolutionary potential of textual politics. It is in confronting the assembled theatre audience with this formal experimentation that the postdramatic can usher in the possibility for a dissensual, democratic collective.

Notes

Introduction

1   Hans-Thies Lehmann, '"Postdramatic Theatre", a Decade Later', in Ivan Medenica (ed.), *Dramatic and Postdramatic Theater Ten Years After: Conference Proceedings*, Belgrade: Faculty of Dramatic Arts, 2011, pp. 31–46, here p. 34.

2   Ibid., p. 34.

3   Ibid., p. 35 (our emphasis).

4   Ibid., p. 36.

5   Giles defines 'generative' action as the particular type of individual action that is required to sustain the forward movement of consequential action that is essential to drama in traditional theories from Aristotle via Hegel to Brecht and Suzanne Langer. See Steve Giles, *The Problem of Action in Modern European Drama*, Stuttgart: Akademischer Verlag Hans-Dieter Heinz, 1981, pp. 3–23.

6   Hans-Thies Lehmann, *Postdramatic Theatre*, trans. Karen Jürs-Munby, London: Routledge, 2006, p. 34.

7   Elinor Fuchs, 'Postdramatic Theatre and the Persistence of the "Fictive Cosmos"', in Medenica, *Postdramatic Theater Ten Years After*, pp. 63–72, here p. 63.

8   Joe Kelleher, *Theatre and Politics*, Basingstoke: Palgrave Macmillan, 2009, pp. 8–9.

9   Lehmann, '"Postdramatic Theatre", a Decade Later', p. 35.

10   Lehmann, *Postdramatic Theatre*, pp. 85, 99.

11   Jan Deck, 'Politisch Theater machen – Eine Einleitung', in Jan Deck and Angelika Sieburg (eds), *Politisch Theater machen: Neue Artikulationsformen des Politischen in den darstellenden Künsten*, Bielefeld: transcript, 2011, pp. 11–28, here p. 12. All translations from German in this Introduction are our own unless otherwise noted.

12   Birgit Haas, *Modern German Political Drama 1980–2000*, Rochester, NY: Camden House, 2003, p. 7.

13 See Jan Cohen-Cruz, 'Motion of the Ocean: The Shifting Face of US Theater for Social Change since the 1960s', *Theatre* 31.3 (Fall 2001), pp. 95–107.

14 Lehmann, '"Postdramatic Theatre", a Decade Later', p. 35.

15 See for instance Shannon Jackson, *Social Works: Performing Art, Supporting Publics*, New York: Routledge, 2011, p. 11. Jackson asserts that, 'rather than paint, clay, or canvas, "intersubjectivity" is itself the substrate of the art event' (ibid., p. 45).

16 Deck, 'Politisch Theater machen', p. 14.

17 Jacques Rancière, *The Emancipated Spectator*, trans. Gregory Elliott, London: Verso, 2009, p. 2.

18 Ibid., p. 2.

19 Erika Fischer-Lichte, *The Transformative Power of Performance: A New Aesthetics*, trans. Saskya Iris Jain, Abingdon: Routledge, 2008, p. 138.

20 Helen Freshwater, *Theatre and Audience*, Basingstoke: Palgrave Macmillan, 2009, p. 3.

21 Referring to film, Müller insists that 'the task is not to make political films, but rather to make films in a political way. That is to say it is about how you manage the material, it is about the form, rather than the content.' Heiner Müller, 'Ich weiss nicht, was Avantgarde ist', in Frank Hörnigk (ed.), *Werke,* Volume 11, Frankfurt am Main: Suhrkamp, pp. 100–13, here p. 104.

22 Deck, 'Politisch Theater machen', p. 14.

23 Kelleher, *Theatre and Politics*, p. 24.

24 Rancière, *Emancipated Spectator*, p. 14.

25 See Karen Jürs-Munby, 'The Vexed Question of the Text in Postdramatic Theatre in a Cross-Cultural Perspective', in Medenica, *Postdramatic Theater Ten Years After*, pp. 83–94, here p. 89.

26 Lehmann, '"Postdramatic Theatre", a Decade Later', p. 33.

27 Deck, 'Politisch Theater machen', p. 22.

28 Kelleher, *Theatre and Politics*, p. 12.

29 Lehmann, *Postdramatisches Theater*, p. 457.

30 Hans-Thies Lehmann, *Das Politische Schreiben*, Berlin: Theater der Zeit, 2002, pp. 16–17. All translations from German are our own unless otherwise noted.

31 Joseph Wood Krutch, *'Modernism' in Modern Drama: A Definition and an Estimate*, Ithaca, NY: Cornell University Press, 1953, pp. 130–1.

32 Jenny Spencer, 'Editor's Introduction', in *Political and Protest Theatre after 9/11: Patriotic Dissent*, Routledge Advances in Theatre and Performance Studies, 19, New York: Routledge, 2012, pp. 1–15, here p. 8.

33 Deck, 'Politisch Theater machen', p. 17.

34 Lehmann, *Postdramatic Theatre*, pp. 37–8.

35 Deck, 'Politisch Theater machen', p. 13.

36 Raoul Hausmann, 'Dada empört sich, regt sich und stirbt in Berlin', in Karl Riha (ed.), *Dada/Berlin: Texte, Manifeste, Aktionen*, Stuttgart: Reclam, 1977, pp. 3–12, here p. 11. See also Hans Richter, *Dada: Art and Anti-Art*, trans. David Britt, London: Thames and Hudson, 1965, esp. Chapter 3.

37 Lehmann, *Postdramatic Theatre*, p. 61.

38 Krutch, *'Modernism' in Modern Drama*, p. 87.

39 Kelleher, *Theatre and Politics*, p. 23.

40 Ibid.

41 Bertolt Brecht, 'The Literarization of Theatre (Notes to the *Threepenny Opera*)', in *Brecht on Theatre, The Development of an Aesthetic*, ed. and trans. John Willett (London: Methuen, 1964), pp. 43–7, here p. 44.

42 Lehmann, *Postdramatic Theatre*, p. 185.

43 Ibid., p. 182.

44 Ibid., p. 25.

45 Brecht, Bertolt, 'Der Dreigroschenprozess: Ein soziologisches Experiment', in *Werke, Band 21*, Frankfurt am Main: Suhrkamp Verlag, 1992, pp. 448–514, here p. 469.

46 See Steve Giles, *Bertolt Brecht and Critical Theory*, Oxford: Peter Lang, 1998, p. 175.

47 Lehmann, '"Postdramatic Theatre", a Decade Later', p. 43.

48 Lehmann, *Das Politische Schreiben*, p. 19.

49 Rancière, *Emancipated Spectator*, p. 6.

50 Ibid., p. 17.

51 Lehmann, *Postdramatic Theatre*, p. 184.

52   Tracy C. Davis, and Bruce McConachie, 'Introduction', in *Theatre Survey*, special issue on audience research 39.2 (November 1998), p. 3.

53   Rancière, *Emancipated Spectator*, p. 11.

54   Ibid., p. 2.

55   Ibid., p. 14 (original emphasis).

56   Ibid., p. 7.

57   Ibid., pp. 2, 5.

58   Peter Boenisch, 'Acts of Spectating: The Dramaturgy of the Audience's Experience in Contemporary Theatre', in *Critical Stages*, 7 (November 2012). Available at: www.criticalstages.org/criticalstages7/entry/Acts-of-Spectating-The-Dramaturgy-of-the-Audiencersquos-Experience-in-Contemporary-Theatre?category=2#sthash.v8w2Pkl3.gZLc0n1r.dpuf (accessed 9 January 2013).

59   Lehmann, *Postdramatic Theatre*, pp. 185–6.

60   Ibid., p. 185.

61   Ernesto Laclauand Chantal Mouffe, *Hegemony and Socialist Strategy: Towards a Radical Democratic Politics*, 2nd edn, London: Verso, 2001, p. 99.

62   Lehmann, *Postdramatic Theatre*, p. 185.

63   Ibid., p. 101.

64   Deck, 'Politisch Theater machen', p. 13.

65   Lehmann, *Das Politische Schreiben*, pp. 14–15.

66   Boenisch, 'Acts of Spectating'.

67   Fuchs, 'Postdramatic Theatre and the Persistence of the "Fictive Cosmos"', pp. 66–8.

68   See Spencer, 'Editor's Introduction', p. 8.

Chapter 1

1   Hans-Thies Lehmann, *Das Politische Schreiben*, Berlin: Theater der Zeit, 2002, pp. 16–17. All translations from German are my own unless otherwise noted.

2   As Jürs-Munby points out in her own written response to Fuchs, the book manuscript was abridged by Lehmann himself for this and other

international translations. See Hans-Thies Lehmann, Karen Jürs-Munby and Elinor Fuchs, 'Lost in Translation?', in *TDR: The Drama Review* 52.4 (2008), pp. 13–20, here p. 18.

3 Elinor Fuchs, 'Postdramatic Theatre (Review)', in *TDR: The Drama Review* 52.2 (2008), pp. 178–83, here p. 182.

4 Ibid., p. 180.

5 Hans-Thies Lehmann, *Postdramatic Theatre*, trans. Karen Jürs-Munby, New York: Routledge, 2006, p. 175.

6 Lehmann, Jürs-Munby, and Fuchs, 'Lost in Translation?', p. 16.

7 Lehmann, *Postdramatic Theatre*, p. 24.

8 Ibid., pp. 24, 27.

9 Ibid., pp. 23–4.

10 Ibid., pp. 24–5.

11 Ibid., p. 33.

12 Ibid., p. 99.

13 Ibid., p. 33.

14 Ibid., p. 33 (original emphasis). A counter-voice here is that of Birgit Haas, who has no interest in a mode of performance that 'place[s] the process of "making sense" of the theatrical event on the shoulders of the spectator'. See Birgit Haas, 'The Return of Dramatic Drama in Germany after 1989', in Denise Varney (ed.), *Theatre in the Berlin Republic: German Drama since Reunification*, Berlin: Peter Lang, 2008, pp. 81–114, here p. 93. Haas traces – and valorises – a resurgence in Germany of a tradition of still 'dramatic drama', to which Brecht's oeuvre belongs, in which the 'postmodern dissolution of text, author and message is replaced by a structured, hierarchical and mimetic dramatic text' (p. 84). Although Haas does not engage theoretically with the issues in the same depth as Lehmann, she seems committed to an understanding of the political that is entirely based on content (i.e. political commitment), precisely one of the conceptions of the political that Lehmann works to challenge.

15 The complexities of this claim are explored in David Barnett's contribution to this book.

16 Lehmann, *Postdramatic Theatre*, p. 33. At times I find Lehmann's expositions in *Postdramatic Theatre* overly totalising of Brecht's quite

complicated and often contradictory – if not dialectical – positions. For a more nuanced approach to Brecht by Lehmann, see 'Der Andere Brecht', in *Das Politische Schreiben.*

17   Lehmann, *Postdramatic Theatre*, p. 180.

18   Although, for the sake of this argument, my emphasis will be on the so-called *formal* aspects of the postdramatic, I find it important to note that, if we are to take Lehmann's dialectical approach seriously, formal questions could never be abstractly divorced from questions of *content.*

19   Lehmann, *Postdramatic Theatre*, p. 50.

20   Walter Benjamin, 'The Author as Producer', in *Understanding Brecht*, London: NLB, 1973, p. 88. The original German text can be found in: 'Der Autor als Produzent', in *Versuche über Brecht*, Frankfurt am Main: Suhrkamp Verlag, 1966.

21   Walter Benjamin, *The Work of Art in the Age of Its Technological Reproducibility, and Other Writings on Media*, Cambridge: Belknap Press, 2008.

22   Benjamin, 'The Author as Producer', p. 93.

23   Ibid., p. 98.

24   Ibid., p. 93 (my emphasis).

25   Lehmann, *Postdramatic Theatre*, p. 105.

26   Ibid.

27   Ibid., p. 18.

28   Ibid., p. 85.

29   Erika Fischer-Lichte, *The Transformative Power of Performance: A New Aesthetics*, trans. Saskya Iris Jain, Abingdon: Routledge, 2008, pp. 39, 40, 44, 147.

30   Ibid., p. 23.

31   Ibid., p. 18.

32   Ibid., p. 9. In many ways, Fischer-Lichte's *event*-character shares much in common with the equally Romantic concept of 'relationality' developed by Nicolas Bourriaud in the field of contemporary visual art. See Nicolas Bourriaud, *Relational Aesthetics*, trans. Simon Pleasance and Fronza Woods, Collection Documents Sur L'art. Dijon: Les Presses du réel, 2002.

33   Marvin Carlson, 'Introduction', in Fischer-Lichte, *The Transformative Power of Performance*, pp. 1–10, here p. 6.

34   Ibid., p. 6.

35   Ibid., p. 44.

36   Ibid., p. 51.

37   Ibid., p. 170.

38   This is the title of Martin Jay's landmark study on the Frankfurt School. See Martin Jay, *The Dialectical Imagination: A History of the Frankfurt School and the Institute of Social Research, 1923–1950*, Berkeley: University of California Press, 1973.

39   Shannon Jackson's recent work also complicates – albeit in different terms – the binarising logics and 'easy' politics of Fischer-Lichte's conception of the relations between the 'aesthetic' and the 'social'. See Shannon Jackson, *Social Works: Performing Art, Supporting Publics*, New York: Routledge, 2011.

40   Fischer-Lichte, *The Transformative Power of Performance*, p. 203.

41   Hans-Thies Lehmann, 'Anagnorisis/Understanding/Performance', paper presented at the symposium 'Conjunctures of Performance and Philosophy: Conversations with Hans-Thies Lehmann and Freddie Rokem', UC Berkeley, 9 March 2010.

42   Lehmann, *Postdramatic Theatre*, p. 182.

43   Ibid., p. 183.

44   Karen Jürs-Munby frames the issue as follows: '[H]ow can theatre represent or refer to "the world" when the world – multiply mediatised and globalised as it is – has become less "surveyable" than ever? Or: what kind of forms of theatre do practitioners find to address the lack of agency in a world without "real" protagonists?' David Barnett, Hans-Thies Lehmann and Karen Jürs-Munby, 'Taking Stock and Looking Forward: Postdramatic Theatre', *Contemporary Theatre Review: An International Journal* 16.4 (2006), pp. 483–9, here p. 488.

45   Lehmann, *Postdramatic Theatre*, p. 175.

46   Ibid., p. 25.

47   Ibid.

48   Ibid., p. 100.

49 David Barnett, 'When Is a Play Not a Drama? Two Examples of Postdramatic Theatre Texts', *New Theatre Quarterly* 24.93 (2008), pp. 14–23, here p. 15 (my emphasis).

50 Lehmann, *Postdramatic Theatre*, p. 101.

51 Ibid., p. 102.

52 Ibid. (my emphasis).

53 Ibid., p. 103 (italics in original).

54 André Eiermann's recent work on the 'reality of illusion' in contemporary theatre extends this discussion in a number of interesting directions. See André Eiermann, 'Introductory Lecture: Realitäten der Illusion im zeitgenössischen Theater', paper presented at the symposium 'TO DO AS IF – Realitäten der Illusion im zeitgenössischen Theater', Justus-Liebig-Universität, Gießen, 6 July 2012.

55 Theodor W. Adorno, quoted in Lehmann, *Postdramatic Theatre*, p. 38.

56 ,Theodor W. Adorno, *Aesthetic Theory*, trans. Robert Hullot-Kentor, Minneapolis: University of Minnesota Press, 1997, p. 59.

57 Hans-Thies Lehmann, *Postdramatisches Theater*, Frankfurt am Main: Verlag der Autoren, 1999, pp. 456–7.

58 Lehmann, *Das Politische Schreiben*, p. 16.

59 Ibid., pp. 16–17.

60 Joe Kelleher, *Theatre & Politics*, New York: Palgrave Macmillan, 2009, p. 34.

61 Ibid., p. 43.

62 Ibid., p. 24.

63 Ibid., p. 29.

64 Alan Read, *Theatre, Intimacy & Engagement: The Last Human Venue*, New York: Palgrave Macmillan, 2008, p. 7.

65 Ibid., p. 6.

66 Ibid., p. 26.

67 Ibid.

68 Jacques Rancière, *The Emancipated Spectator*, trans. Gregory Elliott, London: Verso, 2009, p. 74.

69 Ibid., p. 105.

70 Lehmann, *Postdramatic Theatre*, pp. 179–80.

71 Ibid., p. 180.

72 Ibid., p. 101.

73 Lehmann, *Das Politische Schreiben*, p. 14.

Chapter 2

1 Hans-Thies Lehmann, *Postdramatic Theatre*, trans. Karen Jürs-Munby, Abingdon: Routledge, 2006, p. 33.

2 See Hans-Thies Lehmann, *Das Politische Schreiben: Essays zu Theatertexten*, Berlin: Theater der Zeit, 2002, pp. 219–37.

3 Berliner Ensemble/Helene Weigel (eds), *Theaterarbeit: 6 Aufführungen des Berliner Ensembles*, Dresden: VVV Dresdner Verlag, 1952, p. 434. All translations are my own.

4 See Brecht's poem, '1954, erste Hälfte', in Bertolt Brecht, *Werke: Große kommentierte Berliner und Frankfurter Ausgabe*, Volume 15, Frankfurt: Suhrkamp, 1993, p. 281. Brecht's *Werke* are hereafter referred to in the notes as BFA followed by the volume and page numbers.

5 Meg Mumford, 'Brecht on Acting for the 21st Century: Interrogating and Re-Inscribing the Fixed', *Communications from the International Brecht Society* 29.1 and 2 (2000), pp. 44–9, here p. 47.

6 See Theodor W. Adorno, *Negative Dialektik. Jargon der Eigentlichkeit*, ed. Rolf Tiedemann [=*Gesammelte Schriften*, vol. 6], Frankfurt/Main: Suhrkamp, 2003, p. 168.

7 Ibid., p. 10.

8 Heiner Müller, quoted in Müller and Alexander Weigel, 'Etwas für das Programmheft', in Linzer, Martin and Peter Ullrich (eds), *Regie Heiner Müller*, Berlin: Zentrum für Theaterdokumentation und –information, 1994, pp. 26–30, here p. 29.

9 In the following analysis, I refer to the video recording of the premiere, held in the Akademie der Künste Archive, AVM 33.3595.

10 See aro, 'Nach einer riesigen nationalen Tragödie', *Frankfurter Allgemeine Zeitung*, 16 February 1996.

11 Schleef consulted file 178 in the Brecht Archive. The script he submitted to Barbara Brecht-Schall for permission is available in the Berliner Ensemble Archive in File 190.

12 Franz Wille, 'Der Untergangsdirigent', *Theater heute* 4 (1996), pp. 6–12, here p. 12.

13 [Scharfenberg, Ute], [Documentation of Schleef's *Puntila*], undated, pp. 42, in Akademie der Künste Archive, Inszenierungsdokumentation ID 569.

14 Einar Schleef, quoted in Rolf Michaelis, 'Theater muß man von hinter der Bühne sehen', *Die Zeit*, 29 December 1995.

15 Günther Heeg, 'Herr und Knecht, Furcht und Arbeit, Mann und Frau: Einar Schleefs archäologische Lektüre von Brechts *Puntila*', *Brecht Yearbook* 23 (1997), pp. 147–52, here p. 147.

16 See Lehmann, *Postdramatic Theatre*, pp. 86–7.

17 Esther Slevogt, 'Die Utopie der finnischen Sauna', *die tageszeitung*, 20 February 1996.

18 Peter Hans Göpfert, 'Irgendwie geht es um Klassenkampf', *Berliner Morgenpost*, 19 February 1996.

19 See, for example, Klaus Dermutz, 'Paramilitärische Grundausbildung', *Frankfurter Rundschau*, 20 February 1996.

20 Michael Berger, 'Die Inszenierung', *Die Woche*, 23 February 1996.

21 Göpfert, 'Irgendwie geht es um Klassenkampf'.

22 Ernst Schumacher, 'Wer kennt den wahren Puntila?', *Berliner Zeitung*, 28 February 1996.

23 See Brecht, '[*Messingkauf*: Fragment B 13]', BFA 22: 711.

24 Schleef, quoted in Petra Kohse, 'Gegen die allmähliche Erstarrung', *die tageszeitung*, 20 November 1996.

25 Schleef, quoted in Ulrike Kahle, 'Spiel zwischen Männern', *Die Woche*, 23 February 1996.

26 In the following analysis I draw on the performance I saw at the Deutsches Theater on 5 April 2011. Reviews consulted refer to both the Thalia and Deutsches Theater productions, which were essentially the same.

27 Christine Dössel, 'Was heißt hier zurechnungsfähig?', *Süddeutsche Zeitung*, 12 March 2007.

28 Lehmann, *Postdramatic Theatre*, p. 68.

29 Hans-Dieter Schütt, 'Die totale Ernüchterungszelle', *Neues Deutschland*, 2 November 2009.

30 Thalheimer, quoted in Petra Schellen, 'Puntila ist ein rächender Gott', *die tageszeitung*, 10 March 2007.

31 Thalheimer, quoted in ibid.

32 Brecht, 'Steckels zwei Puntilas', *BFA* 24: 310.

33 Peter M. Boenisch, 'Exposing the Classics: Michael Thalheimer's *Regie* beyond the Text', *Contemporary Theatre Review* 18.1 (2008), pp. 30–43, here p. 31.

34 Simone Kaempf, 'Ein sinnloser Anfall von Nüchternheit', *die tageszeitung*, 12 March 2007.

35 Thalheimer, quoted in Maike Schiller, 'Regieführen ist eine Anmaßung', *Hamburger Abendblatt*, 9 March 2007.

36 See Hans-Thies Lehmann, 'Michael Thalheimer, Gestenchoreograph', in Marion Tiedtke and Philipp Schulte (eds), *Die Kunst der Bühne. Positionen des zeitgenössischen Theaters*, Berlin: Theater der Zeit, 2011, pp. 85–95, for an argument for a more politicised Thalheimer.

37 Lehmann, *Postdramatisches Theater*, p. 190. This quotation does not, to my knowledge, appear in the English translation.

38 Rüdiger Schaper, 'Das Theater und sein Kater', *Der Tagesspiegel*, 1 November 2009.

39 Lehmann, *Postdramatic Theatre*, p. 74.

Chapter 3

1 Hans-Thies Lehmann, *Postdramatic Theatre*, trans. Karen Jürs-Munby, Abingdon and London: Routledge, 2006, pp. 175–87.

2 Ibid., p. 175.

3 See Werner Mittenzwei, *Das Leben des Bertolt Brecht oder Der Umgang mit den Welträtseln*, Volume 1, Berlin: Aufbau Taschenbuch Verlag, 1986, p. 256.

4 Sarah Kane, *Blasted*, London: Methuen, 1996.

5 Peter Handke, *Die Fahrt im Einbaum oder das Stück zum Film vom Krieg*, Frankfurt am Main: Suhrkamp, 1999.

6 Peter Handke, *Journey to the Rivers. Justice for Serbia*, trans. Scott Abbott, New York: Viking Adult, 1997.

7 Friedrich Schiller, *On the Aesthetic Education of Man*, trans. Reginald Snell, Mineola, NY: Dover Publications, 2004.

8 Jacques Rancière, *The Politics of Aesthetics*, trans. Gabriel Rockhill, New York: Continuum, 2004.

9 Jacques Rancière, *Les destin des image*, Paris: La Fabrique éditions, 2003.

10 Jacques Rancière, *The Emancipated Spectator*, trans. Gregory Eliott, London: Verso, 2009, pp. 10–12.

11 Erika Fischer-Lichte, *The Transformative Power of Performance. A New Aesthetics*, trans. Saskia Jayn, London: Routledge, 2008.

12 Ibid., pp. 38–9.

13 Marvin Carlson, *The Haunted Stage. The Theatre as Memory Machine*, Ann Arbor: University of Michigan Press, 2001.

14 Ibid., pp. 6–7.

15 Ibid., pp. 16–51.

16 Ibid., pp. 131–64.

17 Stephen Greenblatt (ed.), *Cultural Mobility: A Manifesto*, Cambridge: Cambridge University Press, 2010.

18 Freddie Rokem, *Performing History*, Iowa City: University of Iowa Press, 2000.

19 Ibid., pp. xii–xiii.

20 Ibid., pp. 111–16.

21 Ibid., p. 117.

22 Ibid., p. 116.

23 Lehmann, *Postdramatic Theatre*, pp. 175–87.

24 Karen Jürs-Munby, 'Introduction', in Lehmann, *Postdramatic Theatre*, pp. 1–15, here pp. 2–3; Lehmann, *Postdramatic Theatre*, pp. 42–5.

25 Unpublished manuscript courtesy of Rowohlt Verlag.

Chapter 4

1 See Theodor W. Adorno, *Ästhetische Theorie*, Frankfurt am Main: Suhrkamp Verlag, 2003 [1970], p. 354.

2 Georg Wilhelm Friedrich Hegel, *Ästhetik* (Die Poesie, III [Die dramatische Poesie], 3, c, α, αα), ed. F. Bassenge, 2nd edn, Undated, Volume II, Berlin-Weimar: Europäische Verlagsanstalt, p. 566.

3 Hegel, *Ästhetik* (Die Poesie, III [Die dramatische Poesie], 3, c, β, αα), p. 581.

4 Hegel, *Ästhetik* (Die romantische Kunstform, Einleitung), p. 490.

5 See Martin Heidegger, 'Einführung in die Metaphysik', § 52, 53 *Gesamtausgabe*, Volume 40, Frankfurt am Main: Vittorio Klostermann, 4th edn, 1976, pp. 153–82.

6 See, for example, Lucien Goldmann, *Le dieu caché ; étude sur la vision tragique dans les Pensées de Pascal et dans le théâtre de Racine*, Paris: Gallimard, 1955.

7 Clifford Geertz, *The Interpretation of Cultures*, New York: Basic Books, 1973.

8 See Jacques Lacan, *Le Séminaire, Livre VII: L'éthique de la psychanalyse, 1959–1960*, Paris: Editions du Seuil, 1986, pp. 285–331.

9 Georges Batailles, *The Tears of Eros*, trans. Peter Connors, San Francisco: City Lights Books, 1989, p. 66.

10 See Gilles Deleuze, *Nietzsche and Philosophie*, trans. Hugh Tomlinson. New York: Columbia University Press, 1983 [1962].

11 See Guy Debord, *Society of the Spectacle*, trans. Donald Nicholson, New York: Zone Books, 1992 [1967].

12 See Book VI of Aristotle, *Poetics*, trans. S. H. Butcher, New York: Dover, 1997.

13 See, for example, Christiane Sourvinou-Inwood, *Tragedy and Athenian Religion*, Lanham, MD: Lexington Books, 2003.

14 Jacques Rancière, 'Schiller und das ästhetische Versprechen', in Felix Ensslin (ed.), *Spieltrieb – Was bringt die Klassik auf die Bühne? Schillers Ästhetik heute*, Berlin: Theater der Zeit, 2006, pp. 39–55.

15 Friedrich Schiller, *Über die ästhetische Erziehung des Menschen in einer Reihe von Briefen* (21. Brief), Stuttgart: Reclam, 2000, p. 86. All translations from German are my own unless otherwise noted.

16 Rancière, 'Schiller und das ästhetische Versprechen', p. 45.
17 Immanuel Kant, *Critique of Judgment*, trans. J. H. Bernard, New York: Hafner Press, § 9, pp. 53–4.
18 Rancière, 'Schiller und das ästhetische Versprechen', p. 43.
19 Ibid.
20 Jacques Rancière, *The Politics of Aesthetics*, trans. Gabriel Rockhill, New York: Continuum, 2006, p. 13.
21 Rancière, 'Schiller und das ästhetische Versprechen', p. 53.
22 Ibid., p. 38.
23 Jacques Rancière, *The Emancipated Spectator*, trans. Gregory Elliott, London: Verso, 2009, p. 22.
24 Sarah Kane, '4.48 Psychosis', in *Complete Plays*, London: Methuen, p. 245.
25 See Heiner Müller, *Gesammelte Irrtümer 2: Interviews und Gespräche*, Frankfurt am Main: Verlag der Autoren, 1990, p. 13.

Chapter 5

1 Hans-Thies Lehmann, *Postdramatic Theatre*, trans. Karen Jürs-Munby, Abingdon and New York: Routledge, 2006, p. 99f.
2 Peter Szondi, *Theory of the Modern Drama*, trans. Michael Hays, *Boundary 2*, 11.3 (1983), pp. 191–230; excerpts from *Theorie des modernen Dramas, 1880–1950*, Frankfurt am Main: Suhrkamp, 1965 [1959].
3 Jacques Rancière, *Aesthetics and Its Discontents*, trans. Steven Corcoran, Cambridge: Polity, 2009.
4 Lehmann, *Postdramatic Theatre*, p. 163.
5 Ibid., pp. 162–7.
6 Ibid., p. 163.
7 Ibid., p. 95.
8 François Cusset, 'Theory (Madness of)', *Radical Philosophy*, 167 (2011), special issue 'From Structure to Rhizome: Transdisciplinarity in French Thought', pp. 24–30, here p. 27.

9   See Gerald Siegmund, *Abwesenheit: Eine performative Ästhetik des Tanzes,* Bielefeld: Transcript, 2006.

10 See André Lepecki, 'Skin, Body and Presence in Contemporary European Choreography', *The Drama Review* 43.4 (1999), pp. 129–40.

11 Gerald, Siegmund, 'Strategies of Avoidance: Dance in the Age of the Mass Culture of the Body', in Peter M Boenisch and Ric Allsopp (eds), *Bodiescapes, Performance Research* 8.2 (2003), pp. 82–90.

12 Una Bauer, 'The Movement of Embodied Thought: The Representational Game of the Stage Zero of Signification in Jérôme Bel', *Performance Research* 13.1 (2010), pp. 35–41.

13 See Sabine Sörgel, *Dance and the Body in Western Theatre: 1948 to the Present*, Basingstoke and New York: Palgrave Macmillan, 2013.

14 Lehmann, *Postdramatic Theatre*, p. 163.

15 Helmut Ploebst, *No Wind No Word – New Choreography in the Society of the Spectacle*, Munich: Kieser, 2001.

16 Boris Groys, *Under Suspicion: A Phenomenology of Media*, trans. Carsten Strathausen, New York: Columbia University Press, 2012.

17 Whereas this production introduced a largely unknown, yet influential moment of Eastern European performance to a Western audience, Janša's *Fake It* (2007) introduced an Eastern European perspective on icons of Western choreography, from Pina Bausch to William Forsythe, Trisha Brown and Steve Paxton: the Slovenian dancers, who had never had the opportunity to actually see these legendary performances themselves as they grew up, reconstructed them by learning them from (mostly pirated) recordings found on the internet. *Fake It* then also invented such a re-enactment of an entirely fictitious choreographer, too, a fabrication which even some scholarly colleagues with whom I attended the performance failed to detect.

18 See Ana Vujanović, 'The Choreography of Singularity and Difference: *And Then* by Eszter Salamon', *Performance Research* 13.1 (2008), pp. 123–30.

19 Karen Jürs-Munby, 'Introduction', in Lehmann, *Postdramatic Theatre*, pp. 1–15, here pp. 7–9.

20 See Ramsay Burt, 'History, Memory, and the Virtual in Current European Dance Practice', *Dance Chronicle* 32.3 (2009), pp. 442–67;

Yvonne Hardt, 'Staging the Ethnographic of Dance History: Contemporary Dance and Its Play with Tradition', *Dance Research Journal* 43.1 (2011), pp. 27–42.

21 Brian Holmes, 'The Flexible Personality: For a New Cultural Critique' (2002). Available at: http://eipcp.net/transversal/1106/holmes/en (accessed 22 September 2012); Luk Boltanski and Eve Chiapello, *The New Spirit of Capitalism*, London and New York: Verso, 2005.

22 Anne Teresa De Keersmaeker and Thierry De Mey, 'The Mutual Infection between Dance and Music', *Theaterschrift* 9 (1995), pp. 202–32, here p. 225f.

23 See Alenka Zupančič, *Ethics of the Real: Kant and Lacan*, London and New York: Verso, 2000. In her important work she brings Lacan and Kant together.

24 See Oliver Marchart, *Post-foundational Political Thought: Political Difference in Nancy, Lefort, Badiou and Laclau*, Edinburgh: Edinburgh University Press, 2007. Similar arguments are pursued in Ernesto Laclau and Chantal Mouffe's approach to political agency and 'agonism', or in the theory of Judith Butler and Leo Bersani. See Judith Butler, Ernesto Laclau and Slavoj Žižek, *Contingency, Hegemony, Universality: Contemporary Dialogues on the Left*, London and New York: Verso, 2000.

25 See Slavoj Žižek, *The Parallax View*, Cambridge, MA: MIT Press, 2006.

26 Jacques Rancière, *The Emancipated Spectator*, trans. Gregory Elliott, London and New York: Verso, 2009.

27 Nicholas Bourriaud, *Relational Aesthetics,* trans. Simon Pleasance, Paris: Presses du Réel, 2002.

28 Slavoj Žižek, *The Ticklish Subject: The Absent Centre of Political Ontology*, London and New York: Verso, 2000.

29 Slavoj Žižek, *Tarrying with the Negative: Kant, Hegel, and the Critique of Ideology*, Durham: Duke University Press, 1993, p. 21.

30 Mladen Dolar, 'Beyond Interpellation', *Qui parle* 6.2 (1993), pp. 75–96.

31 Alenka Zupančič, *Ethics of the Real: Kant and Lacan*, London and New York: Verso, 2000, p. 66.

32 In the contrast of symptomal and fetishistic modes of dramaturgies, I am reworking a prompt from Žižek about *Ideologiekritik,* in Slavoj

Žižek, *In Defense of Lost Causes*, London and New York: Verso, 2008, p. 296f.

33 Ibid., p. 296.

34 Eszter Salamon, post-performance discussion after the performance of *Dance for Nothing* at Black Box, Gasteig, Munich/Germany, 4 November 2010.

Chapter 6

1 The exhibition *documenta X* (1997) provided a critical review of political art in the post-war era and strongly influenced the debates in the field. See Catherine David (ed.), *Politics/Poetics: Documenta X – The Book*, Ostfildern: Cantz, 1997. For the German context, including a discussion of Schlingensief's role in the reorientation process, see Holger Kube Ventura, *Politische Kunst Begriffe*, Vienna: Ed. Selene, 2002.

2 Hans-Thies Lehmann, *Postdramatic Theatre*, New York and London: Routledge, 2006, p. 17.

3 Ibid., pp. 185–6 (original emphasis).

4 For more information on Schlingensief's work see Tara Forrest and Anna Teresa Scheer (eds), *Christoph Schlingensief. Art without Borders*, Bristol/Chicago: Intellect, 2010; Susanne Gaensheimer (ed.), *Christoph Schlingensief: The German Pavilion. 54th Venice Biennale, 2011*, Berlin/New York: Sternberg Press, 2011; and www.schlingensief.com (accessed 16 October 2012).

5 See Schlingensief in Wilhelm Pauli, 'Depressiv, aber heiter', Interview with Christoph Schlingensief, *Die Woche*, 17 May 1996.

6 Schlingensief in Egbert Hörmann and Horst Johnson, 'Unser Mann fürs Grobe', Interview with Christoph Schlingensief, *Prinz*, May 1996. The translation is my own.

7 For images of the production, see the picture gallery at www.schlingensief.com.

8 The translation is my own, based on the video recording provided by the Volksbühne. I would like to thank the Archiv der Volksbühne am Rosa-Luxemburg-Platz in Berlin and the Archiv der Akademie der Künste in Berlin for providing the video recording and further material.

9 See the description of the production at www.schlingensief.com.

10 In some of his later works, Schlingensief invited participants to get more actively involved in determining the project's goals and actions. In *Chance 2000*, the audience could become party members and election candidates and were able to shape the party program and activities according to their own ideas. The *Opera Village Africa* in Burkina Faso provides facilities for education and artistic production, handing over the creative task to the participants.

11 For a discussion of subversive affirmation, see Inke Arns and Sylvia Sasse, 'Subversive Affirmation. On Mimesis as Strategy of Resistance', in Irwin (ed.), *East Art Map: Contemporary Art and Eastern Europe*, Cambridge, MA/London: MIT Press, 2006, pp. 444–55; on over-identification, see Slavoj Žižek, 'Why Are NSK and Laibach Not Fascists?', in Laura Hoptman and Tomáš Pospiszyl (eds), *Primary Documents. A Sourcebook for Eastern and Central European Art Since the 1950s*, New York: Museum of Modern Art, 2002 [1993], pp. 285–8; on *stiob*, see Alexej Yurchak, *Everything Was Forever, Until It Was No More. The Last Soviet Generation*, Princeton, NJ: Princeton University Press, 2006.

12 A personal account of a spectator-participant can be found in Sandra Umathum, 'Theatre of Self-Questioning: Rocky Dutschke, '68, or the Children of the Revolution', in Forrest and Scheer (eds), *Christoph Schlingensief. Art without Borders*, pp. 57–70.

Chapter 7

1 Derek Paget, '"Acting with Facts": Actors Performing the Real in British Theatre and Television Since 1990. A Preliminary Report on a New Research Project', *Studies in Documentary Film* 1.2 (2007), pp. 165–76; Thomas Irmer, 'A Search for New Realities: Documentary Theatre in Germany', *The Drama Review* 50.3 (2006), pp. 16–28.

2 In Britain, the headphone-verbatim form was introduced by British director, Mark Wing-Davey, in his Drama without Paper Workshop (London Actor's Centre 2001). In Australia, Roslyn Oades has worked extensively with an audio-verbatim approach. See Roslyn Oades, 'Creating a Headphone-Verbatim Performance', in Paul Brown (ed.), *Verbatim. Staging Memory and Community*, Sydney: Currency Press, 2010, pp. 84–7. Regarding autobiographical performance, see Deirdre Heddon, *Autobiography and Performance*, Houndmills, Basingstoke and New York: Palgrave Macmillan, 2008. For Rimini Protokoll's theatre of experts see Miriam Dreysse and Florian Malzacher (eds), *Experts of the Everyday. The Theatre of Rimini Protokoll*, Berlin: Alexander Verlag, 2008.

3 Ortrud Gutjahr, 'Interkulturalität als Forschungsparadigma der Literaturwissenschaft. Von den Theoriedebatten zur Analyse kultureller Tiefensemantiken', in Dieter Heimböckel, Irmgard Honnef-Becker, Georg Mein and Heinz Sieburg (eds), *Zwischen Provokation und Usurpation: Interkulturalität als (un)vollendetes Projekt der Literatur- und Sprachwissenschaften*, Munich: Fink, 2010, pp. 17–41, here p. 28. Translations from German in this chapter are our own unless otherwise noted. Gutjahr speaks of this insecurity with regard to the openness of cultural systems. We transfer it to an aesthetic method.

4 David Shields, *Reality Hunger: A Manifesto*, New York: Alfred Knopf, 2010, p. 81.

5 See Erika Fischer-Lichte, 'Theatralität und Inszenierung', in Erika Fischer-Lichte (ed.), *Theatralität*, Tübingen: Narr, 2007, pp. 10–12.

6 Susanne Knaller and Harro Müller, 'Authentisch/Authentizität', in *Historisches Wörterbuch der ästhetischen Grundbegriffe*, Karlheinz Barck and Martin Fontius et al. (eds), *Historisches Wörterbuch der ästhetischen Grundbegriffe*, Stuttgart: Metzler, 2005, pp. 40–65.

7 Meg Mumford, 'Verfremdung', in Denis Kennedy (ed.), *The Oxford Encyclopedia of Theatre and Performance*, Volume 2, Oxford: Oxford University Press, 2003, pp. 1404–5.

8 Janelle Reinelt, 'The Promise of Documentary', in Alison Forsyth and Chris Megson (eds), *Get Real: Documentary Theatre Past and Present*, Basingstoke: Palgrave Macmillan, 2009, pp. 6–23, here p. 9.

9   Pam Morris, *Realism. The New Critical Idiom*, London: Routledge, 2003, p. 6.

10 See Hans-Thies Lehmann, *Postdramatic Theatre*, London and New York: Routledge, 2006, pp. 86–90, here p. 95.

11 See version 1.0 website, www.versiononepointzero.com/index.php/about/ (accessed 10 September 2011). The analysis in this chapter is based on a performance in the 13–17 October 2004 run at Performance Space, Sydney.

12 ibis Hotel Berlin, 17–19 and 21–4 September 2010, Potsdamer Platz. For further information see Rimini Protokoll's website www.rimini-protokoll.de/website/en/project_4677.html and www.ciudadesparalelas.com/menu_aleman.html (both accessed 3 March 2011).

13 Lehmann, *Postdramatic Theatre*, pp. 99–104.

14 Ibid., p. 101.

15 Linda Jaivin, 'Theatre of the Displaced', *The Bulletin* 122.16, website, www.austlit.edu.au/austlit/page/C504878 (20 April 2004, accessed 1 September 2011).

16 John McCallum, '*CMI (A Certain Maritime Incident):* Introduction', *Australasian Drama Studies*, 48 (2006), pp. 136–42, here p. 138. See also Helen Gilbert and Jacqueline Lo, *Performance and Cosmopolitics: Cross-Cultural Transactions in Australasia*, Basingstoke and New York: Palgrave Macmillan, 2007, p. 203.

17 Version 1.0, *CMI (A Certain Maritime Incident)* script, in *Australasian Drama Studies* 48 (2006), pp. 143–76, here p. 147.

18 Caroline Wake, 'Caveat Spectator: Juridical, Political and Ontological False Witnessing in *CMI (A Certain Maritime Incident)*', *Law Text Culture* 14.1 (2010), pp. 160–87, here p. 176.

19 David A. Williams, 'Political Theatrics in the "Fog of War"', *Australasian Drama Studies* 48 (2006), pp. 115–29, here p. 122.

20 Wake, 'Caveat Spectator', p. 170.

21 Paul Dwyer, 'The Inner Lining of Political Discourse: Presenting the version 1.0 Remix of the Senate Select Committee on a Certain Maritime Incident', *Australasian Drama Studies* 48 (2006), pp. 130–5, here p. 132.

22 Ibid., p. 131.

23 See Wake, 'Caveat Spectator', p. 168.

24 Dwyer, 'The Inner Lining of Political Discourse', pp. 134–5.

25 McCallum, '*CMI (A Certain Maritime Incident)*: Introduction', p. 170.

26 Williams, 'Political Theatrics and the "Fog of War"', p. 123.

27 See Theresia Birkenhauer, 'Fiktion', in Erika Fischer-Lichte and Doris Kolesch et al. (eds), *Metzler Lexikon Theatertheorie*, Stuttgart: Metzler, 2005, pp. 107–9.

28 See www.ciudadesparalelas.com/conceptoing.html (accessed 3 March 2011).

29 See www.ciudadesparalelas.com/hoteling.html (accessed 25 March 2012).

30 Ibid.

31 Unpublished letter, dated 18 September 2010.

32 See Wolfgang Iser, *The Fictive and the Imaginary. Charting Literary Anthropology*, Baltimore: Johns Hopkins University Press, 1993, pp. 222–38.

33 See www.ciudadesparalelas.com/hotelale.html (accessed 4 March 2011).

34 See Jan Deck, 'Zur Einleitung: Rollen des Zuschauers im postdramatischen Theater', in Jan Deck and Angelika Sieburg (eds), *Paradoxien des Zuschauens. Die Rolle des Publikums im zeitgenössischen Theater*, Bielefeld: transcript, 2008, pp. 9–19.

35 See Hans-Thies Lehmann, *Das Politische Schreiben. Essays zu Theatertexten*, Berlin: Theater der Zeit, 2002, p. 17.

36 Peter Boenisch, 'Towards a Theatre of Encounter and Experience: Reflexive Dramaturgies and Classic Texts', *Contemporary Theatre Review* 20.2 (2010), pp. 162–72, here p. 171.

37 See Lehmann, *Das Politische Schreiben*, p. 19.

38 Christine Regus, *Interkulturelles Theater zu Beginn des 21. Jahrhunderts: Ästhetik – Politik – Postkolonialismus*, Bielefeld: transcript, 2009, p. 11.

39 Erika Fischer-Lichte, 'Reality and Fiction in Contemporary Theatre', *Theatre Research International* 33.1 (2008), pp. 84–96, here p. 95.

40 Lehmann, *Postdramatic Theatre*, p. 185.

Chapter 8

1 Hans-Thies Lehmann, *Postdramatic Theatre*, trans. Karen Jürs-Munby, New York: Routledge, 2006, p. 178. This chapter is adapted from a chapter in Shannon Jackson, *Social Works: Performing Art, Supporting Publics*, London and New York: Routledge, 2011.

2 Mark Landler, 'Hi, I'm in Bangalore (but I can't say so)', *New York Times*, 21 March 2001, A1, C4.

3 For a lengthier discussion of such topics in relation to other artists see Jackson, *Social Works: Performing Art, Supporting Publics*. I am also currently working with Marianne Weems on a full-length book on the history of TBA to be published by MIT Press.

4 Michael Hardt and Antonio Negri, *Multitude: War and Democracy in the Age of Empire*, New York: Penguin, 2004, p. 108.

5 Saskia Sassen interviewed by Dale Leorke, 'Power, Mobility, and Diaspora in the Global City', *Platform: A Journal of Media and Communication* 1 (July 2009), pp. 103–8, here p. 103.

6 Saskia Sassen, 'Embeddedness of Electronic Markets: The Case of Global Capital Markets', in Karin Knorr Cetina and Alex Preda (eds), *The Sociology of Financial Markets*, Oxford: Oxford University Press, 2005, pp. 17–37.

7 Hardt and Negri, *Multitude*, p. 109.

8 Lehmann, *Postdramatic Theatre,* pp. 185–6.

9 Abdou Maliqualim Simone, 'People as Infrastructure: Intersecting Fragments in Johannesburg', *Public Culture* 16.3 (Fall 2004), pp. 407–29.

10 Ernesto Laclau and Chantal Mouffe, *Hegemony and Socialist Strategy: Towards a Radical Democratic Politics*, 2nd edn, London: Verso, 2001, pp. 98–9 (original emphasis).

11 Ibid., p. 111.

12 Tara McPherson, 'Reload: Liveness, Mobility and the Web', in Wendy Hui Kyong Chun and Thomas Keenan (eds), *New Media, Old Media: A History and Theory Reader*, New York: Routledge, 2005, pp. 199–209, here pp. 200, 202.

13 McPherson, 'Reload', p. 202.

14 Charles McNulty, 'A Dizzying Global Vision', *Los Angeles Times*, 28 February 2004, Available at: http://articles.latimes.com/2004/feb/29/ entertainment/ca-mcnulty29.

15 Marianne Weems, 'Call Centers – TRIP to Bangalore', *Alladeen* Production Files, Unpublished.

16 Mary-Jane Jacob (ed.), *Gordon Matt-Clark: A Retrospective*, Chicago: Museum of Contemporary Art, 1985.

17 Landler, 'Hi, I'm in Bangalore', A1, C4.

18 Ibid.

19 Marianne Weems, Early Script Material, 22 April 2002, *Alladeen* Production Files, unpublished.

20 Marianne Weems, interview with author, 20 January 2009.

21 Marianne Weems, in discussion with author, 10 June 2008.

22 Moe Angelos, in discussion with author, 11 June 2008.

23 Lehmann, *Postdramatic Theatre*, p. 68.

24 Pico Iyer, interview with Dave Weich, 27 March 2000 (available at: powells.com/authors/iyer.html), in Marianne Weems, *Jet Lag* Production Files, Unpublished.

25 Jennifer Parker-Starbuck, 'Lost in Space? Global Placelessness and the Non-Places of *Alladeen*', in Leslie Hill and Helen Paris (eds), *Performance and Place*, London: Palgrave Macmillan, 2006, pp. 155–69, here p. 162. See also Jennifer Parker-Starbuck, 'Global Friends: The Builders Association at BAM', *Performing Arts Journal* 26.2 (2004), pp. 96–102.

26 Parker-Starbuck, 'Lost in Space?', p. 162.

27 Margo Jefferson, 'The Other End of the Phone, Workers Stripped of Their Identities', *New York Times*, 4 December 2003, available at: www.nytimes.com/2003/12/04/ theatre/theatre-review-other-end-phone-workers-stripped-their-identities.html.

28 McPherson, 'Reload: Liveness, Mobility and the Web', p. 202.

Chapter 9

1 Chantal Pontbriand, 'The Eye Finds No Fixed Point on Which to Rest . . .', trans. C. R. Parsons, *Modern Drama* 25.1 (1982), pp. 154–62, here p. 155; Josette Féral, 'Performance and Theatricality: The Subject Demystified', trans. Terese Lyons, *Modern Drama* 25.1 (1982), pp. 170–81, here p. 177 (original emphasis).

2 Hans-Thies Lehmann, *Postdramatic Theatre*, trans. Karen Jürs-Munby, New York and London: Routledge, 2006, p. 134.

3 Ibid., p. 86.

4 Bert O. States, *Great Reckonings in Little Rooms: On the Phenomenology of Theater*, Berkeley: University of California Press, 1985, p. 29.

5 Jacques Rancière, *The Politics of Aesthetics: The Distribution of the Sensible*, trans. Gabriel Rockhill, London: Continuum, 2004, p. 13.

6 Ibid., p. 14.

7 Giorgio Agamben, 'The Face', trans. Vincenzo Binetti and Cesare Casarino, in Giorgio Agamben, *Means without End: Notes on Politics*, Minneapolis: University of Minnesota Press, 2000 [1995], pp. 91–100, here p. 95 (my emphasis).

8 Jacques Rancière, *Disagreement: Politics and Philosophy*, trans. Julie Rose, Minneapolis: University of Minnesota Press, 1999, p. 9.

9 Jacques Rancière, 'The Politics of Aesthetics', *Maska* 19.5/6 (88/89) (Winter 2004), pp. 10–16, here p. 10.

10 Rancière, *Disagreement*, p. 29 (original emphasis). See also Jacques Rancière, *Dissensus: On Politics and Aesthetics*, trans. Steven Corcoran, London: Continuum, 2009, pp. 36–7.

11 Rancière, *The Politics of Aesthetics*, p. 10.

12 Ibid.

13 Ibid., p. 19.

14 Hans-Thies Lehmann, 'The Political in the Post-Dramatic', *Maska* 17.74/75 (2002), pp. 74–6, here p. 76.

15 Lehmann, *Postdramatic Theatre*, p. 22.

16 Ibid., pp. 184–7.

17 Lehmann, 'The Political in the Post-Dramatic', p. 76.

18 Ibid.

19   Tim Etchells, *Certain Fragments: Contemporary Performance and Forced Entertainment*, New York and London: Routledge, 1999, p. 18. See also Peggy Phelan's foreword to the same volume, which borrows Etchells' phrase for its title: 'Performing Questions, Producing Witnesses', pp. 9–14.

20   Ibid., p. 17.

21   Caroline Wake, 'The Accident and the Account: Towards a Taxonomy of Spectatorial Witness in Theatre and Performance Studies', *Performance Paradigm* 5.1 (2009), available at: www.performanceparadigm.net/wp-content/uploads/2009/07/wake.pdf> (accessed 1 November 2012); Jacques Rancière, *The Emancipated Spectator*, trans. Gregory Elliott, London: Verso, 2009.

22   Post-show discussion, Barbican Theatre, 24 June 2010. Participants: Lloyd Swanton, Bruce Gladwin, Sarah Mainwaring, Sonia Teuben, Mark Deans, Scott Price, Nicki Holland. Moderated by Brian Logan.

23   Back to Back Theatre, *Food Court*, theatrical programme, Brussels: Kunstenfestivaldesarts, 2010, p. 14.

24   Post-show discussion, Barbican Theatre, 24 June 2010.

25   This part was originally developed and performed by Rita Halabarec but was played by Teuben in the production I saw.

26   Back to Back Theatre, *Food Court* (unpublished script provided to the author, 2009). The script assigns fictional names to all the characters, but, for simplicity, and because these names are almost never seen or spoken in the play, I will continue to refer to the performers by their real names. I have chosen to use the performers' first names because they indicate gender.

27   Matt Hargrave, 'Pure Products Go Crazy', *Research in Drama Education: The Journal of Applied Theatre and Performance* 14.1 (2009), pp. 37–54, here p. 48 (original emphasis).

28   In reporting on the post-show discussion, I am primarily using Gladwin's comments to represent the position of the company as a whole. My selective reporting does not reflect the extent to which Gladwin deferred to the comments and experience of the actors, who shared the stage with him, and who repeatedly articulated their experience of sharing authorship and ownership of the work.

29 Michael Oliver, *The Politics of Disablement*. London: Macmillan, 1990.
30 Back to Back Theatre, 'Artistic Rationale', available at: http://
    backtobacktheatre.com/about/artistic-rationale (accessed 1 November
    2012).
31 Rancière, *The Politics of Aesthetics*, p. 39.

Chapter 10

1 Hans-Thies Lehmann, 'Wie politisch ist postdramatisches Theater?', in
   Das Politische Schreiben: Essays zu Theatertexten, Berlin: Theater der
   Zeit, 2002, pp. 11–21, here p. 16, originally published in *Theater der
   Zeit*, Nr. 10, October 2001, pp. 10–15. All translations from German in
   this chapter are my own unless otherwise noted. Parts of this chapter
   were first published in German in Karen Jürs-Munby, 'Abraumhalde,
   FaustIn and out: Sekundärdramen', in Pia Janke (ed.), *Jelinek Handbuch*,
   Stuttgart: J. B. Metzler Verlag, 2013, pp. 203–7.
2 Elfriede Jelinek, 'Anmerkungen zum Sekundärdrama', 18 November
   2010, available at: www.elfriedejelinek.com/.
3 Jacques Derrida, 'Marx, das ist jemand', in e-journal *Zäsuren* I (2000),
   pp. 65–6, as cited in Hans-Thies Lehmann, *Das Politische Schreiben*,
   Berlin: Theater der Zeit, 2002, p. 14.
4 Lehmann, *Das Politische Schreiben*, pp. 14–15.
5 Ibid., p. 17.
6 In the Anglophone reception postdramatic theatre has sometimes been
   wrongly identified exclusively with non-text-based practices. See Karen
   Jürs-Munby, 'The Vexed Question of the Text in Postdramatic Theatre
   in a Cross-Cultural Perspective', in Medenica, *Postdramatic Theater Ten
   Years After*, Belgrade: Faculty of Dramatic Arts, 2011, pp. 83–94.
7 Hans-Thies Lehmann, *Postdramatic Theatre*, trans. Karen Jürs-Munby,
   New York: Routledge, p. 17.
8 Gerda Poschman, *Der nicht mehr dramatische Theatertext: Aktuelle
   Bühnenstücke und ihre dramatische Analyse*, Tübingen: Niemeyer, 1997.
9 Lehmann, *Das Politische Schreiben*, p. 21.

10 See also Brandon Woolf in this book.

11 'The Nobel Prize in Literature 2004', Nobelprize.org., 2 February 2013, available at: www.nobelprize.org/nobel_prizes/literature/laureates/2004/.

12 See Lehmann, *Postdramatic Theatre*, p. 18 and p. 24. See also for example Dagmar Jaeger, *Theater im Medienzeitalter: Das Postdramatische Theater von Elfriede Jelinek und Heiner Müller*, Bielefeld: Aisthesis Verlag, 2007.

13 See Karen Jürs-Munby, 'The Resistant Text in Postdramatic Theatre: Performing Elfriede Jelinek's "*Sprachflächen*"', in *Performance Research* 14.1, pp. 46–56.

14 See for example the section on 'Concrete Theatre', in Lehmann, *Postdramatic Theatre*, pp. 98–9.

15 Elfriede Jelinek, *Sprech-Wut,* 19 January 2005, available on Jelinek's homepage at: www.elfriedejelinek.com.

16 Ibid.

17 Evelyn Annuβ, *Elfriede Jelinek: Theater des Nachlebens*, München: Wilhelm Fink Verlag, 2005, p. 11.

18 Ibid., p. 12.

19 Jelinek, 'Anmerkungen zum Sekundärdrama'.

20 Ibid.

21 See David Barnett, 'Resisting the Revolution: Heiner Müller's *Hamlet/Machine* at the Deutsches Theater, Berlin, March 1990', in *Theatre Research International* 31.2 (July 2006), pp 188–200.

22 Karen Jürs-Munby, 'Introduction', in Lehmann, *Postdramatic Theatre*, pp. 1–15, here p. 2.

23 Elfriede Jelinek, 'Das Parasitärdrama', 12 May 2011, available at: www.elfriedejelinek.com.

24 See Cary Wolfe, 'Introduction to the New Edition: Bring the Noise: *The Parasite* and the Multiple Genealogies of Posthumanism', in Michel Serres, *The Parasite*, trans. by Lawrence R. Schehr, Minneapolis: University of Minnesota Press, 2007 [1980], pp. xi–xxviii, here p. xiii.

25 Ortrud Gutjahr, 'Was heißt hier Aufklärung?', in Gutjahr (ed.), *Nathan der Weise von Gotthold Ephraim Lessing: Texterprobungen mit* Abraumhalde *von Elfriede Jelinek in Nicolas Stemanns Inszenierung am Thalia Theater*

Hamburg, [Reihe: Theater und Universität im Gespräch, Bd. 11],
Würzburg: Königshausen und Neumann, 2010, pp. 43–70, here p. 43.

26   Stemann in Benjamin von Blomberg, 'Dem Stück den Hass
zurückgeben'. Benjamin von Blomberg im Gespräch mit Nicolas
Stemann', in *Programmheft des Thalia Theaters zu Gotthold Emphraim
Lessings* Nathan der Weise *mit dem Sekundärdrama* Abraumhalde *von
Elfriede Jelinek*, Hamburg: Thalia Theater, 2009, p. 44.

27   Stemann in Ibid., p. 44.

28   Elfriede Jelinek, *Abraumhalde*, 4 October 2009, available at: www.
elfriedejelinek.com/, henceforth cited as AB.

29   Elfriede Jelinek, 'The Forsaken Place', translated by Margarete Lamb-
Faffelberger, 1 May 2008/21 May 2008, available at: http://a-e-m-gmbh.
com/wessely/famstet.htm.

30   Bärbel Lücke, 'Hermann Brochs *1918. Hugenau oder die Sachlichkeit*
(*Die Schlafwandler*) und Elfriede Jelineks *Abraumhalde*. Zwischen
Zerfall und Restitution religöser und ökonomischer Paradigmen – Eine
Engführung', *Weimarer Beiträge*, 4, 2010, pp. 485–500, here p. 492.

31   Ibid., p. 495.

32   Ibid., p. 493

33   Ortrud Gutjahr, 'Überblick zur Werk- und Auffführungsgeschichte:
Nathan der Weise – Entstehung und Wirkung', in Gutjahr, *Nathan der
Weise*, pp. 25–34, here p. 31.

34   Stemann in von Blomberg, p. 42.

35   Gutjahr, 'Was heißt hier Aufklärung?', p. 63.

36   Herbert Marcuse, 'Repressive Tolerance', in Robert Paul Wolff,
Barrington Moore, Jr. and Herbert Marcuse, *A Critique of Pure
Tolerance*, Boston: Beacon Press, 1965, pp. 81–123, here p. 82.

37   Elfriede Jelinek, 'In Mediengewittern', 28 April 2003, available at:
www.a-e-m-gmbh.com/wessely/fblitz.htm.

38   Gutjahr, 'Was heißt hier Aufklärung?', p. 69.

39   Ibid., p. 68.

40   Serres, *The Parasite*, p. 190.

41   Stemann in '"Dem Stück den Hass zurückgeben – aber auch das
Leben": Ein Gespräch mit Nicolas Stemann und Benjamin von
Blomberg, moderiert von Ortrud Gutjahr', in Gutjahr (ed.), *Nathan der
Weise*, p. 197.

42 Einar Schleef cited in Bärbel Lücke, 'Faust und Margarethe als Untote: Zu Elfriede Jelineks *FaustIn and out (Sekundärdrama zu Urfaust)* – offene/verdrängte Wahrheiten in freiheitlichen Zeiten', in *JELINEK[JAHR]BUCH*, Vienna: Elfriede Jelinek-Forschungszentrum, 2012, pp. 23–62, here p. 30.

43 Ibid., p. 26.

44 Elfriede Jelinek, *FaustIn and out – Sekundärdrama zu Urfaust*, available at: www.elfriedejelinek.com, henceforth cited as FAU.

45 Elfriede Jelinek, *Sports Play*, trans. Penny Black with translation assistance and a foreword by Karen Jürs-Munby, London: Oberon Books, 2012, p. 39.

46 Lücke, 'Faust und Margarethe als Untote', p. 30.

47 Ibid., p. 38.

48 Ibid., p. 41.

49 Announcement of Jelinek's *FaustIn and out* at the Schauspiel Zürich, available at: www.schauspielhaus.ch/haus-service/heute-und-damals/ stucke-archiv/2012/293-faustin-and-out.

50 Serres, *The Parasite*, p. 230.

51 Martin Esslin, 'Goethe's Faust: Pre-Modern, Post-Modern, Proto-Postmodern', in Jane K. Brown, Meredith Lee and Thomas P Saine (eds), *Interpreting Goethe's* Faust *today*, Columbia, SC: Camden House, 1994, pp. 219–27, here pp. 221 and 222.

Chapter 11

1 Hans-Thies Lehmann, *Das Politische Schreiben: Essays zu Theatertexten*, Berlin: Theater der Zeit, 2002, p. 16. All translations from German in this chapter are my own unless otherwise noted.

2 Robert Sokolowski, *Introduction to Phenomenology*, Cambridge: Cambridge University Press, 2000, p. 50.

3 Bert O. States, *Great Reckonings in Little Rooms*, Berkeley, CA: University of California Press, 1985, p. 1.

4 Andy Lavender, *Hamlet in Pieces: Shakespeare Reworked by Peter Brook, Robert Lepage and Robert Wilson*, London: Nick Hern, 2001, p. 44.

5   Hans-Thies Lehmann, *Postdramatic Theatre*, trans. Karen Jürs-Munby, London: Routledge, 2006, p. 22.

6   Stanton B. Garner, Jr, *Bodied Spaces: Phenomenology and Performance in Contemporary Drama*, Ithaca and London: Cornell University Press, 1994, p. 3.

7   Nuki Shigeto, 'Theater', in Hans Rainer Sepp and Lester Embree (eds), *Handbook of Phenomenological Aesthetics*, Dordrecht: Springer, 2010, pp. 331–7, here p. 332.

8   Bruce Wilshire, *Role Playing and Identity: The Limits of Theatre as Metaphor*, Bloomington: Indiana University Press, 1982, p. 12.

9   See States, *Great Reckonings*, p. 7.

10 Maurice Merleau-Ponty, *The Primacy of Perception and Other Essays on Phenomenological Psychology, the Philosophy of Art, History and Politics*, ed. J. M. Edie, trans. W. Cobb, Evanston, IL: Northwestern University Press, 1964, p. 15.

11 Garner, *Bodied Spaces*, p. 2.

12 David Stewart and Algis Mickunas, *Exploring Phenomenology: A Guide to the Field and Its Literature*, Athens, OH: Ohio University Press, 1990, p. 4.

13 Garner, *Bodied Spaces*, p. 4.

14 Alice Rayner, *Ghosts: Death's Double and the Phenomena of Theatre*, Minneapolis: University of Minnesota Press, 2006, pp. xii, xi, xiv.

15 See Lehmann, *Postdramatic Theatre*, pp. 23–4.

16 See Gerda Poschmann, *Der nicht mehr dramatische Text: Aktuelle Bühnenstücke und ihre dramaturgische Analyse*, Berlin: Walter de Gruyter, 1997.

17 See Steve Giles, *The Problem of Action in Modern European Drama*, Stuttgart: Akademischer Verlag Han-Dieter Heinz, 1981, p. 5.

18 Ewald Palmetshofer, 'wohnen. unter glas', in *Theater Theater*, Frankfurt am Main: Fischer, 2010, pp. 267–334, here p. 290, referred to hereafter as W followed by the page number.

19 Ewald Palmetshofer, 'faust hat hunger und verschluckt sich an einer grete', in *Theater Theater*, Frankfurt: Fischer, 2009, pp. 497–555, here p. 519, referred to hereafter as F followed by the page number.

20 Ewald Palmetshofer, 'hamlet ist tot. keine schwerkraft', in *Theater Theater*, Frankfurt am Main: Fischer, 2008, pp. 393–451, here p. 447, referred to hereafter as H followed by the page number.

21 Alfred Schutz, *The Phenomenology of the Social World*, trans. Georg Walsh, London: Heinemann, 1972, pp. 99, 101.

22 Shigeto, 'Theater', pp. 334, 331.

23 Lehmann, *Das Politische Schreiben*, p. 8.

24 Ibid., p. 99.

25 Ibid., p. 85.

26 Ibid., pp. 179–80.

27 Hans-Thies Lehmann, *Postdramatisches Theater*, Frankfurt am Main: Suhrkamp, 1999, p. 457. This paragraph is not included in the English translation.

28 See Lehmann, *Postdramatic Theatre*, p. 32.

29 Ibid., pp. 85–104.

30 Ibid., p. 181.

31 Ibid.

32 Ibid.

33 Ibid, p. 184.

34 Jacques Rancière, *The Emancipated Spectator*, trans. Gregory Elliott, London: Verso, 2009, p. 6.

35 Ibid.

36 See Lehmann, *Postdramatic Theatre*, p. 131.

37 Hans-Thies Lehmann, '"Postdramatic Theatre", a Decade Later', in Medenica, *Dramatic and Postdramatic Theater Ten Years After*, Belgrade: Faculty of Dramatic Arts, 2011, pp. 31–46, here pp. 34–5.

38 Lehmann, *Postdramatic Theatre*, p. 25.

Chapter 12

1 All translations in this chapter are my own unless otherwise noted.

2 Hans-Thies Lehmann, 'Anregungen theoretischer Art zum Umgang mit Texten Heiner Müllers', in Manfred Beilharz, Jan Berg, Heiner Goebbels, et al. (eds), *Heiner Müller Inszenieren. Unterhaltung im Theater,* Berlin: Dramaturgische Gesellschaft, 1987, pp. 5–10, here p. 6.

3   Gerda Poschmann, *Der nicht mehr dramatische Theatertext. Aktuelle Bühnenstücke und ihre dramaturgische Analyse*, Tübingen: Niemeyer, 1997.

4   See, for example, Hans-Thies Lehmann, *Postdramatic Theatre*, trans. Karen Jürs-Munby, London: Routledge, 2006, pp. 21 and 59.

5   David Barnett, *Literature versus Theatre. Textual Problems and Theatrical Realization in the Later Plays of Heiner Müller*, Berne: Lang, 1998.

6   Jacques Rancière, 'Ten Theses on Politics', in his *Dissensus. On Politics and Aesthetics*, ed. and trans. Steven Corcoran, London and New York: Continuum, 2010, pp. 27–44, here p. 38.

7   Georg Wieghaus, *Heiner Müller*, Munich: Beck, 1981, pp. 13–14.

8   Aside from, notably, in the following: Ingeborg Hoesterey, 'Intertextualität als Strukturmerkmal (postmoderner?) deutschsprachiger Prosa', in *Verschlungene Schriftzeichen. Intertextualität von Literatur und Kunst in der Moderne/Postmoderne*, Frankfurt am Main: Athenäum, 1988, pp. 164–96; and Uwe Schütte, *Arbeit an der Differenz. Zum Eigensinn der Prosa von Heiner Müller*, Heidelberg: Winter, 2010.

9   Heiner Müller, *Bildbeschreibung*, in his *Werke* in 12 vols, ed. Frank Hörnigk, Frankfurt/M.: Suhrkamp, 1998–2008 (hereafter referred to as *W*, followed by volume number), *W*2, pp. 112–19 (p. 119): 'in einer abgestorbenen dramatischen Struktur.'

10 Heiner Müller, *Krieg ohne Schlacht*, in *W*9, pp. 7–291, here p. 269.

11 See for example the extensive, but by no means exhaustive, list of performances in Hans-Thies Lehmann and Patrick Primavesi (eds), *Heiner Müller Handbuch. Leben – Werk – Wirkung*, Stuttgart: Metzler, 2003, pp. 404–5.

12 See Jürgen G. Sang, 'Heiner Müller: A Lyric Poet? The Dialectic Process of Aesthetic Self-Recognition', in Gerhard Fischer (ed.), *Heiner Müller. ConTEXTS and HISTORY*, Tübingen: Stauffenberg, 1995, pp. 259–69, here p. 259.

13 Heiner Müller, 'Der Schrecken die erste Erscheinung des Neuen', in *W*8, pp. 208–12, here p. 209.

14 See Katharina Ebrecht, *Heiner Müllers Lyrik. Quellen und Vorbilder*, Würzburg: Königshausen & Neumann, 2001; Marcus Kreikebaum, *Heiner Müllers Gedichte*, Bielefeld, Aisthesis, 2003; and Schütte, *Arbeit an der Differenz*.

15 Jonathan Kalb, *The Theater of Heiner Müller*, Cambridge: Cambridge University Press, 1998, p. 14.

16 Genia Schulz, *Heiner Müller*, Stuttgart: Metzler, 1980, p. 167.

17 Schütte, *Arbeit an der Differenz*, p. 26.

18 Heiner Müller, *Germania Tod in Berlin*, Berlin: Rotbuch/Verlag der Autoren, 1977, p. 28.

19 Heiner Müller, 'Allein mit diesen Leibern', in *W1*, p. 201:

> ALLEIN MIT DIESEN LEIBERN
> Staaten Utopien
> Gras wächst
> Auf den Gleisen
> Die Wörter verfaulen
> Auf dem Papier
> Die Augen der Frauen
> Werden kälter
> Abschied von morgen
> STATUS QUO

20 Janine Ludwig, '"Die Wörter verfaulen/Auf dem Papier" – Heiner Müllers Schreibkrise nach dem Untergang des Sozialismus', *Mauerschau* 2.2 (2009), pp. 29–44, here p. 38. For a thorough discussion of the theme of zombies and other 'undead' creatures in Müller's works, see Hans-Thies Lehmann, 'Heiner Müller's Spectres', in *Heiner Müller. ConTEXTS and HISTORY*, pp. 87–96.

21 Ludwig, 'Die Wörter verfaulen', p. 38.

22 Ibid.

23 Heiner Müller, 'Alone with These Corpses', in *Theatremachine*, trans. Marc von Henning, London: Faber and Faber, 1995, p. 21.

24 Indeed, this is an argument deployed by Jacques Derrida against particular radical democratic utopias, which he regards as never being capable of taking form as anything but a 'democracy to come'. See

Jacques Rancière, 'Does Democracy Mean Something?', in *Dissensus*, pp. 45–61, here p. 59.

25 Ludwig, 'Die Wörter verfaulen', p. 38.

26 Heiner Müller, *Mauser*, in *W4*, pp. 243–60, here p. 255.

27 Müller, *Krieg ohne Schlacht*, p. 246.

28 See, for example, Heiner Müller, 'Der glücklose Engel', in *W1*, p. 53, and the image of the 'Engel der Verzweiflung' (Angel of Despair), in *Der Auftrag*, in *W5*, pp. 11–42, in particular pp. 16–17.

29 Müller, *Krieg ohne Schlacht*, p. 246.

30 Gerrit-Jan Berendse, 'The Poet in a Cage. On the Motif of Stagnation in Poems by Heiner Müller and Ezra Pound', in *Heiner Müller. ConTEXTS and HISTORY*, pp. 249–57.

31 Jacques Derrida, 'Signature Event Context', in *Margins of Philosophy*, trans. Alan Bass, Chicago: University of Chicago Press, 1984, pp. 307–30, p. 316.

32 See Alexandra von Hirschfeld, *Frauenfiguren im dramatischen Werk Heiner Müllers*, Marburg: Tectum, 1999.

33 Müller, *Bildbeschreibung*, p. 119.

34 Berendse, 'The Poet in a Cage', pp. 251–2.

35 Schulz, *Heiner Müller*, p. 168.

36 See, for example, a critical interpretation of Barbara Köhler's response to *Die Hamletmaschine*: Georgina Paul, 'Multiple Refractions, or Winning Movement out of Myth: Barbara Köhler's Poem Cycle "Elektra. Spiegelungen"', *German Life and Letters* 57.1 (2004), pp. 21–32; and Georgina Paul, *Perspectives on Gender in Post-1945 German Literature*, Rochester, NY: Camden House, 2009, pp. 222–36.

37 Heiner Müller, 'Die Form entsteht aus dem Maskieren', in *W10*, pp. 346–63, here pp. 361–2. See also Heiner Müller, 'Heiner Müller über Robert Wilson', in *W8*, pp. 455–9, in particular p. 456.

38 Heiner Müller, 'Fünf Minuten Schwarzfilm', in *W11*, pp. 354–70, here pp. 362–3.

39 Heiner Müller, 'Solange wir an unsere Zukunft glauben, brauchen wir uns vor unserer Vergangenheit nicht zu fürchten', in *W10*, pp. 455–71, here p. 466.

40 Heiner Müller, 'Der Mystery Man', in *W10*, pp. 291–7, here p. 296.

41 Heiner Müller, 'Einen historischen Stoff sauber abschildern, das kann ich nicht', in *W10*, pp. 74–98, here p. 87.

42 Hans-Thies Lehmann, 'Vom Zuschauer', in Jan Deck and Angelika Sieburg (eds), *Paradoxien des Zuschauens. Die Rolle des Publikums im zeitgenössischen Theater*, Bielefeld: Transcript, 2008, pp. 21–6, here p. 26.

43 Lehmann, *Postdramatic Theatre*, p. 135.

44 Ibid., p. 83.

45 Ibid.

46 See, for example, Ferdinand Tönnies's distinction between *Gemeinschaft* and *Gesellschaft*, in Ferdinand Tönnies, *Community and Civil Society*, trans. Jose Harris and Margaret Hollis, Cambridge: Cambridge University Press, 2001, in particular pp. 15–91.

47 Heiner Müller, 'Ich glaube an Konflikt. Sonst glaube ich an nichts', in *W10*, pp. 175–223, here p. 191.

48 Jacques Rancière, *The Politics of Aesthetics*, trans. Gabriel Rockhill, London & New York: Continuum, 2004, p. 13.

49 Rancière, 'Ten Theses', p. 38.

50 Jacques Rancière, 'The Paradoxes of Political Art', in *Dissensus*, pp. 134–51, here p. 140.

51 Rancière, 'Ten Theses', p. 42.

52 Jacques Rancière, 'The Politics of Literature', *SubStance. A Review of Theory and Literary Criticism* 33.1 (2004), pp. 10–24, here p. 14.

53 Rancière, 'The Paradoxes', p. 140.

54 Heiner Müller, 'Fatzer ± Keuner', in *W8*, pp. 223–31, here p. 224.

55 Lehmann, *Postdramatic Theatre*, pp. 145–8.

56 Ibid., p. 148.

57 For a description of varied historical approaches to *The Hamlet Machine*, see Barnett, *Literature versus Theatre*, pp. 93–112. See also David Barnett, 'Some Notes on the Difficulties of Operating Heiner Müller's *Die Hamletmaschine*', *German Life and Letters* 48.1 (1995), pp. 75–85.

58 Lehmann, *Postdramatic Theatre*, pp. 156–7.

59 Ibid., p. 155.

60   Michel Foucault, *The Order of Things*, London and New York: Routledge, 2002, p. 421.

61   See Martin Heidegger's discussion of the distinction between the 'Leib' (living body) and 'Körper' (material, present-at-hand object) in his *Nietzsche: Der Wille zur Macht als Kunst*, *Gesamtausgabe*, Abt. II, Bd. 43. Frankfurt am Main: Klostermann, 1985, pp. 117–18; and his *Zollikoner Seminare: Protokole – Gespräche – Briefe*, ed. Medard Boss, Frankfurt/M.: Klostermann, 1987, p. 116.

62   Erika Fischer-Lichte, *Ästhetik des Performativen*, Frankfurt/M.: Suhrkamp, 2004, p. 139.

63   Heiner Müller, 'Miteinander statt oben und unten', in *W*10, pp. 35–40, here p. 37.

64   Fabian Lettow, '"Geografien." Zum Verhältnis von Geschichte, Landschaft, Sprache und Gemeinschaft in Heiner Müllers chorischem Schreiben', in Theo Girshausen and Günther Heeg (eds), *Theatrographie. Heiner Müllers Theater der Schrift*, Berlin: Vorwerk 8, 2009, pp. 337–50, here p. 349.

65   Heiner Müller, 'Ich weiss nicht, was Avantgarde ist', in *W*11, pp. 100–13, here p. 104.

66   Rancière, *Politics of Aesthetics*, p. 53.

67   Poschmann, *Der nicht mehr dramatische Theatertext*, p. 296.

Notes on Contributors

David Barnett is Reader in Drama, Theatre and Performance at the University of Sussex. He has published monographs on Heiner Müller (Peter Lang, 1998) and Rainer Werner Fassbinder (CUP, 2005), the latter as a Fellow of the Humboldt Foundation. He is currently writing a history of the Berliner Ensemble, a project funded by a British Academy Research Development Award and an AHRC Fellowship. He has written several articles and essays on German- and English-language political and postdramatic theatre.

Peter M. Boenisch is Professor of European Theatre at the University of Kent, where he founded the European Theatre Research Network (ETRN). Recent publications include articles on William Forsythe, Michael Thalheimer, Frank Castorf, Jan Fabre and Flemish Theatre. He is currently writing a monograph, 'Regie: Directing Scenes and Senses in European Theatre', and preparing a book on the German theatre director, Thomas Ostermeier.

Mateusz Borowski teaches cultural studies, queer theory and translation studies at the Department for Performance Studies at the Jagiellonian University, Kraków. He has published, in Polish, *In Search of the Real. New Developments of the European Playwriting of the 1990s* (2007) and, together with Małgorzata Sugiera, *In the Trap of Opposites. Ideologies of Identity* (2012). He is also active as a translator.

Jerome Carroll is Lecturer in German at the University of Nottingham, where he specialises in German history of ideas, aesthetics and modern German theatre. His publications include *Art at the Limits of Perception: The Aesthetic Theory of Wolfgang Welsch* (2006), and articles on recent German theatre (Handke, Müller, Heckmanns) and history of ideas. He is currently working on a monograph on the German tradition of philosophical anthropology from the eighteenth century to the twentieth century.

Antje Dietze is a senior researcher in the PhD Research Training Group 'Critical Junctures of Globalization' at the University of Leipzig, Germany. She received her PhD in Cultural Studies in 2012 with a dissertation on the role of the Volksbühne am Rosa-Luxemburg-Platz in Berlin in post-socialist transition. Her current research focuses on cultural entrepreneurs in the nineteenth century.

Ulrike Garde is Senior Lecturer in German Studies at Macquarie University, Sydney. Her research focuses on Intercultural German Studies, German literature and the performing arts. Her publications include *Brecht & Co: German-speaking Playwrights on the Australian Stage* and, together with Anne-Rose Meyer (eds), *Belonging and Exclusion: Case Studies in Recent Australian and German Literature, Film and Theatre*. Together with Dr Meg Mumford, she is currently co-editing *Rimini Protokoll Close-Up: Lektüren* (Wehrhahn, forthcoming).

Steve Giles is Emeritus Professor of German Studies and Critical Theory at the University of Nottingham. He has published widely on modern drama, critical theory and Bertolt Brecht. He is currently co-editing/translating two volumes of Brecht's theoretical writings for Methuen – *Brecht on Theatre* and *Brecht on Performance* – in the context of a major AHRC project on 'Brecht into English'.

Shannon Jackson is Goldman Professor of Rhetoric and of Theater, Dance and Performance Studies at University of California, Berkeley, where she is also director of the Arts Research Center. In addition to many essays in journals and catalogues, past publications include *Lines of Activity* (2000), *Professing Performance* (2004) and *Social Works: Performing Art, Supporting Publics* (2011). Jackson is currently working with Marianne Weems on a book about The Builders Association to be published by MIT Press.

Karen Jürs-Munby is Lecturer in Theatre Studies at Lancaster University. She translated and introduced Hans-Thies Lehmann's *Postdramatic Theatre* (2006) and has published extensively on postdramatic dramaturgies, modes of acting/performing and relations between text and performance. She has a long-standing research interest in the work of Elfriede Jelinek and is currently writing a monograph on the stagings of her theatre texts by major German directors. She also works as a dramaturg, most recently on the English premiere of Jelinek's *Sports Play* (2012).

Hans-Thies Lehmann is Emeritus Professor of Theatre Studies at the Goethe-Universität, Frankfurt am Main, Germany, and a visiting professor at universities in many countries. His publications include *Theater und Mythos* (1991), *Das Politische Schreiben. Essays zu Theatertexten* (2002) and *Heiner Müller Handbuch* (2004). His seminal work *Postdramatisches Theater* (1999) has been translated into twenty languages. He has recently completed a book entitled *Tragödie und Dramatisches Theater* published by Alexander Verlag in 2013.

Meg Mumford is Senior Lecturer in Theatre and Performance Studies at the University of New South Wales, Australia. She is the author of *Bertolt Brecht* (Routledge, 2009), and co-editor of *Rimini Protokoll Close-Up: Lektüren* (Wehrhahn, forthcoming), and has also published on the work of Marieluise Fleisser, Pina Bausch and Australian verbatim theatre. Together with Dr Ulrike Garde, she is currently researching contemporary Reality Theatre from Germany.

Theron Schmidt is a Lecturer in Theatre and Liberal Arts at King's College London. His writing on contemporary forms of political performance has been published in *Contemporary Theatre Review*, *Law*

312 *Notes on Contributors*

Text Culture and *Performance Research*. He also makes performance as a solo and collaborative artist.

Małgorzata Sugiera is a Full Professor at the Jagiellonian University in Kraków, Poland, and Head of Department for Performance Studies. Her main research fields are performance theory, cultural studies and queer studies. She has published ten books in Polish, recently *Ghosts and Other Returns. Memory – History – Drama* (2006), *Other Shakespeare. New Readings of the European Canon* (2008) and, together with Mateusz Borowski, *In the Trap of Opposites. Ideologies of Identity* (2012). She is also active as a translator.

Michael Wood is an AHRC-funded PhD student at the University of Edinburgh. His doctoral research investigates the relationship between textual politics and audience interaction in a selection of works by Heiner Müller, and considers these in relation to key historical productions of the plays in question.

Brandon Woolf is a theatre maker and doctoral candidate in Performance Studies at the University of California, Berkeley. He is currently based in Berlin, working on a thesis on cultural policy and contemporary performance in Berlin after the end of the Cold War. He has published in *Theatre Journal, TDR: The Drama Review, The Arts Politic* and *HowlRound*.

Index

(NB: Terms such as 'postdramatic theatre' and 'the political', as well as the name of Hans-Thies Lehmann have not been indexed as their mention is ubiquitous throughout the book. End notes have not been indexed. Substantial page ranges and page numbers for whole chapters are indicated in bold font.)

1968 25, 80–1, **129–45**
1989 121, 130, 131, 142, 258
7:84 (McGrath) 147
9/11 2001 2, 131, 219, 246

action/plot 3, 4, 22, 40, 61, 63–5,
        68–9, 109, 182, 212, 239, 249,
        250–1, 256
activism 25, 29, 87
    and Schlingensief's *Rocky
        Dutschke, '68* **129–45**
actors/ performers 9, 50, 80
    as activists in *Rocky Dutschke,
        '68* 130, **135–43**
    'actor-labourers' re-enacting call
        centre training sessions in
        Alladeen 177, 180–1, 183
    disabled 3, 131, 135, 190–1, 197–9,
        202–7
    in Reality Theatre, 150–1, 153–8,
        161–2
    untrained/non-actors 3, 83–5,
        135
    see also real people
Adorno, Theodor W. 11, 12, 20, 28,
        41–6, 51–3, 90
Aeschylus 91
aesthetic 5, 15, 17, 20, 32–3
    autonomy 11, 12, 15, 72–3, 92, 100,
        103–4, 107–8
    experience 45–6, 72–3, 92, 101–2
    and extra-aesthetic realm 23, 41,
        98–9
    interruption of aesthetic
        representation/experience 98,
        103, 107

pleasure 101–2
    and the real 98–100, 210
    see also form
aesthetics,
    materialist 54
    of performativity 83
    and politics **33–46**, 68, 72–6, 85,
        98–104, 192, 256
    of repetition 269–70
Agamben, Giorgio 114, 190
agency 6, 18, 22, 28–9, 197, 240, 245,
        251–4
    and contemporary dance 112, 121,
        122, 123, 126, 127, 128
Althusser, Louis 21, 108, 125–6,
        170–1, 191, 250, 253
Angelos, Moe 181
Annuβ, Evelyn 213–14
Antoine, André 68
appearance 3, 15, 27–8, 102, **190–6**,
        206–7, 214
    'politics of appearance' 191
    see also theatricality
Arab Spring 2
    see also Egypt
Arias, Lola (Rimini Protokoll) 26,
        151, 159
Aristotle 4, 98, 215
Artaud, Antonin 12, 13, 22, 75, 106,
        235
audience 3, 7, 8–9, 29, 70, 72, 74–7
    activation 130, 137–42
    active spectatorship 13, 50
    bodily co-presence of actors and
        spectators 9, 38, 39
    as collective 256–7, 264–7, 270–2

insecurity in Reality Theatre 26–7,
152, **155–64**
involvement/ implication 3, 24,
28, 81, 89, 125, 128, 130, 137,
142–4, 163, 185–6, 194–5, 230
see also relational dramaturgy
memory of 76–7
participation 3, 9, 24, 38, 78–81,
108, 130, 134, 137–8, 141, 143,
266
and spectating relationships 18–20
see also Rancière, 'emancipated
spectator'; reception
authenticity 5
and authenticity effects (A-effects)
in Reality Theatre 148–9,
151–64
autobiographical performance 147,
151, 159
avant-garde 37
heritage of political and
artistic 132, 134
re-enactments of 112, 118–19
see also modernism

Back to Back Theatre,
Food Court 24, 27, 190–1, **195–207**
small metal objects 195–6, 202
Bailey, John 196–7
Ballet Frankfurt 114
Bantzer, Christoph 222
Barbican 200, 202
Barnett, David 15, 16, 20, 41, **47–66**,
170, 255
Bataille, Georges 95
Bausch, Pina 113, 114
Beauvoir, Simone de 226
Beckett, Samuel 105
Bel, Jérôme 116, 123
Cedric Andrieux 121
Véronique Doisneau 121
Benjamin, Walter 7–8, 33, 34, 36–7, 90
Berghaus, Ruth 51
Berliner Ensemble 48–50, 54, 59
Besson, Benno 51

Beuys, Joseph 140
Bible, the 62
Biermann, Wolf 133
Bin Laden, Osama 221, 223
binary oppositions 29, 39, 72, 123,
215, 238
Black Mountain College 116
body/bodies 3, 9, 64, 106, 114–15
and appearance 192, 193, 198–9,
207
and ballet 113, 115
bodiless dance/staging 28, 111–12,
221
and immaterial labour 168–9, 172,
175
in Müller's *Alone with these
Bodies* 260–1, 269–70
phenomenological emphasis
on 235–6
physicality 106, 190, 201
Boenisch, Peter 23–4, 28–9, 63,
111–28, 163
Böhm, Peter 111
Bohrer, Karl-Heinz 92
Borowski, Mateusz 16, **67–86**
Brahm, Otto 68
Brecht, Bertolt 6, 8, 15, 35–7, **47–66**,
90, 169–70, 250–1
actor-character split 155
didacticism 108, 140
epic theatre 13, 17, 35, 50, 59,
68–70, 75, 108
Lehrstück 8, 75, 105, 140
Mr Puntila and his Man Matti 16,
48, **53–66**
post-Brechtian theatre 16, 36,
47–8, 55, 65–6, 170, 171–2,
182, 185, 187
and spectating 13, 36, 47, 158
*Verfremdung/
Verfremdungseffekt* 35, 48, 50,
69, 149, 154, 161, 163
Brook, Peter,
Hamlet 235
Büchner, Georg 147

Builders Association, The 8, 72, 165–6, 169–70, 175–6
    Alladeen 8, 27, 166, **173–88**
    Imperial Motel (Faust) 181
    Jet Lag 181–3
    Jump Cut (Faust) 181
    Master Builder, The 175, 178–9

Cage, John 116, 122, 123
    Lecture on Nothing 117, 124–5, 127
capitalism 17–18, 19, 68, 70, 122, 128, 185, 205, 226, 242, 246–7, 251
    see also globalisation; labour; service economy
Carlson, Marvin 38–9, 76–7
Carroll, Jerome **1–23**, 24–5, **24–30**, **233–54**
Castellucci, Claudia and Romeo 114
character 3, 4, 6, 13, 22, 65, 212, 249, 250–1, 256, 268
    actor-character split 155, 157
    in The Builders Association's *Alladeen* 173–4
    in Palmetshofer's plays 239–40, 241, 247–8, 253
    played by disabled actors in Back to Back's *Food Court* 202–3
    reappearance in dance 112
    in Schleef's *Puntila* 54–7
    in Thalheimer's *Puntila* 61–4
Charmatz, Boris 116
    Flip Book 121
Chekhov, Anton 13–14, 49
Childs, Lucinda *Dance* 112
choreography 114–15, 117, 119, 121, 122
chorus 54, 57–8, 105
    Jelinek's 'one person chorus' 226–7
Cichowski, Joel 179
Cleater, John 179
Cohen-Cruz, Jan 6
communism,
    fall of the Berlin Wall and Eastern Bloc 2, 70, 129

community,
    conflict between individual and community 91
    local 82, 85
    in Palmetshofer's plays 241–2, 253
    and participatory theatre 143
    of spectators 266–7, 271
    and theatre 19, 73, 100, 109
    see also audience as collective
conflict 40, 62, 67–8, 74, 90–2, 95–7, 105
consciousness 46, 91, 211, 236–7, 242, 263
    class 16, 59
    consciousness raising 142, 228
    false 171
    political 126, 138, 238, 240
    see also tragic consciousness
contingency (of subjectivity, identity, history etc.) 29, 38, 121, 123, 124, 125, 128, 172, 187
Corneille, Pierre 94
Crowhurst, Donald 181
Cunningham, Merce 116, 121, 122, 123

Dadaism 13, 141
Dambrain, Cédric 111
dance **111–28**
    classical ballet 113–15
    concept dance 116
    and drama 113–15
    within the postdramatic paradigm 113–18
    without dancing bodies 111–12
Deans, Mark 196, 199, 200–2, 203–4
Debord, Guy 18, 194, 251
Deck, Jan 7, 9, 11, 12
democracy 7, 21–2, 89, 150, 256–7, 264, 265, 267, 270–1
Derrida, Jacques 14, 23, 209–10, 261
Desmond, Norma (character) 136–7, 144
Deutsches Theater Berlin 53, 257, 264

dialectics, dialectical relations 4, 15
  and contemporary relational
    dramaturgies 123–4, 128
  Lehmann's dialectical
    method 33–6, 39, 44
  negative 34, 51–3
  and (post-)Brechtian theatre
    48–60, 62, 65–6, 75, 170,
    182, 185
dialogue (dramatic) 1, 6, 212, 249
  in Back to Back Theatre's *Food
    Court* 196, 199, 203
  in Jelinek's *FaustIn and out* 226,
    228
  in Müller's work 265, 272
  in Palmetshofer's plays 239, 240,
    244, 253
  return of in dance 28, 112
Dietze, Antje 25, 27, **129–45**
Diller + Scofidio 181–2
disability 24, 29, 190–1, 195–9, 203,
    204–7
  see also actor/performer,
    disabled
discourse (political/public) 10, 11, 18,
    22–3, 43, 70, 231, 249
disruption/interruption (of the
    aesthetic, the dramatic,
    political consensus etc) 22–4,
    43, 45–6, 98, 163, 210–11, 217,
    224, 225, 230–1, 257
dissent (*dissensus*) 22, 26, 74, 192,
    211, 256, 267, 272
documentary art/theatre 6, 26, 87,
    147, 152
Dolar, Mladen 125
drama 1, 4, 6, 16, 17, 19, 256
  crisis of 13–14, 68
  and dance 113–15
  and postdramatic theatre 33–7, 41,
    211, 215–16, 231
    see also Jelinek, post-drama;
      secondary drama
  and Reality Theatre 150

  and theatricality 189–90, 193–4
  and tragedy 89, 97, 105
  unable to represent reality 17–18,
    40, 44
dramaturgy,
  in contemporary dance 115
  'dramaturgy of the fetish' 127
  reflexive 'dramaturgy of the
    symptom' 117–18, 124,
    126–8
  relational dramaturgy 124–8
  epic as classical 35
  of the spectator 89
  visual 190, 201
Drössel, Christine 60
Duncan, Isadora 115
Dutschke, Rudi 25, 130, 132, 134–6,
    138, 139, 144
DV8 114

Eastern Europe 120–1
Ebrecht, Katharina 258
Egypt,
  demonstrations in Cairo 87–9
Elevator Repair Service,
  Gatz 25
Elizabeth I 213
energy/ energetic theatre 11–12,
    114–15
Engels, Friedrich 49
Enlightenment 29, 59, 73, 93, 127,
    147, 217, 224–5
Ensslin, Gudrun 213
Etchells, Tim 195, 197
event (theatre as) 5, 10, 24, 38–40,
    45, 75–6, 116, 190, 209, 231,
    250
  see also situation

fable *see* story
Fabre, Jan 107, 114
  Crying Body, The 106
feminism 213, 225–6, 227
Féral, Josette 189, 205

fiction 3, 80
  fictive cosmos 4, 5, 16, 22, 25, 35,
    41, 111, 113, 148, 151, 210,
    235, 239, 249, 251
  and reality, indecidability of 148,
    151–2, **158–64**
financial crisis 2, 212, 227–8
Fischer-Lichte, Erika 9, 38–41, 75–6,
    164
Forced Entertainment 71, 120, 154
Foreman, Richard 71
form (aesthetic/artistic) 3, 7, 15–16,
    33, 34, 36–46, 72, 85, 209, 231
  of dance 116
  of text 255, 271–2
Forsythe, William 114, 122
Foucault, Michel 191, 270
Freie Bühne 68
freie Theaterszene (independent
    theatre scene) 2
Freud, Sigmund 127
Fried, Michael 74
Fritzl, Elisabeth 223, 226, 227
Fritzl, Josef 218, 219, 223
Fuchs, Elinor 4, 25, 31–3, 35, 36, 39
Futurism 13

Garde, Ulrike 24, 26, **147–64**
Garner, Stanton B. 237
Gay Sweatshop 69
Geertz, Clifford 94
genre 10, 257–9, 271–2
Gestus 48, 50, 58
Giles, Steve **1–30**
Gladwin, Bruce 195–7, 202, 203
globalisation 8, 17, 21, 29, 40, 67, 122,
    128, 166–70, 173–4, 177–8,
    179–81, 182–3, 187–8, 241,
    245, 250
Gob Squad 71, 119
Godard, Jean-Luc 271
Goethe, Johann Wolfgang von,
  Faust 26, 226, 230
  Urfaust 217, 226

Gogol, Nicolai,
  Government Inspector, The 82
Graham, Martha 115
Greenblatt, Stephen 77, 85
Greenspan, Alan 221
Groys, Boris 117
Gutjahr, Ortrud 224, 225

Haas, Birgit 6
Hage, Ghassan 155
Halabarec, Rita 198, 201, 203
Handke, Peter,
  *Voyage by Dugout, or the Play on
    the Film about the War* 70–1
Hardt, Michael 167–8
Hargreaves, Matt 202–3, 204
Hebbel, Christian Friedrich 98
Heeg, Günther 55
Hegel, Georg W. F. 85, 90, 91–2, 95–7,
    123, 125
Heidegger, Martin 93
Henning, Marc von 260
history 3, 5, 16, 28, 54, 59–60, 71–2,
    78–86, 90, 92
  in Müller's *Alone with These
    Bodies* 260–4, 269, 270
  return of in dance 112, 119–21,
    124, 127–8
  schism between subject and
    historical process 250, 253–4
Hochhuth, Rolf 68, 69, 147
Hofmannsthal, Hugo von 94
Hölderlin, Friedrich 97
Holland, Nicki 198–202
Holocaust 79, 80, 222
Hostettler, Sarah 229

Ibsen, Henrik,
  Doll's House, A 213
  Master Builder, The 175, 178
  Pillars of Society 213
identity 3, 86, 120, 124, 128, 148,
    191, 239, 242, 243, 246–8,
    254

ideology 28, 52, 55, 59, 71, 74, 108,
        170–1, 191, 253, 266
    and hegemony 171
illusion (dramatic) 4, 8, 12, 19, 169,
        190, 193–4
intercultural encounters 163–4
interruption *see* disruption
intertextuality 120, 211, 212–13,
        214–15
Ionesco, Eugène 86
Iyer, Pico 182–3

Jackson, Shannon 8, 21, 26, **165–88**
Janša, Janez 120, 124, 127
    Monument G2 118–19
Jefferson, Margo 186
Jelinek, Elfriede 25–6, 211, 212
    Abraumhalde **217–25**, 231
    FaustIn and out 217, **225–31**
    'parasitic drama'
        (*Parasitärdrama*) 216–17
    post-drama 212–14
    secondary drama
        (*Sekundärdrama*) 25, 211,
        214–17, 220, 226, 230–1
    Sports Play 226
    Ulrike Maria Stuart 213
    *What happened to Nora after She
        Left Her Husband* 213
Jooss, Kurt 113, 114
Jovanović, Dušan,
    Monument G 118–19
Judson Dance Theater 115
Jürs-Munby, Karen **1–30**, 25, 31, 120,
        209–31

Kaegi, Stefan (Rimini Protokoll) 26,
        151, 159
Kalb, Jonathan 258
Kane, Sarah 107
    4.48 Psychosis 106
    Blasted 70–1, 106, 210–11
    Phaedre's Love 211
Kant, Immanuel 100–2, 125

Kantor, Tadeusz,
    Wielopole, Wielopole 86
Kaprow, Alan,
    18 Happenings 112
Karge, Manfred 51
Keersmaeker, Anne Teresa De 114,
        122
Kelleher, Joe 5, 10, 14, 44–5
Khan, Keith (*motiroti*) 176
Kierkegaard, Søren 97
Kipphardt, Heinar 68, 69
Klata, Jan,
    Government Inspector, The 82
    H. 82
    Transfer! 77–9, 81–6
Klinder, Stephen 156–7
Knopp, Felix 223
Kohl, Helmut 131
Krasnoff, Sarah 181
Kreikebaum, Marcus 258
Kresnik, Johann 113, 114
Kristeva, Julia 114
Krutch, Joseph Wood 11, 13

La Fura del Baus 71
Laban, Rudolf 115
labour 7, 8, 27, 42–3, 170–2, 178–9,
        185
    of disabled actors in theatre 204–5
    immaterial (affective, etc.) 8,
        166–9, 179–81
Lacan, Jacques 6, 95, 112, 117, 123,
        125–7, 249
Laclau, Ernesto 21, 22, 170–3
Laibach 141
LaLaLa Human Steps 114
Langhoff, Matthias 51
language,
    meaning-making 150
    of media 71
    mediation by 21, 22
    in Müller's *Alone with These
        Bodies* 260, 262, 265, 268
    norms of 12

in Palmetshofer's plays 239, 240
referential and poetic
function 161–2
Lauwers, Jan 114
Lavendery, Andy 235
law, abstract 95–6
Le Roy, Xavier 116
Giszelle 119, 121
Le Sacre du Printemps 121
Lehmen, Thomas 121
Leiris, Michel 95
Lepage, Robert,
Hamlet 235
Lepecki, André,
18 Happenings (re-enactment) 112
Trio A (re-enactment) 112
Les SlovaKs 120, 124, 127
Journey Home 119
Lessing, Gotthold Ephraim,
Emilia Galotti 63
Nathan der Weise 26, 215,
217–25
Lettow, Fabian 271
Li, Jinrong 161–2
Limon, José 114
Littlewood Joan 68, 147
Lock, Édouard 114
Lücke, Bärbel 218, 226, 227
Ludwig, Janine 260, 261
Lukás, Georg 3, 90
Lyotard, Jean-François 11

McCarthy, Paul,
Bunker Basement 220
Piccadilly Circus 220
McGrath, John 147
McPherson, Tara 174, 186
Maertens, Miriam 229
Matta-Clark, Gordon 178
Mainwaring, Sarah 199–202, 203–4
Mantero, Vera 116
Mao Zedong 50, 51
Marchart, Oliver 123
Marcuse, Herbert 224

Marxism 7, 21, 51–2, 127, 166–7,
213, 262
and post-Marxism 21, 170–3
Mary Queen of Scots 213
meaning 3, 5, 7, 11, 17, 29, 77, 150,
212, 233, 235–6, 263, 265–7
indeterminacy of 4, 9–10, 20, 253
from meaning to energy in
dance 114–15
see also semiotics
media /mass media/mediatisation 18,
21–2, 40, 70, 117, 148, 168–9,
212, 217, 225, 246, 250, 251
see also technology
Meinhof, Ulrike 213
memory 3, 27, 76–7, 82–6, 120, 164,
222, 238
remembrance 89, 135
Merleau-Ponty, Maurice 236
Mey, Thierry De 122
Meyerhold, Vsevolod 13, 69–70
Mickunas, Algis 237
Middle East 222, 225
mimesis 14, 17, 41–2
Mnouchkine, Arianne,
1789 77–81, 85–6
modernism 11, 12
monologue 105, 203, 215, 226, 246–8
Monstrous Regiment 69
Morris, Pam 149
motiroti (arts group) 176, 180
Mouffe, Chantal 21, 22, 170–3
Müller, Heiner 9, 10, 52, 54, 107, 109,
133, **255–72**
Alone with These Bodies 10, 256,
259–64, 268–71
Description of a Picture 257, 258,
263
Germania Death in Berlin 259
Hamletmachine 211, 215, 268, 269
Hamlet/Machine 215
Horatian, The 257
Krieg ohne Schlacht
(autobiography) 261

Mauser 261
Scab, The / *Wagepresser, The* 264
Task, The /*Mission, The* 268
Wolomkolamsker Chaussee 105
Mumford, Meg 24, 26, 50, **147–64**

Nachbar, Martin 121
National Socialism 131, 133, 212, 221
   neo-Nazism and xenophobia 131,
      212
naturalism 13
Needcompany 114
Negri, Antonio 167–8
Neue Slowenische Kunst 141
New German Cinema 131
Newson, Lloyd 114
Nietzsche, Friedrich 12, 14, 22, 92,
      95, 98
norms/normative structures 28–9, 252
   cultural norms and values 22–3,
      96, 99
   see also *Sittlichkeit*
   of discourse 23, 28
   of language 12, 28
   social and political 24, 233

Oliver, Michael 205
O'Neill, Eugene 49

Palmetshofer, Ewald 24, 234, 253–4
   faust hat hunger etc 239, 241–6
   hamlet ist tot. keine schwerkraft 239,
      241, 243, 245–8
   wohnen. unter glas 239–41, 243–4,
      246–7
parallax view 45, 124, 128
parasitic politics 26, 213, 216–17,
      225, 230–1
Pařízek, Dušan David,
   Faust 1–2 with *FaustIn and
      out* 217, 228–31
Parker-Starbuck, Jennifer 185
perception 20–1, 104, 149, 168–9,
      182, 183, 210, 235–6
   politics of 15, 164, 168–9, 194

performance,
   performance art/live art 38, 97,
      116, 130, 189
   Performance Studies 39
   and theatre 189, 194–5
   phenomenology 25, 123, 233–8
      components of theatre and
         corporeal experience 234–6,
         239
   as 'discipline of the
      imagination' 236–7, 240
   phenomenal body 270
   and theatre 237–8
Pirandello, Luigi 13–14, 222
   *Six Characters in Search of an
      Author* 13, 57
Piscator, Erwin 13, 69–70, 147
Ploebst, Helmut 117
polis state (ancient Greek) 90–1, 96,
      98–9
'political theatre' 1–2, 6, 16, 35, 44,
      67–70, 81, 169, 250
Pollesch, René 240, 241
Pontbriand, Chantal 189
Poschmann, Gerda 210, 239, 255,
      271–2
postmodernism 48, 116, 121
   postmodern theatre/dance 1, 6,
      117, 122
   and uncertainty 51–2, 66
presence 116, 126, 174
   more than representation 38, 249
   see also audience, bodily
      co-presence
Price, Scott 198, 201–2
production 7–9, 18, 36–8, 42–3,
      169, 193, 205, 210, 215, 228,
      251–2
   of images 20, 130, 194
progress 26, 29, 230–1

Racine, Jean 91, 94
Rainer, Yvonne,
   18 Happenings (re-enactment) 112
   Trio A (re-enactment) 112

Rancière, Jacques 8, 9, 18–19, 22, 24,
44, 45–6, 72–6, 100–4, 109,
112, 251, 256, 271
'distribution [partition] of the
sensible' 73, 100–1, 103, 113,
128, 191–5, 206, 267
'emancipated spectator' 8, 74, 86, 125
'police'/'policing' 191–2
'representational regime of art' 113
'stultifying' logic/dramaturgy
10–11, 126
rationality/rationalism 93, 96, 102
anti-rationality 11, 14
Rayner, Alice 237–8
Read, Alan 44, 45
real 5, 148, 189
and aesthetic sphere 98–100
'irruption of the real' 6, 41, 190, 249
and phenomenology 237, 243
real people 3, 147–8, 151, 160
see also Reality Theatre
reality-status of performance 7, 12,
14–15, 20, 249–50
versus representation 5–6, 23–5,
27–8, 39–46, 117–18, 172, 189,
194–5, 238–9
see also fiction, and reality; Reality
Theatre
realism 6, 13, 49
reality (external/social and political/
economic) 14, 15, 16–18,
20–1, 26, 40–2, 50, 65–6, 68, 76,
108, 109, 149, 152, 156, 164,
212, 237–8, 249, 250–1, 251–2
Reality Theatre 26–7, **147–64**
reception 8–9, 18, 24, 74, 77, 109, 163
see also audience
Red Army Faction (RAF) 136, 213
re-enactment,
of avant-garde pieces 112, 118–21
of call centre training in
Alladeen 177, 183
in *Rocky Dutschke, '68* 134–5, 137–8
reflexivity (of performance) 116, 117,
120, 123, 124, 126–8

Regus, Christine 164
representation 4–8, 10–12, 22–4, 30,
65–6, 190, 203, 209–10, 251
and advanced capitalism 17
anti-representationality in
contemporary dance 116
and ballet 113, 115
and conceptuality 10–12, 235, 250
and language/discourse 22
means/modes/process of 36–8,
42–3, 47, 67, 85, 149
and presentation 11, 199
and spectatorial hierarchies 19–21
and tragedy 92, 95, 97, 98–100
and 'unpresentness' 214, 231
versus corporeal experience 235–6
versus the real *see* real, versus
representation
see also presence, more than
representation
responsibility/response-ability
99–100, 168, 194, 196, 210
revolution 136–8, 246, 261, 262–3, 272
French 78–81
see also activism
Rimini Protokoll,
Call Cutta in a Box 21
Chambermaids (*Ciudades Paralelas/
Parallel Cities Project*) 26–7,
151, 158–64
'experts of the everyday' 3, 5, 149,
159
Roccigiani, Graciano 'Rocky' 138
Rois, Sophie 134, 135–7
Rokem, Freddie 79–81
Rosas 114
Rousseau, Jean-Jacques 100
Rudolph, Sebastian 222, 223

Salamon, Eszter 119, 124, 126–8
And Then . . . 120
Dance for Nothing 118, 123–5
Hungarian Dances 120
Tales of the Bodiless 28, 111–12
Sassen, Saskia 167

Scharfenberg, Ute 54
Schauspiel Zürich 217, 228
Schechner, Richard 71
Schiller, Friedrich 72–3, 91, 100–4,
    109
    Maria Stuart 213
Schleef, Einar 11, 16, 226, 227
    Puntila and his Man Matti **53–61**,
    64–6
    Westerners in Weimar 54
Schleyer, Hanns-Martin 136
Schlingensief, Christoph 25, 27,
    130–2
    African Opera Village 131
    Chance 2000 (political
        party) 131–2
    Church of Fear 131–2
    Please Love Austria 131
    Rocky Dutschke, '68 129–45
Schmaering, Oliver,
    Seefahrerstück 86
Schmidt, Theron 24, 27, **189–207**
Schöne, Maja 223
Schopenhauer, Arthur 97
Schulz, Genia 258, 263
Schütt, Hans-Dieter 61
Schütte, Uwe 258.
Schutz, Alfred 243
Schütz, Bernhard 138
semiotics 122
    'density of signs' 190
    semiotic aspects (of theatre) 7, 10,
        20–1
    semiotic body 270
    theatrical signifiers in Reality
        Theatre 150–2
sensory experience 11, 12, 15,
    64, 102, 143, 234–6, 250
    see also phenomenology
Serres, Michel 216, 225, 231
service economy 167–8, 177–8,
    179–81, 187–8
Shackleton, David John (Vice Admiral
    of the Australian Navy) 154–5

Shakespeare, William 91, 94, 206
    Hamlet 57, 82, 215
    Macbeth 94
    Richard III 94
Shields, David 148
Shigeto, Nuki 235, 248
site/location of performance 3, 134,
    159, 160, 195–6, 202, 228
Sittlichkeit 91, 95–6
situation (of theatre) 5, 7, 10, 16, 20,
    23, 24, 89, 107, 108, 116, 130,
    143, 190, 194, 252, 266
Situationism 141, 194
Slevogt, Esther 56
Societas Raffaello Sanzio 71, 114
society, social and political
    issues 2–3, 16, 49, 66, 72–3,
    129, 131–2, 163, 171–2, 192,
    239, 252–3
    information society 166, 185
    social aspects of theatre 5, 7, 15,
        20, 209, 256, 264, 266–7
    see also audience, as a collective
    'social and political
        theorising' 32–3, 35
    social turn 7, 9
    socially critical art 131, 144
    see also reality
Sokolowski, Robert 234
Soliman, Laila 9
    No Time for Art 87–9, 100, 107,
        108
Sophocles,
    Antigone 91–2, 93, 95, 218
spectacle 18–20, 148, 194–5, 197,
    207
    'society of the spectacle' 97, 117,
        194, 251
    see also Debord, Guy
Spencer, Jenny 11
Stallone, Sylvester,
    Rocky 138
Stan's Café 120
states (theatre of) 61–5, 182

States, Bert O. 190, 235–6
Stemann, Nicolas,
  Nathan der Weise with
  Abraumhalde 217, 218, **220–5**
Stewart, David 237
story (fable) 1, 4, 17, 25, 28, 35–6,
  49–50, 55, 64, 179, 182, 235,
  248, 250
  storytelling 83–4
Strauss, Richard,
  Alpensinfonie 61
Strindberg, August 13
subject/subjectivity 28–9, 101–2, 105,
  107, 191, 236–7
  and agency 250–2
  and contemporary dance 112, 119,
  121–3
  interiority 240–2, 243–8, 252, 254
Sugiera, Małgorzata 16, **67–86**
Surrealism 13

technology 27, 166–7
  new media 174–6, 184–8
  technical support *see* service
  economy
Teuben, Sonia 198–202, 203
text 5, 9–10, 29, 55–6, 64–5, 150,
  210–11, 269
  dramatic 5, 14
  main text and secondary text 272
  metatext 153–6
  'no longer dramatic' 210–11, 212,
  215, 239, 255
  'textual politics' 255–6, 271–2
  to be read on stage 200
Thaemlitz, Terre 111
Thalheimer, Michael,
  Emilia Galotti 63
  *Herr Puntila und sein Knecht
  Matti* 16, 53, **60–6**
Thalia Theater Hamburg 53, 217
Théâtre du Soleil (Mnouchkine),
  1789 77–81, 85–6
Théâtre Libre 68

Theatre of the Everyday 69
Theatre Workshop (Littlewood) 147
theatricality 14–15, 27–8, 44, 74, 150,
  153, 189–90, 193–4, 195–6,
  206–7
tolerance 26, 29, 218, 224
tragedy / the tragic 5, 53–4, 59–60,
  61, 63, 65, **89–100**, **105–9**
  consciousness 227
  experience 93, 95, 97–9, 105
  and ritual 98
  'tragische Weltanschauung' 94
  transgression 92–5, 106
Tragelehn, B. K. 51
Troubleyn 114

Ultima Vez 114
Umfunktionierung (functional
  transformation) 7–8, 37–8
understanding (cognitive/
  conceptual) 11, 17, 18, 99,
  101–3, 163–4, 198, 236
utopia 23, 42–3, 260–3

Vandekeybus, Wim 114
verbatim theatre 5, 147, 152–3, 154
version 1.0
  *CMI (A Certain Maritime
  Incident)* 26, 150–1, 152–8,
  159, 161
Vinaver, Michel 68
Virillo, Paul 181
Vogl, Joseph 227–8
Volksbühne 129, 135

Wake, Caroline 155, 195
Walser, Franziska 229
Weber, Samuel 251
Wedekind, Frank,
  Erdgeist 12
Weems, Marianne (The Builders
  Association) 175–6, 178–83,
  187
Weigel, Helene 48

Weiss, Peter 68, 69, 147
Investigation, The 26
Wieghaus, Georg 257
Wigman, Mary 113
Wilder, Billy,
Sunset Boulevard 136
Wille, Franz 54
Williams, David 153, 155
Wilshire, Bruce 236
Wilson, Robert 21, 264
Einstein on the Beach 112
Hamlet 235

Wood, Michael 10, **255–72**
Woolf, Brandon 7–8, 15, 23, **31–46**
Wooster Group, The 71, 77, 119, 120,
154, 183
To You, the Birdie! (Phèdre) 211
Wuolijoki, Hella 54

Zaidi, Ali (*motiroti*) 176
Ziółkowska, Patrycia 223
Žižek, Slavoj 112, 117, 123, 124,
125–8
Zola, Émile 13

9972656R00193

Printed in Germany
by Amazon Distribution
GmbH, Leipzig